Agency and Change

Can we *make a difference* by changing the organizations we inhabit? *Agency and Change* remaps the limits and possibilities of change agency in organizations, clearly shifting the focus from increasingly outmoded debates on agency and structure to new practice-based discourses on agency and change.

The book presents a critical and selective interdisciplinary exploration of discourses on agency and change in organizations using two overarching conceptual continua: *centred agency–decentred agency* and *systems–processes*.

This allows the classification of four competing discourses:

- *Rationalist discourses* focus on intentional agency, expert knowledge and the management of organizational change.
- *Contextualist discourses* examine emergent patterns of strategic change and the bounded nature of strategic choice.
- *Dispersalist discourses* address the growing challenges of organizational complexity and chaos as well as providing new models of organizational learning, sensemaking agency and 'communities of practice'.
- *Constructionist discourses* explore the limits of human agency as discourse while affirming new possibilities for change and transformation.

This book is essential reading for all those interested in the origins, development and future prospects for change agency in an organizational world characterized by ever increasing complexity, risk and uncertainty.

Raymond Caldwell is Reader in Organizational Change at Birkbeck College, University of London. His research interests include organizational change theories, change agency and leadership, and the role of the HR function in the management of change.

Understanding Organizational Change

Series editor:
Dr Bernard Burnes

The management of change is now acknowledged as being one of the most important issues facing management today. By focusing on particular perspectives and approaches to change, particular change situations, and particular types of organization, this series provides a comprehensive overview and an in-depth understanding of the field of organizational change.

Titles in this series include:

Organizational Change for Corporate Sustainability
A guide for leaders and change agents of the future
Dexter Dunphy, Andrew Griffiths and Suzanne Benn

Reshaping Change
A processual perspective
Patrick Dawson

Agency and Change
Rethinking change agency in organizations
Raymond Caldwell

Agency and Change

Rethinking change agency
in organizations

Raymond Caldwell

Routledge
Taylor & Francis Group

LONDON AND NEW YORK

First published 2006 by Routledge
2 Park Square, Milton Park,
Abingdon, Oxon OX14 4RN

Simultaneously published in the USA and Canada
by Routledge
270 Madison Ave, New York, NY 10016

Routledge is an imprint of the Taylor & Francis Group

© 2006 Raymond Caldwell

Typeset in Times New Roman by
GreenGate Publishing Services, Tonbridge, Kent
Printed and bound in Great Britain by MPG Books Ltd, Bodmin

British Library Cataloguing in Publication Data
A catalogue record for this book is available from the British Library

Library of Congress Cataloging in Publication Data
A catalog record for this book has been requested

ISBN10: 0-415-32676-1 (hbk)
ISBN10: 0-415-32677-X (pbk)

ISBN13: 9-78-0-415-32676-6 (hbk)
ISBN13: 9-78-0-415-32677-3 (pbk)

Contents

Series editor's preface   vii
Preface   ix
Acknowledgements   xi

1 Introduction   1
  • Four discourses   5
  • Plan of the book   13
  • A note for readers   17

2 Agency and change   19
  • Introduction   19
  • Centred and decentred agency   22
  • Systems and processes   23
  • Conclusion   26

3 After Lewin, after modernism: rethinking change agency   28
  • Introduction   28
  • Rationality and change: from Lewin to Argyris   33
  • Diffusing expertise: Schein on process consultation   39
  • In search of autonomy   45
  • Reflexivity: redefining knowledge and practice   49
  • Conclusion: after Lewin, after modernism   53

4 Pettigrew and contextualism: organizational change and
  strategic choice   60
  • Introduction   60
  • Process and processual analysis   66
  • In search of contexts   71

- Strategic change and strategic choice: leading change   77
- Theory, practice and engaged scholarship   81
- Discussion: the legacy of contextualism   84
- Conclusion: contextualizing contextualism   88

5 The edge of chaos: complexity theory and organizational change   92
- Introduction   92
- Complexity theories: four core concepts   97
- Beyond order: from systems to processes of change   100
- Evolution and adaptiveness   107
- Systems and agent-based interaction   112
- Decentred agency   115
- Discussion   116
- Conclusion   120

6 From Foucault to constructionist discourses: change without agency?   122
- Introduction   122
- Discourse and the subject   126
- Power/knowledge and resistance   129
- Embodiment and identity   133
- Self-reflexivity and ethics   137
- Discussion: agency and change   139
- Conclusion   145

7 Things fall apart?   149
- Future research   150
- Things fall apart?   162
- Postscript   167

References   168
Index   183

Series editor's preface

It is an accepted tenet of modern life that change is constant, of greater magnitude and far less predictable than ever before. For this reason, managing change is acknowledged as being one of the most important and difficult issues facing organizations today. This is why both practitioners and academics, in ever-growing numbers, are seeking to understand organizational change. This is why the range of competing theories and advice has never been greater and never more puzzling.

Over the past 100 years, there have been many theories and prescriptions put forward for understanding and managing change. Arguably, the first person to attempt to offer a systematic approach to changing organizations was the originator of Scientific Management – Frederick Taylor. From the 1930s onwards, the Human Relations school attacked Taylor's one-dimensional view of human nature and his over-emphasis on individuals. In a parallel and connected development in the 1940s, Kurt Lewin created perhaps the most influential approach to managing change. His planned approach to change, encapsulated in his three-step model, became the inspiration for a generation of researchers and practitioners, mainly – though not exclusively – in the USA. Throughout the 1950s, Lewin's work was expanded beyond his focus on small groups and conflict resolution to create the Organization Development (OD) movement. From the 1960s to the early 1980s, OD established itself as the dominant Western approach to organizational change.

However, by the early 1980s more and more Western organizations found themselves having to change rapidly and dramatically, and sometimes brutally, in the face of the might of corporate Japan. In such circumstances, many judged the consensus-based and incrementally-focussed OD approach as having little to offer. Instead a plethora of approaches began to emerge that, whilst not easy to classify, could best be described as anti-OD. These newer approaches to change were less wary than OD in embracing issues of power and politics in organizations; they did not necessarily see organizational change as clean, linear and finite. Instead they saw change as messy, contentious, context-dependent and open-ended. In addition, unlike OD, which drew its inspiration and insights mainly from psychology, the newer approaches drew on an eclectic mix of sociology, anthropology, economics, psychotherapy and the natural sciences, not to mention the ubiquitous postmodernism. This has produced a range of approaches to change, with suffixes and appellations such as emergent, processual, political, institutional, cultural, contingency, complexity, chaos, and many more.

It is impossible to conceive of an approach which is suitable for all types of change, all types of situation and all types of organization. Some may be too narrow in applicability whilst others may be too general. Some may be complementary to each other whilst others are clearly incompatible. The range of approaches to change, and the confusion over their strengths, weaknesses and suitability, is such that the field of organizational change resembles more an overgrown weed patch than a well-tended garden.

The aim of this series is to provide both a comprehensive overview of the main perspectives on organizational change, and an in-depth guide to key issues and controversies. The series will investigate the main approaches to change, and the various contexts in which change is applied. The underlying rationale for the series is that we cannot understand organizational change sufficiently, nor implement it effectively, unless we can map the range of approaches and evaluate what they seek to achieve, how and where they can be applied, and, crucially, the evidence which underpins them.

Bernard Burnes
Manchester School of Management
UMIST

Preface

The history of the concept of 'agency' in organizational change theory over the past fifty years makes dismal reading. From a position of unbounded optimism that organizational change could be managed as a rational or planned process with a transparent agenda, we now confront restructured workplaces characterized by new forms of flexibility, hyper-complexity and chaos in which the nature, sources and consequences of change interventions have become fundamentally problematic. How did this occur and what implications does it have for our understanding of agency and change in organizations? Should we assume that rationalist concepts of change agency are no longer viable, or should we welcome the plural and promising new forms of 'decentred agency' emerging within organizations?

This book presents a selective interdisciplinary exploration of competing disciplinary discourses on agency and change in organizations, classified into *rationalist, contextualist, dispersalist* and *constructionist* discourses. Rationalist discourses give priority to intentional agency, concepts of planned change and the possibilities of strategic action. Contextualist discourses focus on processes of 'emergent' change and the bounded nature of strategic change and strategic choice in organizations. Dispersalist discourses focus predominantly on non-linear complex systems of self-organization and learning processes in organizations, which allow new forms of 'sensemaking' agency, 'distributed leadership' and 'communities of practice' to emerge. Constructionist discourses decentre human agency within discourses or 'discursive practices' over which human actors appear to have little rational or intentional control.

The four discourses will be analytically explored by reference to two overarching conceptual continua: *centred agency–decentred agency* and *systems–processes.* This meta-theoretical schema is designed to help delineate a shift away from the increasingly problematic agency and structure dichotomy and towards a more intensive focus on *agency and change.* However, this schema must be treated with caution. While the search for synthetic categories helps to map the meta-theoretical terrain of change agency and organizational change, the growing plurality of discourses challenge the social scientific ambitions of the research field to be objective, cumulative or unified. It is concluded that the future for applied research on change agency in organizations is characterized by new opportunities for empirical investigation and intervention, but also mounting threats to the epistemological rationale of research practice.

Acknowledgements

Some sections of the book have appeared in R. Caldwell, 'Things Fall Apart? Discourses on Agency and Change in Organizations' in *Human Relations*, Volume 58, Number 1, 2005.

1 Introduction

- **Four discourses**
- **Plan of the book**
- **A note for readers**

What should the unit of analysis of 'agency' be in organizational change theory? Is it possible to integrate competing concepts of agency into a coherent theory of organizational change? Can we have theories of organizational change without purposeful or intentional concepts of agency?

Fifty years ago these perplexing questions were often answered positively. Archetypes of agency were identified with models of rational actors and organizational change was conceived as a process that could be effectively planned and managed to achieve instrumental outcomes. A classic exemplification of this rationalist view is Lewin's concept of the 'change agent' as an expert facilitator of group processes of planned change, although his original concept has gone through many reformulations within various traditions of organization development theory and consultancy practice (Schein 1988).

Outside the organizational development tradition, however, over-rationalized models of agency and organizational analysis have been challenged from their very inception, both theoretically and practically. Simon's (1947) persuasive critique of decision-making processes in complex organizations is still a classic starting point for 'processual' and 'contextualist' attacks on the rationalism propounded by corporate planners, functional specialists and other experts (Mintzberg 1994; Pettigrew 1997). His work also anticipated later ideas on 'logical incrementalism' and 'emergent' concepts of strategy and organizational change, although this has rarely been acknowledged (Quinn 1980).

Challenges to rationalism, planned organizational change and expertise have also emerged from far-reaching transformations of the workplace over the past two decades. During the 1980s post-Fordist models of organizational flexibility and new modes of information technology radically undermined the idea that organizational success depended on traditional bureaucratic modes of workplace authority, stability and control (Castells 2000). Managerial agency and leadership was no longer identified primarily with the traditional roles of instructing, directing and controlling work processes. Instead, managers and leaders were now expected to encourage 'commitment' and 'empower' employees to be receptive to culture change, technological innovation and enterprise. The new vehicles for this 'dispersal' or distribution of change agency were new self-managed teams, quality circles and task groups, which acted as internal agents of transformation and change, as well as sources of distributive knowledge and expertise (Nonaka 1994; Nonaka and Takeuchi 1995).

This overall picture of a gradual shift or dispersal of change agency in organizations towards decentred groups or teams has been popularized in concepts of the 'learning organization' and more recently in the idea of 'communities of practice' (Senge 1990, 2003; Wenger 1998). Although the genealogy of these concepts is complex, they broadly conceive of organizations not as top-down structures of rational control, but as loosely coupled systems, networks or processes of learning and collective knowledge creation that devolve autonomy to agency at all levels (Dierkes et al. 2001). These ideas are, of course, partly a recognition of the fact that central hierarchical control has declined in many organizations and that large-scale organizational change is simply too complex and high-risk for any one group or individual to lead. It is in these terms that proponents of the learning organization have rejected the bureaucratic and mechanistic idea that organizations 'need change agents' and leaders who can 'drive change' (Senge 1999). Instead, leadership and change agency become identified with the systemic self-organization of learning by broadening leadership theory to encompass participative models of learning across the whole organization.

One finds similar ideas of the dispersal and decentring of agency within complexity theories of organizations. These theories have become increasingly influential over the past decade, as managing change has become synonymous with coping with the challenges of chaos (Anderson 1999; Fitzgerald and Van Eijnatten 2002). Although complexity and chaos theories have their origins in physics, computer science and mathematical biology, they have often been transposed into discussions of organizational change as well as broader ideas of the 'hyper-complexity' of network organizations and societies, and concepts of 'disorganised capitalism' (Brown and Eisenhardt 1997; Anderson 1999; Urry 2003). In all these theories the central idea is that dynamic systems are in a constant state of self-organizing stability–instability, which allows them to adapt and change. This occurs through 'dissipative structures' or devolved networks of information interchange that allow order and chaos, continuity and transformation to occur simultaneously, and without the hidden hand of purposiveness or central control. Effectively, 'order is free' since it appears to emerge from simple bottom-up processes or rules that create non-linear dynamics of bounded instability (Kauffman 1993). Applied to organizational change theory these ideas have encouraged a rejection of conventional rationalist subject–object dichotomies of knowledge creation, concepts of 'centred agency' and a reinterpretation of organizational change and change agency as an emergent, self-organizing and temporal process of communication and learning (Stacey 2001; 2003).

While this brief history of the growing diversity and plurality of forms of agency in organizations can be plotted in relation to transformations of the workplace, it can also be delineated in terms of an overall transition from rationalist epistemologies of agency to the increasingly fragmented discourses of 'social constructionism' and 'organizational discourse' analysis (Gergen 2001a; Grant *et al.* 2004). Rationalist epistemologies of agency have, of course, a long and complex intellectual genealogy in philosophy, but broadly they are characterized by a belief in human beings as rational subjects or autonomous actors who can act in an intentional, predictable and responsible manner toward predetermined goals or planned outcomes (Davidson 2001; Giddens 1984). These assumptions are essential in creating 'objective' ideals of rational scientific knowledge and its application to human action and practice, including universal ideals of ethical behaviour. Rationalist epistemologies are therefore scientific, prescriptive and interventionist. In contrast, the multi-various forms of social constructionism invariably undermine science and rationalism and with it ideals of agency and organizational change centred on rationality (Foucault 1994). Not only does knowledge of the natural world not have a predetermined structure or laws discoverable by rational investigation, but also ideas of 'human action', 'personality', 'intentionality' and 'agency' are equally problematic. For social constructionists and organizational discourse theorists, all forms of knowledge, understanding and action are culturally and historically relative and must therefore be situated within competing discourses (Hardy 2004).

This brief historical and epistemological overview of the nature of agency and change in organizations charts a profound and increasingly disconcerting transformation. From a position of great optimism regarding the practical efficacy and potential emancipatory role of rational action, expert knowledge and 'change agency', we now confront a plurality of conflicting ideals, paradigms and disciplinary self-images that are increasingly difficult to meld together in any coherent manner. We must ask how this fragmentation occurred, and what epistemological implications it has for understanding the future prospects for modes of agency and change in organizations, as well as concepts of practice. Should we give up the search for an 'integrated paradigm' or interdisciplinary ideal of change agency that goes beyond the Babel of increasingly competing discourses and the disparate contingencies of practice? Or, should we accept the plurality of discourses and the eclecticism of practice as itself a positive affirmation of new and more positive ideals of decentred agency?

This book presents a selective, synthetic and critical historical review of some of the literature and empirical research on agency and change in organizations. The review, however, is not strictly chronological and takes the form of a heuristic classification of change agency and organizational change theories using two conceptual continua: *centred agency–decentred agency* and *systems–processes* (see Figure 1, p. 5). Centred agency refers to intentional forms of rational and autonomous action, while decentred agency refers to emergent and 'embodied' forms of action that are enacted through practice. Systems define the relatively ordered and stable properties of organizations conceived as 'structures', while processes encompass emergent aspects of organizational change and instability. The poles of each continuum are conceived generically as analytically useful contrast concepts that reconfigure the familiar, if increasingly problematic, dichotomy between agency and structure (Giddens 1984).

The agency–structure dichotomy invariably reproduces varieties of ontological or epistemological polarity: *agency without structure* (i.e. voluntarism) or *structure without agency* (i.e. determinism), as well as many intermediate theoretical variants. The two continua are designed to avoid this polarity, while shifting the analytical focus from agency and structure to *agency and change*. The theoretical rationale for this shift is briefly outlined in Chapter 2, which begins by examining Giddens' (1984) classic reformulation of agency and structure as the 'duality of structure'. While a case is made for a move away from the agency–structure dichotomy, it is argued that we must retain multi-faceted conceptions of agency related to change (Caldwell 2005b).

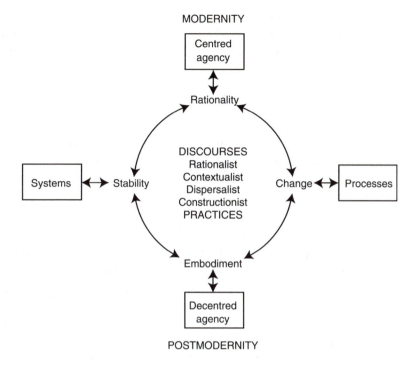

Figure 1 *Discourses on agency and change in organizations*

Four discourses

The four discourses can be broadly defined as follows.

Rationalist discourses identify intentional action and agency with rationality, expertise, autonomy and reflexivity, and this is amplified in the corresponding idea that human behaviour and organizations are ordered or 'functional' systems that can be subject to planned change or expert redesign, even in the face of resistance.

There is a vast range of rationalist discourses of intentional and teleological agency in the social sciences, from rational choice models of economic action to cognitive theories of instrumental behaviour. In the field of organization change theory, however, the most influential rationalist discourses on change agency have their origins in the influential work of Kurt Lewin (1947, 1999), although his ideas have gone through many reformulations within the various traditions of organizational development (OD) research and practice. Broadly, the four key attributes of an intentional or centred concept of change agency are invariably synonymous with the Lewinian legacy and the OD tradition: *rationality* and *expertise*, and to a lesser extent, *autonomy* and *reflexivity*.

Contextualist discourses *conceive human agency as embedded in emergent processes of organizational change that are not predetermined by internal structural contingencies or external environmental factors, but are rather the outcomes of non-linear, multi-level and incremental transition processes open to choice by human agents who operate within contexts of 'bounded choice' defined by competing group interests, organizational politics and power.*

Broadly conceived contextualist discourses have a long and distinguished academic lineage, crossing a range of disciplinary fields and assuming many sub-varieties. One can find genealogical links between Simon's (1947) critique of 'objective rationality' in complex organizations, Child's (1972) call for 'strategic choice' in understanding organizational contingencies, and the more recent work of Mintzberg (1994) on 'strategy as craft'. However, the most influential recent exponent of a contextualist approach within the organizational and strategic change fields is undoubtedly Pettigrew (1987, 1997). His programmatic intent is to create 'theoretically sound and practically useful research on change', that explores the 'context, content, and processes of change together with their interconnectedness through time' (Pettigrew 1987: 268). This was conceived as a direct challenge to 'ahistorical, aprocessual and acontextual' approaches to organizational change; especially planned change approaches, managerial ideals of control, and the variable-centred paradigms of organizational contingency theories. Moreover, Pettigrew appeared to create a new strategic change–strategic choice variant of contextual analysis that can be characterized as *incrementalism with transitions;* an approach that sought to pragmatically accommodate both continuity and discontinuity in organizational change processes.

Dispersalist discourses *locate agency as a decentred or distributed team or group activity of self-organizing learning, operating outside conventional hierarchical structures or control systems, and this allows organizations as complex systems of learning and knowledge creation to cope with innovation as well as the challenges of increasing organizational complexity, risk and chaos.*

There is an enormous and increasing variety of dispersalist discourses, from notions of organizational learning and 'sensemaking' agency to complexity theories of agent-based interactions in 'complex adaptive systems' (Anderson 1999; Weick 1995). At the heart of many of these discourses is the idea of leadership and agency, organizational change and development as decentred or distributed team processes. These are certainly not new ideas, but their significance has grown enormously over the past two decades (Gronn 2002). There are a number of factors that partly explain this development. The reduction of central hierarchical control in organizations has resulted in a growing emphasis on project and cross-functional teams as mechanisms to achieve greater horizontal coordination across organizational divisions, units and work processes. This is also associated with a shift towards information-intensive and network organizations with 'distributed intelligence', creating new opportunities for knowledge creation and innovation at multiple levels (Nonaka and Takeuchi 1995). In addition, the emergence of flexible forms of manufacturing and supply chain management founded on flexible 'economies of scope', rather than Fordist economies of scale has allowed greater potential for decentralized decision-making. It is against this background that Castells (2000) has provided a powerful and often positive overview of the tensions between hierarchies and networks, centralizing and decentralizing control in the emergence of new network organizations and societies. Others have, however, viewed the restructuring of managerial control negatively: 'the dispersal of management away from managers entails no more than a dispersal of instrumental rationality' (Grey 1999: 579).

Constructionist discourses *abandon subject–object distinctions and the corresponding agency–structure dichotomies; there are no objective scientific observers or autonomous actors, but only socially constructed worlds of fragmented cultural discourses, practices and fields of knowledge in which the possibilities for 'embodied agency' and organizational change are fundamentally problematic.*

Constructionist discourses are enormously diverse, partly because of their embrace of epistemological 'perspectivism' and their multiple points of intersection with the various intellectual movements of 'poststructuralism' and 'postmodernism'. This makes it almost impossible to disentangle the various strands of constructionist discourses (Gergen 2001a). There are, however, at least four concerns that help define the programmatic intent of constructionism:

Anti-rationalism. Most forms of social constructionism are hostile to the claims of reason and rationalism, both as a foundation for knowledge of the world of things and as a guide to human conduct. Constructionism argues that rationalism is neither a foundation of truth nor a basis for self-knowledge, moral conduct or political emancipation; it is simply one discourse among many.

Anti-scientism. Constructionism holds that the 'laws' or 'facts' of the natural and human sciences are constructions within discourse that could be otherwise. Science is not a cumulative or progressive understanding of 'how the world is', nor does its knowledge of laws or facts predetermine how the natural or human sciences will evolve (Hacking 1999).

Anti-essentialism. Constructionists hold that there are no essences or inherent structures inside objects or people. Just as nature is not immutably fixed by entities designated as 'atoms', 'cells' 'molecules', so human subjects are not predetermined objects with discoverable properties such as 'human nature', 'intentionality', 'free will' or 'personality'. These nominalist entities do not have an existence outside of socially constructed discourses.

Anti-realism. Constructionalists deny that the world has a fixed or pre-determined reality discoverable by empirical observation, theoretical analysis or experimental hypothesis. There can be no truly objectivist or realist epistemologies founded on the subject–object and appearance–reality dichotomies that have characterized the history of Western rationalist thought.

These statements (minus any hint of invective) represent very broad meta-theoretical characterizations of constructionist positions. As such their implications will vary enormously in relation to the disciplinary fields, research traditions, or theoretical perspectives within which they are developed. Nevertheless, these statements broadly indicate that most constructionist discourses are compatible with the long tradition of relativism and nominalism in Western philosophy (Hacking 1999: 83).

While the four discourses are defined as 'pure types', they assume a multiplicity of forms, some of which may overlap with apparently competing discourses. For example, the shift within the OD tradition towards the concept of the learning organization has meant that its parameters overlap with dispersalist discourses; in this sense ideas of planned organizational change and system-wide organizational learning are often reinforcing. Similarly, contextualist discourses can be defined by 'emergent' or 'processual' perspectives, which may blend into ad hoc appropriations of constructionist ideas, especially if they are identified with a process ontology of change as becoming and ideas of knowledge as discourse. Ultimately if one pushes contextualism too far from its comforting empirical anchorages it can become constructionist.

Discourses are, of course, by their very nature enormously complex (Alvesson and Karreman 2000). They range from the apparently context-free textual and conversational analysis of meaning to context-specific micro or macro discourses of 'power/knowledge' within discursive practices that may be critical or interpretative (Foucault 1994, 2000). It is not possible or necessary to examine all these forms of discourse. Here the primary focus is on *disciplinary discourses* that address issues of the role of 'agency' in organizational change. Disciplinary discourses are broadly defined as forms of language, meaning and interpretation representing and shaping relatively coherent social, cultural or disciplinary fields of academic knowledge creation and practice that embody contextual rules about what can be said, by whom, where, how and why. Disciplinary discourses are therefore forms of 'rarefaction' designed to limit or exclude those who cannot speak authoratively (Foucault 1994).

This definition emphasizes the plurality of disciplinary discourses, but it does not assume that all that exists are discourses about discourses (Foucault 1991). Many 'scientific' discourses may be characterized by patterns of self-referential circularity and indeterminism; and constructionists are right when they claim that: 'there are no claims to truth that can justify themselves' (Gergen 1999: 227). But this does not mean that 'truth' is 'simply rendered irrelevant' to discourse. Disciplinary discourses of knowledge and science can be subject to critical self-scrutiny and empirical interrogation in terms of their own claims to knowledge or objectivity, as well as their related moral and political implications. Because such discourses may 'refer to' ideas, concepts, objects or actions that embody human activities, patterns of meaning and knowledge they can take on a *real, naturalistic* or even a *deterministic* efficacy in human practices. This matters in terms of what we believe, understand, and how we act in the world: they matter because they have consequences and so 'truth' as a fragile criterion of discourse does matter.

Although the review of the four discourses is deliberately interdisciplinary, it cannot hope to encompass all the various paradigms and traditions of research and practice within each set of discourses. For example, the review does not discuss societal, collectivist or broader macro-models of change agency associated with formal institutions or social and political movements. There is also no discussion of agency versus non-agency differences and the broader issues of naturalism in the social and human sciences (Latour 1987; Barnes 2000). Nor is it possible to explore psychoanalytical concepts of *agency* within the analyst–patient relationship. Instead, the primary focus is on the exploration of the relationship between change agency and organizational change.

But how do we define the scope of 'change agency' in organizations? One possibility in answering this question is to follow discourses of intentional or centred agency and define change agency as the capacity of internal or external human *actors* within organizations, individually or in groups, to consciously choose to use their knowledge, skills, power, expertise or reflexivity to sponsor, initiate, enact, direct, manage or implement a specific change idea, process, initiative, project or complete programme of change which impacts directly or indirectly on the efficiency or effectiveness, values or culture of an organization and the behaviour or actions of its members. This definition broadly assumes that change agency is a sub-type of rational action and expert intervention. Is this definition adequate? Can it cope with the relationship between agency and change within constructionist discourses of decentred agency? No – it cannot.

An adequate theorization of change agency in organizations requires emergent models of 'agency' that are not limited to rationalist notions of intentional agency which situate action and meaning within essentially individualist concepts of *rationality, expertise, autonomy* and *reflexivity*. It also requires models of agency that go beyond notions of decentred agency founded on *discourses* of *power/knowledge, embodiment,* and *self-reflexivity* (see Chapter 2). If change agency is identified primarily with models of centred agency it can become synonymous with the exercise of expert knowledge and power within structures as systems that order, control and potentially dominate human beings. If change agency is identified primarily with non-intentional or 'embodied action' it can become diffused within temporal processes of organizing that may have only a marginal impact on practice or outcomes and may limit change to the rhetorical negotiation and renegotiation of meaning within discourses of power (Gergen 1999, 2001a). One form of change agency is authorized by knowledge, expertise and power and a belief in the legitimacy of its moral and political ends, while the other seeks to transgress, redefine or de-rail the relationship between knowledge, expertise and power in the search for new innovative forms of organizing or new patterns of social transformation. An adequate account of change agency must leave room for both: for rational intervention in 'managing change' and for the freedom to question, challenge and repudiate the meaning and goals of organizational change as well as the intervention techniques and expert tools used to achieve it. Ultimately, change agency is a synthetic category of creative human action. Its true ontological and epistemological centre of gravity lies in the enactments of practice that never fully conform to the intentional action models of rationalism or the purely self-referential limitations of reflexivity and embodiment within constructionist discourses.

Capturing the enormous complexity and potential scope of change agency in organizations is clearly a daunting and perhaps impossible task. The classification of the four discourses is therefore simply an attempt to provide an overarching meta-theoretical framework for exploring the nature of agency and change that straddles different and competing disciplinary discourses. The meta-theoretical task is essentially conceived as an overall attempt to: 1) gain a better understanding of competing disciplinary discourses and the diversity of theories; 2) develop an overall perspective on the nature of agency and change in organizations; 3) explore the difficulties in developing multi-disciplinary theories or models of organizational change (Van de Ven and Poole 1995), and 4) indicate, where appropriate, future avenues for empirical research.

While the four discourses provide a way to explore the meta-theoretical terrain of agency and change in organizations, they do not offer the prospect of a 'grand theory', meta-narrative or a new paradigm. A parallel search for synthesis has constantly been reinvented in sociological explorations of agency and structure, but without any success in achieving theoretical integration; and there are lessons here for other disciplines (Bourdieu 1990; Giddens 1984; Archer 2003).

One key theoretical lesson is not to separate organizational change and agency. When Van de Ven (1987) sets out the conditions for a robust theory of organizational change he demonstrates just how difficult it is to achieve this ambition. Such a theory must simultaneously demonstrate:

> a) how structure and individual purposive action are linked at micro and macro levels of analysis; b) how change is produced both by the internal functioning of the structure and by the external purposive action of individuals; c) stability and instability; and d) how time can be included as a key historical metric.

> (summarized by Chia 1999: 213)

This is an admirably inclusive set of requirements, and it appears to avoid many familiar traps. But what emerges when Van de Ven and Poole (1995) finally formalize these requirements into four 'process' models of organizational change (*life cycle*, *teleological*, *dialectical* and *evolutionary*) is a theorization that virtually excludes agency in the form of purposive or intentional action as a category of analysis, even though this is the very 'subject' foundation of their epistemology. Ultimately, it is impossible to have adequate theories of organizational change without including theories of agency.

Paradoxically, similar dangers are apparent in the emerging synthetic ambitions of constructionism and, in particular, various forms of 'organizational discourse' analysis (Gergen 2001a; Grant *et al.* 2004). Organizational discourse analysis often seeks to consolidate the exploration of 'talk', 'text' and 'relational dialogue' as a precursor to change through discourse, even though these discourses invariably sidestep purposeful action and under-theorize models of embodied agency. Taken in a strongly nominalist direction the key assumptions are that discourse and organizational change can apparently be theorized without a concept of agency and that organization/organizing only exists as discourse (Gergen 1992, 1999; Reed 1998). Of course, not all organizational discourse theorists would agree with this view. Interestingly, the forms of organizational discourse that do seek to re-incorporate agency invariably return to Giddens' 'structuration theory', although this reprise throws up almost as many problems as it appears to resolve (Heracleous and Hendry 2000: 1269). Currently, however, there is not even the remotest prospect of a synthetic 'recontextualization' of an overall 'order of discourse' that would somehow link micro-discourses on decentred agency to a more grandiose macro-level structural analysis of social order or social change: a move from discourses to *Discourse*. The strength of organizational discourse as an exploration of organizational change is its enormous plurality (Heracleous and Barrett 2001).

What are the broader implications of this frustrated search for synthesis? Perhaps the most important implication is that the oppositions and relationships between the concepts and dichotomies explored within a cultural or disciplinary field of discourse cannot be stated universally (Abbott 2001). Instead, the formulation and reformulation of concepts of agency and change depend on the specific theoretical discourses or practices within which they occur (Foucault 1994). Moreover, social 'scientific' knowledge of agency is itself a socially constructed discourse and practice that may simply reproduce old dichotomies in the conceptual language of an apparently new paradigm (Hacking 1999). This epistemological dilemma presents a challenge not only to rationalism and purposeful action, but also to many versions of social constructionism which appear to affirm the nominalism of discourse analysis while somehow claiming to 'critically' transcend the dichotomies that underpin their often debilitating theorization of agency. In this respect, critical discourse analysis is always in danger of sliding from nominalism to realist reductionism or, worse still, a variant of monistic idealism (Gergen 2001a).

Plan of the book

Chapter 1. This chapter has given a brief overview of the scope and limitations of this book. It has outlined the four discourses that form the interpretative schema for the exploration of agency and change, and it has tried to indicate the potential multiplicity of theoretical and empirical forms of change agency in organizations.

Chapter 2. This chapter begins a sociological dialogue with Giddens' work that recurs throughout the book. Giddens' classic examination of 'agency and structure' is the natural starting point for an exploration of agency and change. However, the overall critical aim of the chapter is to provide a brief summary of the theoretical rationale for a shift from the debates over agency and structure towards a more intensive exploration of agency and change (Caldwell 2005b). This provides the unifying sociological thematic of the book as well as a programmatic research challenge for the exploration of the four discourses. Some readers, however, who want to go directly to the substantive exploration of the four discourses, may wish to skip this chapter.

The four middle chapters (3 to 6) focus on specific issues related to the four discourses. These chapters are primarily concerned with depth rather than coverage. They drill down into the rich vein of a specific disciplinary discourse or the work of a specific author, rather than surveying the surface terrain. A more comprehensive review of each set of discourses would require a far more ambitious study that this one, and a lot more time and energy.

Chapter 3. This chapter begins the substantive task of rethinking the concept of 'change agency' by an exploration of Kurt Lewin's work. There have been virtually no serious attempts to explore the broader meaning and significance of change agency in Lewin's work, or to trace the genealogy of its many reinventions within the organizational development and action research traditions. This is a fateful omission. Change agency is central to Lewin's commitment to rational action and democratic values, his belief in expert knowledge as reflexive feedback, and his overall liberal idealism regarding the self-reflective mediation of theory and practice, knowing and doing, science and action. Change agency is also central to the key ideas of 'action science', 'process consultation' and 'reflective practice' propounded by many of the leading advocates of the OD tradition; most notably Argyris (1982), Schein (1988) and Schön (1983). But is a Lewinian-inspired idea of change agency still viable within the OD tradition or change management theory? In this chapter the limitations of Lewin's concept of the change agent and its various reinterpretations are examined through an exploration of the four major conceptual components implicit in rationalist discourses of 'centred agency': *rationality*, *expertise*, *autonomy* and *reflexivity*. It is argued that this disciplinary discourse is no longer sustainable because it is based on an understanding of organizational change that is linear, rational and expert driven. If the action research and OD traditions are to find new models of change agency they must rethink the dualisms of subject–object, research–practice, knowledge–action that have plagued their understanding of agency and change for decades. This requires a far-reaching search for new practice-based and distributive models of decentred agency, rational inquiry, moral discourse and knowledge creation.

Chapter 4. This chapter provides a long-overdue examination of contextualism through a detailed critical examination of the work of Andrew Pettigrew (1987, 1997). Pettigrew is the leading proponent of a contextualist discourse on organizational change and strategic choice. But what is contextualism? Does it offer a coherent challenge to opposing models of organizational change that emphasize rationalism, causal contingences or the efficacy of structure over agency? Here it will be argued that contextualism as a theory of the 'embeddedness' of agency and change in organizations has four major weaknesses. First, contextualism does not provide a coherent understanding of organizational structure–organizational change as a dynamic interplay between systems and process, continuity and change. Instead, contextual analysis highlights the processual nature of organizational change, while underplaying the potentially macro or broader system characteristics of organizational structures. A truly coherent theory must seek to incorporate both. Second, Pettigrew uses the idea of 'outer and inner' context to undermine structural/system concepts of organizations or their environments, effectively turning context into a holistic image of organizational change processes that are primarily incremental, open-ended and indeterminate. Organizational change therefore invariably appears as *incrementalism with transitions*. Third, Pettigrew's focus on the micro-dynamics of organizational politics and power is designed to emphasize constraint while simultaneously undermining determinism and emphasizing choice. Yet, paradoxically, it also underplays the exploration of leadership and change agency in organizations. In this respect contextualism, despite its emphasis on agency and choice, does not offer a 'contextual theory of leadership', or an understanding of the processes of leading change. Fourth, contextualism does not provide a theory of practice, and so its claims to provide 'practically useful knowledge' and a liberal model of engaged scholarship are difficult to sustain. Finally, it will be concluded that contextualism needs to be contextualized as the rhetorical discourse of *Homo Academicus* (Bourdieu 1988). As such it is not a coherent theoretical challenge to rationalist models of organization and strategic change, but rather a modest reaffirmation of the virtues of scholarship, individual choice and liberal humanism.

Chapter 5. This chapter explores complexity theories as just one of the numerous and growing varieties of dispersalist discourses on agency and change in organizations. Complexity theories of organizations have become enormously influential partly because they offer system-based concepts for exploring non-linear change and the 'hyper-complexity' of network organizations and societies as well as the growing challenges of simultaneously managing order and chaos within 'informational capitalism' (Castells 2000). However, recent attempts to re-work chaos and complexity theories of natural systems as 'process', 'interactional' or 'network' versions of 'complex adaptive systems' are partly attempts to reconnect systems theory with the idea of 'decentred agency' (Anderson 1999; Stacey 2001). Rather than macro-structural models of system change, complex adaptive systems attempt to theorize agent-based models of decentred agency as modes of self-organization. This requires a shift from the generative rules of systemic entities to the self-organizing 'schemata' of interaction between agents: a precarious move from systems as structural entities at the edge of chaos to systems as 'processes' of change founded on decentred agency. Is this apparent shift in the organizational focus of complexity theory credible or convincing? Can complexity theories offer a theory of agential dispersal, distributed leadership and change agency in organizations that keeps at bay the spectre of chaos – the collapse of the virtuous system coupling of chaos–order? To answer these questions two overlapping sets of questions are explored. First, can complexity theories reconcile the concept of 'system' as a functional entity with a 'process' or evolutionary overview of organizational change? What happens if one takes away the functionalist and evolutionary assumptions of system concepts and replaces them with a processual ontology of change (Chia 1999; Van de Ven and Poole 1995)? Second, is the concept of 'agency' in complexity theory simply the outcome of self-organizing rules of micro-interaction? Does this decentring of agency mean that individuals cannot exercise autonomy or reflexivity in the choice of ends? Conversely, if agents are free to follow their own self-organizing rules how is order and change possible? Will self-organization as agential dispersal lead to a reinstatement of chaos as the antithesis of order? After briefly examining these questions it is concluded that complexity theories of agential dispersal in organizations are in serious danger of falling apart as they stray into the territory of constructionist discourses of decentred agency and a processual ontology of change.

Chapter 6. Michel Foucault's work appears to mark an important break with conventional ontological dualism, epistemological realism and rationalist and intentional notions of individual action and human agency. In these respects his ideas have had an enormous influence on constructionist discourses as well as postmodern organization theory and analysis. In particular, Foucault's ideas have lead to a rejection of agency–structure dichotomies and a move towards process-based ontologies of 'organizing/changing' that create a new problematic of *change without agency*. While this has often provoked a counter-reaction against the corrosive influence of postmodernism, there have been few attempts to explore how the decentring of the subject within constructionist discourses is related to new, more positive and potentially emancipatory discourses that redefine the relationship between agency and change in organizations and society. Does the fall of the subject also allow for the creative emergence of a multiplicity of new forms of agency? Here it will be argued that Foucault's legacy can be re-conceptualized as a theorization of the decentring of agency consisting of four key components: *discourse, power/knowledge, embodiment* and *self-reflexivity*. Redefined within Foucauldian constructionist discourses, decentred agency can lead to new possibilities for the creation of 'embodied agency' and the dispersal of agency in organizations. It will be concluded, however, that Foucault-inspired constructionist discourses and organizational theory leave us with few answers on how to reconnect decentred agency with change agendas derived from its apparent conceptual opposite: the activist, politically engaged and potentially autonomous epistemological and moral subject of Enlightenment rationalism and humanist discourses. Until Foucauldian organizational theory and constructionist discourses re-engage with rationalist discourses of intentional agency they will remain fundamentally flawed in their theorization of the relationship between agency and change in organizations and societies.

Chapter 7. Finally, the theoretical implications of a temporal, fragmented and non-cumulative understanding of knowledge and action for the future of change agency as a research field are discussed. It is concluded that as organizational theories of change and human agency become more fragmented it is becoming increasingly difficult to construct an ideal of change agency as a basis of knowledge, action or practice.

The plan of the book clearly reflects its scope and limits. But if every act of selection is by definition an act of exclusion this should not be taken as derogative. Many authors deserve a much more extensive treatment, but that would be a very long book. Nor should the selection process be assumed to be purely idiosyncratic – although one cannot completely avoid this criticism. A whole chapter on the work of Andrew Pettigrew and contextualism may seem excessive homage to some readers, while an engagement with complexity theory and organizational change may seem far removed from an exploration of change agency. There is, however, a strong rationale for selection in that chapters 3 to 6 address the core issues of theorizing agency and change central to each of the four sets of discourses. In terms of an overall sequence it is also appropriate that the book essentially begins with Giddens and ends with Foucault, for they provide powerful theoretical counter-images of agency.

A note for readers

As a search for synthesis this book presents particular problems for readers – and for the author. At least four should be noted.

First, the focus is primarily theoretical. The aim is to clear pathways through a confusing terrain and map out new areas for more detailed empirical investigation. In clearing pathways one has had to explore epistemological and ontological issues of 'agency' and 'change' that may appear remote from the practice of change agency, and this is likely to be frustrating for some readers. By way of an apology one can only say that the empirical challenge as mapped out here will be taken up in a complementary volume to this study.

Second, the book is a curious mix of intradisciplinary and interdisciplinary ambition, with the result that disciplinary boundaries are often ignored. Change agency as a hybrid subject area is treated as a sub-field of organizational theory, which is in turn a sub-discipline of sociological theory. It is also explored across the conventional domains of organizational development practice, the less conventional arena of strategic change, as well as within the potentially synthetic paradigm of complexity theory. Treating these discourses in a unifying problem-solving manner does not make for easy reading. The ideal reader, however, is one who wishes to engage with these competing discourses and build bridges between them.

Third, the true disciplinary centre of gravity of this book is sociological rather than an extension of management thought, although the overarching commitment is to 'practice' above all, rather than the virtues of grand sociological theorizing. Giddens and Foucault figure prominently in this book but they are not the heroes within the narrative; the real heroes are those in search of creative new methods and strategies of change through practice. Some readers may find this judgement disconcerting, others will welcome it.

Fourth, and finally, there is a constant tendency to take a long view of the issues discussed and this introduces an historical note of scepticism with regard to the present. Change agency theory has not come a long way over the past fifty years and this presents an unpalatable message for those who wish to further theory and practice. For those readers looking to the future, however, the challenge is to rethink the subject and reinvent practice.

2 Agency and change

- **Introduction**
- **Centred and decentred agency**
- **Systems and processes**
- **Conclusion**

It is analytical to the concept of agency: (a) that a person could have acted otherwise and (b) that the world as constituted by a stream of events-in-process independent of the agent does not hold out a predetermined future.

(Anthony Giddens)

Introduction

Most attempts within the social sciences to link 'agency' and 'change' are informed not only by the search for the possibilities of intentional or reasoned 'choice', but by an ideal that choice can *make a difference.* When Giddens famously identifies 'agency' with the capacity 'to have acted otherwise' he also identifies choice with the *power* to make a difference: 'the transformative capacity of human agency is the capability of actors to intervene in a series of events so as to alter their course' (Giddens 1976: 111). Agency is a necessary condition of intentional conduct and a requirement for the ability to effect change: actors can act against external structures and systems to transform them (Habermas 1987). For Giddens (1984) the power of intentional action and the power of change are ontologically and epistemologically connected in an individualistic ideal of agency as choice.

Yet, paradoxically, Giddens' claim that choice can and should make a difference is rarely extended into an exploration of its apparent opposite, the heterogeneous possibilities of 'decentred agency': agency that is not primarily informed by intentional choice or the outcome of the unintended consequences of rational action (1976: 77). Giddens appears to recognize this problem when he argues that intention, reason and motive are misleading terms: 'the reflexive monitoring of conduct only becomes the statement of intentions, or the giving of reasons, when actors either carry out retrospective enquiries into their own conduct or, more usually, when queries about their behavior are made by others' (1976: 156). But in a later reformulation of this retrospective interpretation of intention, Giddens appears to suggest a broader exploration of the nature of agency: 'Agency refers *not* to the intentions people have in doing things but to their capacity of doing things in the first place' (Giddens 1984: 9, emphasis added). What are these first order capacities, if they are not intentional forms of rational action (Bourdieu 1990)? Are they 'embodied' forms of action without prospective intent? Or, are they 'practices' that exist as action unfolds? Is agency possible without a concept of intention (Foucault 1991)? Giddens does not give adequate answers to these difficult questions.

The absence of answers is partly related to Giddens' (1993) need to explore the limits of intentionality while defending it from the perceived threat of decentred agency. If decentred agency takes hold then human actors may become the mere bearers of anonymous structures over which they have little control. 'A decentring of the subject must at the same time recover that subject as a reasoning, acting being' (Giddens 1982: 8). This is the spectre of 'structuralism' and 'post-structuralism' that confronted Giddens in his early work, rather than the more recent challenges of constructionism and organizational discourse analysis which seek to dispense with the agency and structure distinction altogether (Gergen 2001a).

Giddens' concern with preserving a relatively strong notion of intentionality partly explains the limitation of his concept of agency (Emirbayer and Mische 1998). One of the clearest indications of this limitation is evident when Giddens (1984) explores agency in relation to 'structure' rather than in relation to change. At first this seems a rather curious focus, given his emphasis on the transformative capacity of agency (Giddens 2000). But it soon becomes clear that Giddens has to re-establish a broadly open-ended relationship between structure and intentional conduct if he is to establish a counter-force to determinism – those forces that undermine the possibilities of activistic agency and the project of modernity (1990a). This intent is crystallized in Giddens' 'structuration' theory.

Structuration theory is a sustained attempt to establish the relationship between agency and structure as one of *identity* or synthetic 'duality'. Structuration refers to both the temporal processes of *producing–reproducing* structures and the epistemological identification of agency and structure (Giddens 1990b). This involves a rejection of the holistic and essentialist idea of 'structure' as systems of integrated normative regulation over time (Parsons 1951). It also involves a rejection of micro–macro distinctions and the individual versus society dualism that have plagued classical sociological discourses of social order and social action. Instead, Giddens proposed that the relationship between agency and structure is one of interaction, or what he terms (somewhat misleadingly), the '*duality of structure*'. Structures are dualities because they are both the 'medium and outcome' action (1979: 5). Moreover, because structure as a process-based construct is sustained by interaction it is apparently open to change and this involves a rejection of the determinism implied by evolutionary and old style structuralist or systems concepts of order and collective agency: '*All reproduction is necessarily production* … and the seed of change is there in every act which contributes towards the reproduction of any ordered form of social life' (Giddens 1976: 102, emphasis in original).

While Giddens' ideas appeared to bring agency back into sociological theory, especially after the abstract 'structural-functional' legacy of Parsons' (1951) social systems theory, his work rarely offers new empirical or practical insights into how agency transforms 'structure'. What emerges instead is a meticulous focus on how agency routinely *reproduces* structures, while these structures remain indeterminate (Barnes 2000). Giddens partly ends up in this position because he draws a confusing distinction between 'systems' as reproduced social relations and 'structures' as rules and resources that actors use (1984: 157). A more coherent approach would be to conceive of structures as both systems and processes. But Giddens cannot envisage this possibility because he wants to argue both that 'social systems' do not have fixed structures, and that structures have no reality other than as instantiated social practices or the memory traces of actors' conduct. With this processual formulation Giddens appears to dissolve the dualism of agency and structure by collapsing structure as system into structure as temporal processes of agential interaction or practice: 'In structuration theory structure has always to be conceived as a property of social systems, "carried" in reproduced practices embedded in time and space' (Giddens 1984: 170). Reinforcing this indeterminacy of structure, agency as practice appears to *produce* itself while again remaining indeterminate: actors reproduce or transform structures, somehow 'remaking what is already made in the continuity of *praxis*' (1984: 171; emphasis in original). In this formulation we are never sure where structure and agency begins and ends. Nor are we clear as to what Giddens means by practice.

What are the sources of these equivocations? Part of the problem is that Giddens appears to identify 'structure' with the 'inherent indeterminism of social reproduction', and as such, it appears as a 'medium' of interaction with no substantive or persistent properties over time that can be clearly identified, analysed or changed (Layder 1987). In effect, structures as possible systems of reproduction have essentially a virtual existence in that they are the temporal manifestations of the ongoing processes of actor interaction. Critics of Giddens' work have often pointed to this under-theorization of 'structure' as an over-reaction to systems concepts, but it is often forgotten that this problem applies equally to the indeterminate nature of agency. Agency lacks determination because its primary function is the denial of determinism, including any hint of naturalism: agents can 'produce' their agency in that they are the objects of their own temporal self-constitution through 'practice'. While this activistic embrace of practice has positive connotations for action, it is still unclear how practice moderates the implicitly intentional and rationalist presuppositions of Giddens' notion of agency (Bourdieu 1990).

One of the most striking consequences of Giddens' reformulation of the agency–structure dichotomy is that he offers a process-based theory of the 'duality of structure', but no corresponding exploration of the *duality of agency* (Sztompka 1993). How is agency produced and reproduced through temporal processes of intentional self-constitution and embodied forms of social action and practice? Again the failure to explore this question is somewhat surprising in that Giddens appears to privilege the efficacy of agency *against* structure: agency is the affirmation of the possibilities of choice in the face of any system determinism. This leads to an abstract, even vaguely voluntaristic, affirmation of agency that appears to exist outside of time or history (Giddens 1984). In this sense Giddens simply claims that agents have 'power' to act, to change structures, especially by using their reflexive knowledge. But it is unclear how this occurs or what heterogeneous forms agency takes. Ultimately, Giddens' work is a particularly disappointing theorization of agency and change, especially given his passionate belief that human actors, even the most powerless, can change the social world by virtue of their ability to become empowered (Layder 1987).

Centred and decentred agency

One way of partly avoiding some of the potential entrapments and paradoxes of Giddens' over-activistic or intentional concept of agency is to focus on both modes of rational or 'centred' agency versus forms of embodied and 'decentred' agency. In other words we are interested in treating agency as a mediated category of creative action, as a form of action enacted in practice. The continuum of 'agency' that partly defines this area of mediation and practice can be briefly summarized as follows.

Centred agency is defined by four key characteristics of individual action: 1) *rationality* or intentionality in defining the direction or outcomes of behaviour – although all action involves unintended consequences; 2) *expertise/knowledge* or the 'causal power' to influence, shape or control events; 3) *autonomy* or the freedom to make voluntary choices about ends and act to attain them, including, if possible, ethical responsibility for their consequences – unfortunately 'rationality' and 'autonomy' are not synonymous (Giddens 1976: 154); and 4) *reflexivity* or the ability to critically reflect upon knowledge and conduct, both practically and morally. These are generic characteristics of agency in general, but they are constrained by the central problematic of agency: the uneven distribution of power in organizations and societies.

Decentred agency is the potential antithesis of the primarily individual, rational, expert or action-centred analysis of agency. Like centred agency, decentred agency has a multiplicity of forms. Within the nominalist frameworks of constructionist discourses it can, however, be identified by the following four generic characteristics: 1) *discourses* or rhetorics embedded in collective behaviours, social practices or political ideologies that undermine the teleological and normative possibilities of individual 'rational' action; 2) *power/knowledge* which expresses the underlying prejudgements or bias within discourses of knowledge that undermine the possibility of objectivity, and create a symbiosis between expertise and power (Foucault 1994); 3) *embodiedness* created by the culturally habitual, determined, pre-conscious, intuitive, involuntary or improvisatory nature of all human actions and the inability of actors to predict outcomes, master the 'logic of practice', or take full ethical responsibility for their actions (Bourdieu 1990); 4) *self-reflexivity* created by the growing awareness of the 'self' as a problematic socio-cultural construction that must be subject to self-scrutiny in uncovering the possibilities of knowledge and human identity (Gergen 2001a). While these characteristics of decentred agency often define the remit of constructionism in the social and human sciences, they can also lead in the opposite direction towards a resurgence of 'naturalism' (Barnes 2000: 151).

Systems and processes

The continuum of *centred–decentred agency* provides a useful meta-theoretical heuristic for differentiating the concept of 'agency' into its multiplicity of forms. Similarly, the continuum of 'structure' as *systems* and 'structure' as *processes* is an attempt to explore a long-standing issue in organizational theory: how does one account for the reciprocal relations between perceived order and ongoing change? Or more precisely, how can the apparent analytical asymmetry between organizational structures (systems) be reconnected with organizational changes (processes)?

If it is possible to rethink the old dichotomy between stasis and change, what implications does this have for understanding agency? Most attempts to capture the nature of organizational structure have used atemporal or static categories allied to system ontologies and realist epistemologies (Luhmann 1995). In contrast, many attempts to explore organizational change tend to use temporal categories allied to process ontologies and 'interpretative' models of action (Giddens 1984). Atemporal structural categories are often very misleading because they can lead to essentialist ideas of societies or organizations as purely mechanistic, systemic or functional entities outside of time or history (Parsons 1951). Systems are external structures 'out there'. Introducing change into this reading of structure usually becomes a mechanistic exercise at overlaying change on to structure. Change inevitably becomes identified with linear, multi-linear or broader evolutionary patterns of change defined by causal events, predictive movements or teleological processes leading from one stable stage or state to another (Van de Ven and Poole 1995). Parsons' (1951) structural-functional theory is a classic example of structure as system entity and change as 'moving equilibrium'.

Attempts to avoid a realist notion of structure as a system entity with hypothetical properties usually gravitate towards an ontological view of structuring or 'structuration' as a temporal process: as the activity of organizing (Giddens 1984). Giddens' work is a powerful expression of this position and it is animated by a consistent hostility to the atemporal nature of systems ideas. This viewpoint makes sense in capturing the processual nature of organizational structure. However, the analysis of organizational change using temporal categories can be misleading because they define change as a seamless and continuous process of interaction that situates the past and present, the before and after, in ongoing processes of becoming (Chia 1999). Taken to its logical conclusion, process-based ideas of temporality can lead to concepts of social and organizational change as always emergent processes created by perpetual change and always open to the future (Giddens 1984). Ontologically this understanding of temporality is sound, but epistemologically it is vacuous; it invariably defines change as constant and indivisible, but it does not explain when, how or why change occurs. Recent attempts to define change as 'becoming' have therefore ended in attempts to replace a systems ontology of structure with a process ontology of change (Chia 1999; Tsoukas and Chia 2002). Taken to its extreme the ontological opposition of systems and processes amounts to a recipe for futile rhetoric and polemic.

One way out of this dilemma is to argue that static and temporal categories are not either/or choices. Ontologically systems and processes are inseparable, but epistemologically they can be analytically differentiated in developing a temporal theorizing of 'structure' that can accommodate both continuity and discontinuity. The schematic continuum of *structure as systems* and *structure as processes* is an attempt to do this. Organizational structure–organizational change is conceived as the temporal interplay between systems and processes, continuity and discontinuity. Any adequate theory of organizational structure must by definition involve a theory of organizational change (Luhmann 1995: 347). In this sense, there is an intrinsic reciprocal relationship between structure as systems and structure as processes (Levi-Strauss 1966: 73).

Here systems and processes will be very broadly defined as follows.

Systems refer to the ordering of human social behaviour, action or meaning into relatively coherent or stable self-organizing patterns of recursive or iterative reproductive interaction which can be conceived as forming entities or 'objects' that can be classified and examined in terms of their hypothetical properties, boundaries, levels, inter-relationships and continuity over time. These systems and sub-systems may be conceived as consisting of highly integrated functional parts or forming loosely coupled networks within networks (Luhmann 1995). Systems can also be explored in terms of the relational properties of 'deep structures' in the form of language systems, rules, codes, symbols or signs (Levi-Strauss 1966). Overall, the analysis of systems is primarily concerned with synchronic issues of structural stability and continuity, although system models can accommodate evolutionary patterns of change as well as significant discontinuities (Parsons 1951).

Processes refer to the temporal, emergent and contextual patterning of interaction and communication between individuals and groups within and across internal and external organizational boundaries. These processes are invariably characterized by non-linearity, unpredictability and uncertainties with regard to outcome (Giddens 1984). The analysis of processes is primarily concerned with the contextual analysis of change as it unfolds through slow incremental transition processes over time, although process models of organizational change do sometimes include change that is bumpy, abrupt or transformational.

The idea of structure as an emergent property of systems *and* processes does not seek to resolve the debates over agency and structure. Instead, it makes it clear that structure as systems/processes are inseparable and that structure is not reducible to individual purposeful or intentional action. Conversely, it is an argument against the transformation of structures into purely realist system entities: structure is both/and, systems and processes; it oscillates between order and disorder, linearity and non-linear change. A more extended exploration of these ideas is provided elsewhere (Caldwell 2005b).

Conclusion

Giddens' work is a key reference point for any exploration of the agency–structure dichotomy in organizational theory and management practice (Whittington 1992; Reed 1997; Heracleous and Barrett 2001). For the purposes of this study, however, the dichotomy of agency and structure needs to be reconfigured by refocusing on the problematic relations between 'agency' and 'change'. This requires a differentiation of agency into a 'centred' and 'decentred' continuum and a re-conceptualization of 'structure' as consisting of both 'systems' and 'processes'. Implicit in this framework is the view that an adequate exploration of change agency must involve a theoretical clarification of organizational change.

Using the two continua of *centred agency–decentred agency* and *systems–processes* (see Figure 1, p. 5) it is possible to create a meta-theoretical framework for exploring four discourses that straddle different and competing disciplinary discourses within the social sciences about the nature of change agency and organizational change. The four discourses are classified as *rationalist, contextualist, dispersalist* and *constructionist*. Rationalist discourses give priority to centred agency, concepts of planned change and the possibilities of strategic action. Contextualist discourses focus on processes of 'emergent' change and the bounded nature of centred agency in organizations. Dispersalist discourses focus predominantly on systemic or self-organizing processes of learning in organizations, while giving autonomy to new forms 'conjoint agency', 'sensemaking', 'distributed leadership' and 'communities of practice' (Weick 2001; Wenger 1998). Constructionist discourses decentre human agency within discursive practices over which human actors appear to have little rational or intentional control.

The arrows in Figure 1 indicate that discourses are only nominally distinct; they emerge at the intersections of overlapping concepts. The map therefore has an essentially heuristic value, although it may serve a useful didactic purpose in reformulating discourses on change agency and organizational change.

The meta-theoretical framework is also important because it holds out the possibility of a narrative leading from long-standing disputes over rationalism and autonomous agency to current issues of mounting organizational complexity, chaos and the 'decentring of agency'. At this level, the issue of the directionality of organizational change can be conceptualized as a transition from debates over the nature of 'modernity' versus 'post-modernity' or 'first modernity' versus 'second modernity' (Beck 1992, 2000; Giddens 1990a). As these debates intensify, however, there is growing concern that 'agency' as a category may be lost in postmodernist explorations of subjectivity, self-reflexivity and identity (Lash 2003). While this book argues for an overall move away from the agency–structure dichotomy, it also argues for the need to retain more constrained, creative and contingent conceptions of agency related to change.

3 After Lewin, after modernism: rethinking change agency

- Introduction
- Rationality and change: from Lewin to Argyris
- Diffusing expertise: Schein on process consultation
- In search of autonomy
- Reflexivity: redefining knowledge and practice
- Conclusion: after Lewin, after modernism

Introduction

The idea of 'change agency' within the organizational development (OD) and action research traditions has its origins in the pioneering work of Kurt Lewin (1890–1947), the polymorphous founding father of experimental social psychology and small group research (1946, 1947, 1951). It was Lewin who first strongly advocated a new activist agenda for the researcher as a facilitator or consultant of group processes of rational persuasion and reflective practice, although the idea has gone through numerous transmutations within the various traditions of organizational development, action research and management consultancy practice (Tichy 1974; Armenakis and Bedeian 1999; Fincham 2001; Reason and Bradbury 2001; Kipping and Engwell 2002).

While many of Lewin's most influential ideas, such as 'planned change', 'resistance' and his ubiquitous three-fold model of unfreezing, changing and refreezing behaviour, have all been subject to reinterpretation or ridicule in almost equal measures, his concept of change agency has rarely been seriously addressed, either by his admirers or traditional critics (Burnes 2004). This is a curious omission. Change agency is central to Lewin's rationalist epistemology of action and reflexivity, his belief in expert knowledge as feedback, his commitment to rational persuasion and his overall goal to integrate theory and practice, science and action in the service of democratic values and ideals (Lewin 1997, 1999; Reason and Bradbury 2001).

As the OD tradition has developed, however, change agency as an overarching concept and mode of practice has become somewhat lost. The growing absorption of OD as a sub-field of change management and leadership theory, the proliferation of faddish intervention techniques, the focus on delivery, value and measures of effectiveness, and the overall downgrading of 'theory' as an appendage to consultancy practice and professional competency have all contributed to the gradual eclipse of a once valuable and potentially critical concept (Worren *et al.* 1999; Bradford and Burke 2004; Caldwell 2005a).

Compounding this neglect, most recent historical explorations of the OD field and its future have rarely mentioned change agency as a topic, and Lewin's legacy appears to have been safely canonized and forgotten. This seems all the more surprising in a context in which OD appears to be entering a 'crisis' over its disciplinary identity, academic validity, practical relevance and moral virtues (Bradford and Burke 2004). Against this background Greiner and Cummings (2004) have recently argued that it 'is the time for a serious reevaluation of OD and its future' (p. 383). It would appear, however, that the current internal re-evaluations of OD by its professional advocates does not really take historical reflection on the intellectual origins of the field very seriously. Certainly, there have been no attempts to explore the origins and theoretical limits of core OD concepts such as change agency.

A rethinking of change agency is central to any exploration of the current crisis facing OD. This requires that the present internal focus on practice issues and the normative rebuilding of disciplinary boundaries and self-defences needs to be broadened (Bradford and Burke 2004). One must ask more perplexing ontological and epistemological questions. Are Lewin's ideas of change agency still relevant or valid in a context where postmodernist and constructionist discourses have undermined ideas of 'agency' and the conceptual efficacy of theory and practice divides (Gergen 2003; Hardy 2004)? Is the appropriate starting point for an epistemology of agency 'I think' or 'I do': the rational reflection of intentional action or the iterative discourses of practice (Reason 2003: 113)? Can science or practice be reconciled or bridged in a concept of agency centred on an ideal of organizational change that is linear, rational and expert-based (Tsoukas and Chia 2002; Clegg *et al.* 2005)? Is there any possibility of objective self-reflection on 'practice' (Schön 1983)? Perhaps we should abandon a concept of reflexivity based on feedback between theory and practice and face up to the ontological insecurity that reflection on the presuppositions of knowledge and action is locked in interests, practices and rhetorical discourses that can never be epistemologically secure (Lash 2003)?

In this chapter the Lewinian legacy is critically re-examined, both through a close reading of his major writings and the major first generation 'modernist' interpreters of his work that have extended, revaluated or departed from his ideas, most notably, Argyris (1982), Schein (1988) and Schön (1983). Understanding the intellectual genealogy of ideas is important and the true greats of the OD tradition must be treated with regard rather than sidelined under the presumption that their work has been eclipsed by cumulative or additive disciplinary advancements. The overall focus, however, is not biographical or chronological; others have successfully traversed that historical territory many times, at least with respect to Lewin's work, although a convincing history of the OD tradition has yet to be written (Marrow 1969; Watson 1978; Cooke 1999; Metraux 1992; Kipping and Engwell 2002; Greiner and Cummings 2004). Nor is the concern to provide a re-appraisal of Lewin's influential ideas on planned change in the face of competing models (Burnes 2004). This is a well-worn path that usually leads to counterpoising models of organizational change as 'transformational', 'emergent' or 'processual' (Dumphy and Stace 1993; Pettigrew 1997). Instead, the analytical objective will be to clarify the theoretical limitations of Lewin's concept of change agency by exploring the four major conceptual components implicit in modernist discourses of 'centred agency': *rationality, expertise, autonomy and reflexivity.* These four overlapping components will provide the focus and sequence for a critical analysis that is both an exercise in intellectual genealogy and analytical investigation. The overall goal is to trace the origins and legacy of the key concept of change agency in the OD tradition and re-evaluate its significance after modernism.

Modernist or rationalist discourses of intentional or centred agency are still ubiquitous in the social sciences, whether they take the form of rational choice models, theories of individual action or models of economic behaviour (Smelser 1992; Barnes 2000). While these theories and models are enormously diverse, they tend to have four common elements: 1) *rational* behaviour or action as a universal conceptual construct tends to take priority over the exploration of the competing rhetorics, values and interests involved in the creation of knowledge; 2) it is assumed that social scientific knowledge and *expertise* are synonymous with the realist understanding of 'reality'; 3) the extension of *autonomy* as rational individual action and choice is identified with the goals of social scientific knowledge; 4) the exploration of *reflexivity* is limited to reflection on the methodological protocols of knowledge and professional expertise rather than an exploration of the underlying presuppositions and discursive constitution of social scientific knowledge (Johnson and Duberley 2003).

All four of these components are reproduced in various guises and disguises within Lewin's work and the various overlapping pathways of the OD and action research traditions. Each component will be critically examined.

Rationality. Lewin's rationalist conception of planned change as a process of movement from one relatively stable state to another facilitated by the intervention of a change agent is still prevalent in OD and the rhetoric of change management consultancy (Berglund and Werr 2000). This idea will be criticized because it is based on a system model of intentional action and reflective feedback that underplays the processual, non-linear and iterative nature of change. For Lewin (1997) the change agent is a rational actor who defines, directs and manages feedback during the implementation of change. Essentially what is missing from this model is a relational, interactional or broader practice/discourse-based understanding of organizational change as processes in which multiple change agents enact their own goals, interests or values as potentially autonomous actors in an open dialogue (Wenger 1998).

Expertise. Lewin's idea of the change agent or 'action researcher' as an expert who can rationally and objectively explicate the relationship between knowledge and action is based on a model of research *into* action that treats the value presuppositions of knowledge as unproblematic. Lewin (1999) assumed that the objectivity of scientific knowledge as democratic knowledge is given. This carries the ever-present danger within the OD and action research traditions of transforming democratic virtues and liberal humanism into rationalist dogmatism – the one best way of designed or planned change. Despite attempts by later OD practitioners to moderate the epistemological uncertainties of knowledge and action by an explication of 'double-loop learning' (Argyris 1976) and the process dynamics of the 'consultant-client relationship' (Schein 1988), OD has been unable to formalize an ideal of democratic knowledge creation. Instead, an ideal of participative involvement as a form of democracy in action is increasingly subordinated to the intervention techniques of organizational change management with the result that genuine discursive 'communities of inquiry' cannot emerge (Reason 2003: 106).

Autonomy. Because Lewin's model of centred agency implicitly gives more autonomy to change agents, leaders and managers in setting group ends and values, it undermines concepts of individual self-determination and choice: *the possibilities of knowledgeable agents to act otherwise* (Giddens 1984: 256). The danger of making autonomy an outcome of intentionality is that it reduces the possibilities of choice to the rational autonomy of action: it is turned into what it was meant to be a counterforce against – the arbitrary or irrational use of coercion, power or domination. Paradoxically, irrationality as choice and 'resistance to change' becomes the counterforce against which change agents within the OD tradition must struggle to affirm their rationalist ideals and democratic ethos (Argyris 1982). This paradox has been almost completely lost as OD morphs into change management consultancy.

Reflexivity. Lewin the epistemological rationalist could not conceive of a decentring of agency within action research, conceived as dialogue or discourse, and so his model of reflexivity as feedback *from* practice is purely a methodological tool that never resolves the theory and practice divide that is the central ambition of all his work. This difficulty is reproduced in the OD and action research traditions as tensions between *epistemologies of knowledge* and *epistemologies of practice* (Schein 1988; Schön 1995). Despite the erosion of positivist modes of inquiry these tensions are still very much alive and they continue to revolve around notions of instrumental knowledge versus participative models of agency (Schein 2002; Bradford and Burke 2005). They are unlikely to be resolved, however, unless OD and action research practices can fuse processes of 'knowing' and 'doing' as discourses of knowledge within potential communities of inquiry (Reason 2003: 110).

It will be concluded that Lewin's ideal of change agency as centred agency is no longer sustainable. It leads to reinforcing ideas of *rationality, expertise, autonomy* and *reflexivity* that cannot resolve the new challenges posed to the OD and action research traditions. From within these traditions existing claims to mediate theory and practice look increasingly problematic; partly because they remain tied to a subject–object *episteme* of knowledge production and participative involvement, and partly because professional practice rarely matches up to an ideal that is both objective and democratic – there is always an intrinsic tension between 'objectivity and solidarity' (Rorty 1995: 28). Reinforcing these challenges, the precarious boundaries of the OD tradition are now beginning to implode in the face of disparate consultancy practices that allow instrumental technique, rhetoric and power to legitimize claims to expertise (Kipping and Engwell 2002). If the OD and to a lesser extent the action research traditions are to find a new model of change agency they must rethink the dualisms of subject–object, research–practice, knowledge–action that have plagued their understanding of agency and change for decades (Nowotny *et al.* 2001; Reason and Bradbury 2001; Worley and Feyerherm, 2003). They must begin a synthetic search for new practice-based, distributive and dispersed models of decentred agency, rational inquiry, moral discourse and knowledge creation.

Rationality and change: from Lewin to Argyris

Lewin's work created a framework for a profoundly rationalist approach to change agency and organizational change. All three of his core concepts of 'force field analysis', 'group dynamics', and 'action research' involved an overriding search for a rational and participative methodology of behavioural change (Lewin 1997, 1999). These ideas have, however, often been misrepresented and misinterpreted by Lewin's critics and admirers (Burke 2002).

Force field analysis, borrowed primarily from analogies of physical systems, was based on the assumption that group behaviour is held in a 'state of quasi-stationary equilibrium' by a constellation of equal and opposite dynamic forces that can be measured in terms of their strength and direction (Lewin 1999: 34). These relatively stable structures of group behaviour form homeostatic systems that can be subject to change by processes of rational interventions operating through *negative* or compensating feedback mechanisms.

While this model allows Lewin to explore 'change and constancy as relative concepts', it also allows him to conceive of feedback as a way of indirectly pushing a fluid and changeable system towards a rational goal. At its most schematic, negative feedback entails comparing the current state of a behavioural system to a desired state, and then moving the system in a linear direction that minimizes the differences between the two. In effect, change is a linear or evolutionary transition process in which one state of quasi-stationary equilibrium is sequentially replaced by another (Van de Ven and Poole 1995).

The idea of system change as a linear or evolutionary process also decisively informed Lewin's three-stage process of 'unfreezing, moving and refreezing' behaviour into a new quasi-stationary state: 'by adding forces in the desired direction or by diminishing opposing forces' (1999: 280). Formalized within the OD tradition this idea of intended change has become synonymous with various multi-phase models for matching 'recommended phases/steps for change agents to follow in implementing change (i.e. phases within which change agents act) with stages in understanding change (i.e. stages through which change targets progress)' (Armenakis and Bedeian 1999: 304). Organizational development models of planned organizational change therefore tend to conceive of the change 'process' as the explicit realization of rational goals (Berglund and Werr 2000).

An evolutionary concept of quasi-stationary equilibrium also underpins Lewin's idea of 'resistance' to change as a dynamic within a system of forces: 'Only by relating the actual degree of constancy to the strength of forces toward or away from the present state of affairs can one speak of degrees of resistance or stability of group life in a given respect' (Lewin 1947: 13–14). Essentially, resistance is a systems concept that allows Lewin to conceive patterns of continuity and discontinuity within relatively static structures of group behaviour (Dent and Galloway Goldberg 1999). In this respect, behavioural change is not conceived as intrinsically emergent or processual, but rather as a planned process requiring the intervention of a change agent who acts to steer the process of incremental change towards a predefined end. Ultimately, Lewin's rational systems model of linear change is expert-centred in that the 'change agent' or action researcher acts as a feedback mechanism ensuring sequential transitions between states of stability while helping to diffuse or dissipate resistance.

Most interpreters of Lewin's work have consistently ignored the system presuppositions that underpin his three-phase model of change, as well as the rationalism that informs his concept of change agency as a feedback mechanism (Bradford and Burke 2005). This has serious consequences in exploring the ambitions of Lewin's theoretical enterprise, for without an integrative overview it is very difficult to offer an appreciation of the holistic scope and eclectic range of Lewin's interests, as well as the limitations of his work.

One illuminating example of the narrow reading of Lewin's work is the lack of focus on his psychological interpretation of human agency; still a common feature of OD as a theory of personal change and organizational learning (Senge 2003). It is often forgotten that the close integration between Lewin's systems-based model of change and his concept of the change agent as expert arises from a profoundly rationalist view of human agency that lacks psychological depth or ambiguity with regard to meaning, learning or identity (Bradford and Burke 2004: 370). This is perhaps most evident when one compares Lewin's model of the change agent as expert with Freud's psychoanalytical conceptions of the analyst–patient relationship.

In Freud's (1968 [1938]) work the patient mentally and symbolically refers to the analyst as 'the subject that is supposed to know': the person who knows what is happening to them, why it is happening, and how they can be cured (p. 174). Yet Freud's 'meta-psychology' also incorporated an interest in patient 'self-discovery', and this went beyond the purely specialist remit of expert knowledge, although he warned against treating the analyst as helper, adviser or teacher (Freud 1968 [1938]: 174–5). For Freud the analytic relationship is not just founded on a doctor–patient dynamic, but it is also based on a relationship between two autonomous and knowledgeable individuals, one who can enable the other to express their rational understanding of unconscious desire.

Freud's prescriptive ideal of knowledge and expertise as both a means of 'cure' and a mode of rational self-enlightenment is at the core of Lewin's concept of the change agent. However, Lewin the experimental psychologist was strongly critical of Freud's psychoanalytic methodology. He rejected psychoanalysis because he believed it offered purely historical explanations of behaviour that lacked scientific rigour; Freud did not offer systematic theoretical concepts, operationalized through experimental procedures that would establish 'general laws'. For Lewin it is not the psychoanalytical history of the 'unconscious' that influences behaviour but only the 'existing facts' of behaviour in the present, and these can be subject to change through experimental procedures and participative discussion (1999: 69). In Lewin's judgement, if one accepts psychoanalytic theory 'one would have to assume an immense rigidity of acquired structures within a living being' (Lewin 1999: 70). He argues instead that it is only current behaviours and 'conscious experience' that really matter, and these can be changed by group behaviour. For Lewin this means that the dialogue between analyst and patient could be transposed into potentially consensus-seeking 'group processes' that encouraged 'rational' decision-making or goal-directed action and learning. This amounts to an essentially phenomenological inspired exploration of various forms of 'discursive' and 'practical' consciousness, thereby undermining any concern with motives and especially unconscious motivation – both are common features of rationalist

constructs of intentional agency (Giddens 1984: 7). Moreover, by
identifying rationality with both individual and group behaviour, Lewin
appeared to offer a practical synthesis of individual–group dynamics that
avoided Freud's association of the individual with rationality and the
collective with 'irrationality' (Freud 1972 [1921]). It is in this sense that
one can understand Lewin's emphatic claim near the end of his life that:
'Freud was wrong and Marx was right' (Watson 1978: 178).

One must, of course, treat this provocative claim with considerable
caution. Lewin may have placed more emphasis on 'group dynamics' and
system-based concepts rather than individualism, but his work does not
explore 'social fields' of collective behaviour using structural or
organizational concepts, except in an incidental manner, and he certainly
has no concept of collective agency (Lewin 1999: 34). More importantly,
despite his rejection of psychoanalysis the tensions within Freud's
methodology between analyst and patient were reproduced in Lewin's
work and the instrumental problem-solving logic of action research. For
although the processes of group dynamics were participatory, they could
not be managed without the 'expert' intervention of the trained facilitator
or 'change agent'. This created an epistemological asymmetry between
the individual or group as an 'object' of investigation set apart from the
investigator (Danziger 1990). The history of organizational development
theory and practice is a history of repeated failures to come to terms with
the ambiguities and paradoxical nature of 'change agency' as both an
expert or rational intervention and an 'emancipatory' or democratic
process of group involvement that challenges irrationality, power and
injustice (Greiner and Cummings 2004: 384).

After Lewin one of the most dramatic illustrations of the persistent
tensions between change agency as rational intervention and
emancipatory practice are to be found in the seminal work of Chris
Argyris (1982, 1985, 2003). Argyris (1985) was both directly and
indirectly influenced by Lewin's legacy, and especially his moral
imperative to further the causes of democracy and social justice (Bokeno
2003). Like many of the early leading figures of the OD tradition,
Argyris was above all a rational moralist.

In recently summing up the *vita contemplative* of his distinguished
academic career, Argyris states boldly that his research began with 'a
dedication to reducing injustices' and creating 'liberating alternatives'
within organizations: 'I assumed that justice and seeking truth
represented unbounded good' (2003: 1178). He discovered, however, that

these goals were constantly frustrated and threatened by human behaviour:

> If people create injustices when they are trying to prevent them or to reduce them, then people must be skilled at producing the very conditions that they abhor. If they are skilled at reducing their liberating alternatives, then they are skilled at producing inner contradictions.
>
> (Argyris 2003: 1179)

In effect, people create defensive routines and 'self-sealing patterns of escalating error' that ensure stable and change-resistant systems of behaviour (Argyris 1985: 61).

Argyris was deeply perplexed by defensive routines not only because they blocked positive change, but also because they called into question the foundations and validity of rational inquiry and rational persuasion. By acting in an apparently unpredictable and irrational manner through self-censorship people indulge in self-deception. But unlike Lewin who sought to partly resolve 'resistance to change' through system-based processes of participative group dialogue, Argyris locates the primary sources of resistance within the cognitive construct of a 'defensive reasoning mindset' (2003). It is this mindset that appears as the central threat to rational inquiry:

> If people can choose to be unpredictable, then how will we ever develop a science of human action which can predict and generalise? What makes this dilemma solvable is that people cannot normally be unpredictable to themselves ... Behind every major action is a process of reasoning, no matter how automatic and spontaneous the action appears to be ... Our task therefore is to discover the reasoning processes people use to make themselves unpredictable.
>
> (Argyris 1982: 14)

To discover reasoning within the unpredictable and intentionality within the unintended consequences of human action, Argyris (1976, 1982) draws two classic distinctions, one between 'single-' and 'double-loop' learning and the other between explicit or 'espoused theories' of action and tacit 'theories-in-use' that appear to exist outside of rational awareness. In single-loop learning people are trapped in their defensive routines of 'skilled incompetence and skilled unawareness' and so they cannot progress towards double-loop learning which explores new possibilities for effective action (Argyris 2003: 1184). This form of learning is both normative and prescriptive because it maintains that insights and explanations are connected with practical action that produces particular effects. Similarly, Argyris (2003) maintained that rational inquiry into tacit theories-in-use, rather than espoused or rhetorical theories, could yield universal cause–effect explanations of why human actors in organizations, no matter what their position in the hierarchy, 'produce the same counterproductive consequences'. For example, managers espouse rational theories of strategic action and open dialogue, but they engage in processes of collusion, self-deception and cover-up that subvert rationality. By discovering these omnipresent patterns of single-loop learning and the fundamental causality of theories-in-use, Argyris (1982) believes that he can make organizations and human action more rational, more predictable, and more subject to desirable change.

Paradoxically, however, the defensive routines of single-loop learning and espoused theories are also embedded in the 'normal science' models of expert knowledge:

> It is the researchers who are in unilateral control over the methods used; who define the criteria of victory; and who design research conditions that minimize the expression of feelings, especially of doubt, bewilderment, and at times anger at being dominated by researchers in the name of validity.
>
> (Argyris 2003: 1182)

Nevertheless, Argyris maintains that his methodological ideal of double-loop learning and action research as a form of privileged self-reflection on practice will allow forms of participative inquiry to emerge that have scientific validity. The practitioner as change agent somehow becomes a mechanism for redesigning 'mental models' by exposing the disjunction between what people and researchers say they are doing and what is *really* guiding their behaviour: the defensive reasoning mindsets within both organizations and the research process itself. For Argyris the participative dimension of action research is not a fundamental challenge to objective validity, but a reaffirmation of the foundations of action science.

While Argyris's either/or dichotomies of behaviour appear to leave more room for the unpredictable, irrational and emotional as well as for self-reflection on practice, they represent an even stronger embrace of rationalism than envisaged by Lewin. If Lewin had a flat, one-dimensional notion of the human personality, Argyris overlays this with a developmental notion of subjectivity as a cognitive-psychological mechanism of learning and goal-directed rational action. This extends the scope of rationality further by arguing that the unpredictable (i.e. the irrational) can be made transparent through the retrieval of the 'hidden programs' or the real foundations of defensive behaviours. With this cognitive and explanatory notion of rational action as centred agency that can be made transparent in predictable patterns, Argyris identifies action science with expert knowledge of the causality of human behaviour. His methodological project therefore becomes an attempt to uncover the existence of defensive reasoning, discovering its causes and outcomes through the meticulous and forensic exploration of human beings as skilled incompetents involved in their own self-deception (Argyris 1982). But by identifying rationality with an epistemological ideal of effective and predictable action counterpoised against the unpredictable, Argyris (2003) is in constant danger of treating defensive reasoning as irrational resistance and thereby undermining the critical scope of reflexivity. In this respect, Argyris again goes further than Lewin in allowing expertise a privileged status in defining how theory relates to practice, and science to action.

The relentless drive of Argyris's work towards prescriptive rationalism partly explains the curious mix of dogged optimism and realistic pessimism that runs through his work. He affirms ideals of reason and the possibility of 'actionable knowledge' grounded in moral values, but he is constantly frustrated by 'skilled incompetence' as a rhetorical counter-image: *why are people not rational, why do they not learn?* This tension may also explain why Argyris's work has invoked contradictory evaluations: 'I have had many experiences where the positivist saw me as being too humanistic and where the humanist saw me as a closet positivist' (Argyris 2003: 1189). Like Lewin, his intellectual progenitor, Argyris is both, a humanist and a positivist. But with more faith in science and a methodology for unmasking defensive routines rather than trust in group behaviour or involvement, he states a stronger case for expert knowledge over participation. As a consequence his work marks a continuation of and break with Lewin's work. In Argyris's action science the OD tradition begins to lose not only its faith in unbounded reason and unbounded good, but also its faith in change agency as a form of action and involvement that will produce liberating alternatives.

Diffusing expertise: Schein on process consultation

Although the concept of the change agent as expert (or action researcher) offering rational persuasion or objective knowledge has its fateful origins in Lewin's work, it has gradually been differentiated and reformulated within the OD tradition to cover a whole array of expert interventions in the management of a change effort (Beckhard 1969; Burke 2002). Some of these interventions are technical while others emphasize the role of the consultant as educator, analyst or counsellor. As the OD tradition has evolved, however, a growing tension has emerged between instrumental models of expertise and the ideal of the consultant as 'helper' involved in transferring expertise to the client. This tension is prefigured in Lewin's work, but it is rarely examined in terms of its central problematic: the conflict between change agency as a participative activity that diffuses expertise and an expert-centred ideal of consultancy practice (Kipping and Engwell 2002). Instead, many OD practitioners often ignore this conflict or assume a pragmatic stance towards practice.

One of the few serious attempts to partly address the issue of transferring or diffusing expertise, at least indirectly, has been proposed by Schein (1988, 2002), especially in his later work. As a first generation OD practitioner Schein's work grew out of a desire to counteract scientific management and static bureaucratic models of organizational life, although he was never averse to seeing the harsh instrumental connection between rational persuasion, behavioural change and expertise (Schein 1961). What is intriguing, however, is that Schein's later work has become synonymous with a paradigmatic process-oriented model of consultancy intervention contra-expertise that emphasizes a 'helping' role of the change agent, yet this role is still strongly grounded in a normative commitment to expert intervention techniques. Somehow Schein (1996) appears to fuse process consultation, expertise, management learning, and change agency in a potent mix. Even though process interventions have evolved within the OD tradition to cover an increasingly disparate variety of expert techniques, the idea that the consultant can help or empower the client to lead and manage change is still an enormously important focal point of OD and many action research interventions as specialist forms of change management practice (Dickens 1998; Schein 2002; Worley and Feyerherm 2003). Despite this continued influence, however, one central interpretative question remains unanswered in Schein's work: does he allow for the possibility of 'agency' to emerge from the dialogue between participants or is it circumscribed by the expert intervention techniques and rhetoric of the process consultant?

When Schein begins to define the remit of the process consultant role in his major two-volume study of *Process Consultation* (1987, 1988) he strongly emphasizes the importance of client self-awareness: 'The process consultant seeks to give the client insight into what is going on around him, within him and between him and other people' (1988: 11). To achieve these insights the process consultant must become involved in 'process consultation', defined as 'a set of activities on the part of the consultant that helps the client to perceive, understand, and act upon the process events that occur in the client's environment'(1988: 11). Schein suggests, however, that this helping relationship is less traditionally expert-centred (e.g. doctor–patient) in that the consultant seeks to act as an 'unbiased' facilitator positively involved in consultative or consensus-seeking interventions based on feedback and group ownership. Ultimately, the aim of process consultation is to help the client gain the expertise and skills to solve their own problems (Schein 1988: 19). In this sense the attributes required in this process role are broadly synonymous with the soft techniques of 'process consultation': listening, providing feedback, counselling, coaching, and inter-group dynamics, rather than instrumental knowledge (Schein 1988: 11). Moreover, although the process relationship may unfold in planned stages (e.g. entering, data gathering, diagnosis), the process consultant is also preoccupied with reducing involvement, terminating the consulting relationship and avoiding client dependence – at least in principle.

But is Schein's formulation of process consultation really an adequate model for participation and the diffusion of expertise? Does he locate change agency in the *processes of participation* or the *expert intervention techniques* employed by the process consultant? In other words, is agency an emergent aspect of 'process consultation' as dialogue or discourse or is 'agency' an intentional category of expert intervention?

In Lewin's work these questions are unresolved, if less problematic, because the tensions between knowledge and participation are partly subsumed by his overarching faith in science and his systems model of the change process. But once the invariably non-linear processes of process consultation rather the linear stages of the change process (i.e. unfreezing, change and refreezing) or expert knowledge becomes the object of investigation and self-reflection the issue becomes much more perplexing and confusing. Schein partly recognizes this difficulty. In particular, he highlights the inherent dangers of assuming that consulting interventions only occur after data gathering or diagnostic stages: 'The correct assumption is that every act on the part of the process consultant – even the initial act of deciding to work with the organization – constitutes an intervention' (1988: 142).

Yet despite Schein's heightened awareness of the complexity of intervention, he leaves many questions unresolved. It is often unclear, for example, if Schein places his faith in the expert techniques of process consultation because he believes the process consultant has a specific theory of organizational change, or simply because he has a workable set of process techniques, including a rhetoric of rational persuasion (Berglund and Werr 2000). At other times, the role of the process consultant as change agent appears to emerge within the normative-participative or discursive relationship between client and consultant rather than as an activity grounded in expert knowledge or process techniques (Schein 1988: 48). Alternatively, if the process consultant uses participative techniques purely because they are assumed to be instrumental techniques that work, this may simply reinforce a pragmatic relationship of expert dependence (Berglund and Werr 2000: 636). Further confounding these unresolved questions, Schein (1988) appears to pursue process consultation techniques not because they are justified or verified by causal efficacy or measures of effectiveness, but because they amplify a prescriptive ideal of rationality. In this respect, Schein appears to be implicitly restating the system presuppositions of the OD tradition from Lewin onwards: measures of effectiveness are secondary because the functioning of systems of behaviour is a pre-given normative construction that requires no formal justification.

Curiously, Schein often appears oblivious to these broader issues and he is notably less concerned with question of self-reflection than other OD practitioners, even though he makes the intervention process the 'object' of investigation. Process consultation appears transparent, even resistance-free, despite the fact that it is an ongoing accomplishment concerned with unmasking distorted communication and negative interpersonal dynamics (Schein 1988). In contrast, when Argyris (1982) ponders expertise he is concerned with how experts can push previously acquired mental models, knowledge and techniques below the surface of self-awareness, so that they become undiscussable or unquestionable – effectively blocking double-loop learning. This danger applies with equal force to Schein's work. If change agents as process consultants automate their expertise in taken-for-granted techniques of intervention they too can become trapped in single-loop learning. Unfortunately, Schein does not face up to the difficulty of breaking out of this vicious cycle of reflexivity, by questioning his rhetoric of expertise or his rationalist commitment to 'process consultation'.

Despite his pioneering focus on 'process', Schein's work appears to end up in an unsatisfactory reflexive cul-de-sac. For although he emphasizes transferring or diffusing expertise to the client, the process consultant still operates in an expert-consultancy or diagnostic role, partly because he instrumentalizes process and partly because the organizational development practitioner must be able to demonstrate general consultancy skills and an instrumental knowledge of OD tools and techniques (Cummings and Worley 2005). How does Schein end up in this curious position of positively affirming the transfer of expertise while restating a powerful case for expert knowledge? There are perhaps two main reasons, and again their intellectual genealogy stretches directly back to Lewin's model of organizational change and change agency.

First, Schein claims that his model of process consultation is founded on the view that 'all organizational problems are fundamentally problems involving human interactions and processes' (1988: 12). This partly explains why he rejects 'static' structural models of organizational change interventions that focus only on implementing changes to formalized roles, functional levels or routine procedures. Nevertheless, Schein does not abandon a system model of organizational change or a functionalist reading of 'organizational culture'. Rather, he identifies 'process' with 'systems' or structures of behaviour independent of their interactional, processual or discursive properties: 'it is possible to abstract the interpersonal processes evident in a group independent of the actual people in these processes' (1988: 17). And he adds: 'These processes of relating to others have a decisive influence on outcomes and must themselves become objects of diagnosis and intervention if any organization improvement is to occur …' (1988: 17). Moreover, if these processes are repeatable or stable as 'structured processes' then it is possible to distinguish them from more transient processes characterized by instability or discontinuity. For example, 'organizational culture' forms a repetitive system of structured processes and functional symbols defining prevailing attitudes, values and conventional expectations of interpersonal behaviour (Schein 1990a). While this allows an exploration of the 'processes' of repetitive behaviour within system entities and the use of symbols by leaders to facilitate change, it does not lead to an exploration of how these ongoing processes of behaviour come into being or change over time (Tsoukus and Chia 2002). The truncated theoretical logic of this problem is again set up in Lewin's system models of group dynamics, planned change and the rationality of human behavioural change, but Schein's methodology of process consultation does not resolve the issues. Essentially what is missing in Schein's rationalist and system-based model of process consultation is any sense of how participants interact in constantly enacting new forms of behaviour rather than simply acting out pregiven roles or system goals. In this sense his work lacks a theory of practice.

Second, because the expertise of the process consultant reproduces the epistemological asymmetry between the system of observed repetitive behaviour and the people within it, the consultant operates as a feedback mechanism outside the system, yet is still able to treat feedback as an 'object' (i.e. process) of disinterested intervention (Ulrich 2003). The implications of this model of process consultation are made clear when Schein claims that clients are analogous to actors fulfilling pregiven roles while the process consultant remains off-stage as a mere observer. Schein also argues that as the drama of process consultation unfolds, the process consultant must be able to re-write their scripts according to the 'stream of feedback signals they get from their clients' (Schein 1987: 82). Again, what is missing from this model of process consultation is the iterative idea of process as 'becoming', as an ongoing mode of discourse, improvisation, practice, and meaning creation between potentially equal participants in an open dialogue. In this respect, the absence of a theory of practice in Schein's work is reinforced by the absence of a theory of how inclusive dialogue unfolds.

The unresolved tensions between change agency as a dialogue enacted in practice versus a model of expert knowledge and intervention techniques have rarely been seriously explored within the OD tradition (Tichy 1974; Armenakis and Bedeian 1999). At first reading Schein's work appears enormously promising in this regard because it envisages the diffusion of expertise to the client: change agency can be a participative and iterative activity rather than a purely expert-centred process. But Schein still maintains that the process consultant's theory, methods and intervention techniques are autonomous objects that exist outside the discursive relationships and performative practices involved in the change process. Just as the process consultant can be separated from the observed 'structured processes' of organizational behaviour, so the 'process consultation' process can be treated as an object of expert diagnosis and intervention. In effect, Schein's model of process consultation is the formalization within consultancy practice of Lewin's instrumental model of *change agency* as intentional action, rational expertise and system change, rather than an exploration of its potentially participative and discursive counter-image: the interpersonal exploration of the processual, relational and practice-based aspect of human agency as discourse, narrative or dialogue. It is no surprise then that Schein's model of process consultation is under-theorized: it provides a limited model of the diffusion of expertise and says very little about broader issues of rationality, autonomy and reflexivity. With Schein's work a powerful template was set for the implosion of the OD tradition into a disparate set of instrumental process techniques and design tools (Schein 2002). The consequences of this are most clearly apparent in the continued (although not irreversible) slide of the OD tradition into a 'tool kit' for practitioners (Worley and Feyerherm 2003: 113).

In search of autonomy

Within the OD tradition 'rational autonomy of action' or the classic issue of individual rational choice appears to be invested primarily in the change agent as expert and in the practice-oriented models of action research. As a consequence, there is limited discussion of the expansion of rational autonomy by knowledge or the ability of individuals freely to choose rational ends: both key requirements of a concept of agency and change (Giddens 1984). This curious absence can partly be traced back to Lewin in which the rationality of the group takes precedence over the individual as an explanatory framework, and choice is reduced to potentially participative methods of group learning towards a predetermined end circumscribed by the change agent. Effectively, autonomy can be subsumed by the idea that ends are given: human choice is synonymous with objective knowledge made transparent through rational persuasion within the context of group dynamics. This idea is also evident in the various stands of the OD tradition which appear to suggest that autonomous individuals and groups operating within learning organizations freely choose ends in relation to holistic goals or transcendent ends. For example, Senge (2003) identifies autonomy with 'commitment' to shared values or overarching moral ideals, although he allows leaders to exercise self-determination by setting goals for others – a theme that is replayed continually within the OD tradition (Bennis 1969; Schein 1990a). But if individuals, rather than leaders or change agents, have limited autonomy to choose ends and organizations or groups are not simply systems with pregiven goals (e.g. adapativeness, rational consensus), then the neutral benevolence of OD as a participative methodology of behavioural change becomes fundamentally problematic.

This issue raises a central question: what precisely is the goal of OD as an experimental science of practice, *persuasion or empowerment*? If it is only rational persuasion, then the OD tradition may be in danger of becoming purely an instrumental technique of control with agendas set by others: leaders, managers or consultants. This self-abnegation would also leave it with very little to say on the vast range of moral issues raised by its expert ideal of scientific practice. For the continuum of persuasion can lead from rationality to coercion, and all sorts of congeries in between – including ideological manipulation.

Alternatively, if OD and action research are identified with empowerment then they become a potential mechanism for 'joint consultations' or 'communities of inquiry' within an agreed ethical framework (Reason and Bradbury 2001; Reason 2003). This would appear to partly concur with Lewin's inspiring but vague notion of action research as a microcosm of a free and democratic society, a sort of mini-theory of participation and consensus in operation.

> The only hope ... for a permanent foundation of successful social management, and particularly for a permanent democratic society of the common man, is a social management based to a high degree on a scientific insight which is to be accessible to the many.
>
> (Lewin 1999: 334)

But this admirable liberal ambition often remains oblique and it appears unrealistic without a definition of what 'autonomy' is. Only in the most idealized forms can OD and action research offer rational consensus-seeking interventions within 'orders of democracy' free of manipulation, power or coercion (Gergen 2003).

The uncomfortable complicity between reason, persuasion and coercion is rarely mentioned in the historiography of the OD and action research traditions, but it constantly reappears in new and sometimes insidious forms (Cooke 1999; Schein 1999). One of the most illuminating and disturbing illustrations of the dark side of reason can be found in Schein's early work on *Coercive Persuasion* (1961): a minor, if long-forgotten classic. This study grew out of his investigations of Chinese Communist Party techniques of ideological indoctrination and brainwashing of Western prisoners during the Korean war (Cooke 1999). Some of these indoctrination techniques had uncomfortable affinities with OD practices. Schein recognized this overlap between rational persuasion and rational coercion in his interpretation of various OD techniques of behavioural change, but he valiantly sought to draw a realist distinction between means and ends:

> I am not drawing these parallels in order to condemn some of our approaches, rather my aim is just the opposite. I am trying to shown that Chinese methods are not so mysterious, not so different and not so awful, once we separate the awfulness of the communist ideology and look simply at the methods
>
> (1962: 97)

This distinction between 'bad' ideology and potentially 'good' rational technique is profoundly ambiguous precisely because Schein remains committed to a 'general theory of attitude change' that allows the change agent as expert to achieve desirable 'ideological change'. This scientific belief in a potentially neutral technique allows the change agent the illusion of a universal ideal that justifies the benevolence of a rational end; an end that can just as easily succumb to ideological manipulation.

Again the sources of this confusion over means and ideological ends, science and politics are apparent in Lewin's work. In one of his early, pre-war essays questioning the Tayloristic degradation of human labour through manipulation and control, he affirmed the possibility of a more positive reading of scientific management:

> Applied psychology could just as well put itself one-sidedly into the service of the humanization of labour, consider only beauty and convenience, and completely disregard the profitability of work. It is by nature merely a method that could serve any goal in changing work processes.
>
> (1999 [1920]: 308)

This belief in neutral technique becomes in Lewin's later work the positive moral imperative of the expert or leader who purses rational knowledge in the service of acceptable political ends. For example, in his post-war writings Lewin appears to believe that both the change agent and the democratic leader must exercise persuasion to further liberal democracy (Lewin 1948: 50). He has no doubt about the role of the democratic leader in 're-educating' post-war German society, just as he has few doubts about the role of action research as a form of positive 'social engineering'. Lewin therefore never appears to question the moral and practical goals of rationalism: 'to make fascists into democrats and Americans more tolerant of minorities' – a theme with disturbing contemporary resonance (Wetherall 1996: 43). What Lewin did not realise, however, is that such apparently self-evidently moral ends are in danger of ideological reversal without an ideal of autonomy that goes beyond the rationalism of scientific objectivity and expert knowledge. Those attempts to restore Lewin's 'left credentials' as if they were subverted by the OD canonization of his work should be wary of such complicity between objectivism, dogmatic reason and expertise (Cooke 1999; van Eltern 1992).

Schein's reinterpretation of Lewin's three-stage unfreeze/change/refreeze model of behavioural change reveals the dangerous possibilities of an expert-driven model of change in which 'choice' is problematic. At the core of this model is an idea of the individual self as an integrated sub-system of values, beliefs and attitudes within a force field of group

dynamics than can be systematically controlled. Unfreezing forces of
resistance to change within the personality not only becomes a process
of negative group feedback envisaged by Lewin, but a de-stabilizing of
the individual's self-image through psychological 'disconfirmation' and
'de-programming' (Lewin 1999: 281). This allows 'the creation of guilt
or anxiety … and the provision of psychological safety', effectively
breaking down the forces of resistance to change while allowing the
possibility of a new quasi-state of personality reintegration and system
stability to re-emerge. If this instrumental approach to change
contained for Lewin (1999: 279) the twin dangers of turning a
participative process towards 'high pressure methods' and means into
ends, the reality of changing behaviour for Schein is simply not
possible without coercion: 'What is cruel and coercive about this
process is the control which the agent of change exerts over the
individual in the process of undermining and destroying his social
supports' (1962: 97). Moreover, the move from 'unfreezing' to 'change'
is not possible without adding further potentially coercive forces in the
desired direction of change, although this tends to be identified with
the positive affirmation of new 'role models' or learning desired
behaviours, rather than an attack on resisting forces. Finally, Schein
conceives the refreezing stage as 'helping the client reintegrate the new
point of view into the total personality and self-conception' (1988: 93).
Just as Lewin has limited theoretical space for autonomy outside
system discourses of behavioural change and the feedback mechanisms
of group dynamics, so Schein appears to have no convincing concept of
choice that can conceive of rational persuasion free of coercion or
power.

These practical and moral dilemmas are still just below the surface of OD
practice, and they invoke different responses (Bradford and Burke 2005).
Some OD practitioners have almost inevitably fallen back on a positive
conflation of instrumental expertise and power:

> The OD consultant strives to use power that is based on rationality, valid
> knowledge, and collaboration and to discount power based on and channelled
> by fear, irrationality and coercion. The latter kind of power leads to
> augmented resistance to change, unstable changes, and dehumanised irrational
> conflicts.
>
> (Bennis 1969: 79)

In contrast, action research practitioners influenced more by collaboration
than knowledge have sought to stretch the participative ethos into
'communities of inquiry' defined by participative self-organization

processes of communication between equal partners in an open dialogue (Reason and Bradbury 2001). In these terms, Kemmis (1991, 2001) argues forcefully that in action research there is only room for equal participants:

> In genuinely critical action research, all participants must take on genuinely collaborative roles, as members of, not outsiders to, the research work, even if roles within groups are differentiated. The projects should be collaborative projects governed by open dialogue and decision making in a group committed to examining its own values, understanding, practices, forms of organization and situation
>
> (Kemmis 1991: 123)

But do either of these approaches stand up to critical scrutiny, do they really propose a credible principle of 'autonomy' that clarifies the possibility of choice within contexts defined by power and limited reflexivity (Rorty 1995: 28)? Just as it is dangerous to use power in the service of reason, so it is equally dangerous to assume that knowledge creation and collaboration are free from coercion (Reason 2003: 113).

Reflexivity: redefining knowledge and practice

Lewin's work was profoundly inspired by an attempt to rethink the theory and practice divide. He believed that the traditional divisions in the natural sciences between theoretical research and applied experimental methods were beginning to break down and this had far-reaching implications for the integration of social scientific inquiry (1947, 1999). What he envisaged was a fusion of science and practice that integrated research and practice through system-oriented feedback processes of reflexivity that transformed *research into action*. It is this ambition that was captured in Lewin's most often quoted and mis-quoted remark: 'There is nothing so practical as a good theory' (1999: 336).

During the golden era of applied behavioural science that began in the 1950s and lasted well into the 1970s, Lewin's mission for OD appeared to be reflected in the relatively close connection between research and practice (Bunker *et al.* 2004: 405). This all changed during the last two decades as the epistemological relationship between the object of research and the researcher began to fall apart (Johnson and Duberley 2003: 1281). Some OD researchers now worry that 'the field will continue to rely on knowledge derived from practice that is distinct from theory', while others believe that the 'widening gap' between academic researchers and practitioners interested in technique can be closed by a new focus on practical relevance (Worley and Feyerherm 2003: 108; Bunker *et al.* 2004: 419). Curiously, however, these emergent debates within the OD field have rarely engaged with the broader 'reflexive turn' (Weick 1999) of organizational theory and management research.

Although the idea of self-reflection, or in its modern guise, 'reflexivity', is important in Lewin's work it tends to be underdeveloped as a theoretical concept. There are two important reasons for this lack of theoretical clarification.

First, theory and research are conceived as a scientific enterprise for producing 'general laws' of behaviour and 'useful' knowledge that can be applied to practical social problems. The development of these laws and their application involve actions in the real world by individuals and groups concerned with promoting change. OD in the early forms of 'action research' therefore entailed a political commitment to desirable social change through the transformation of social scientific knowledge into practice. In these respects, Lewin had few doubts about the secure foundation of knowledge and its prescriptive application and so he never really felt the imperative to develop his notion of self-reflection on practice.

Second, the research process should in principle be participative, involving both the action researcher or change agent and the subjects of the change process. But because change as a linear process occurs within 'systems' of behaviour, the change agent performs a privileged feedback role in moving the system from one state to another. In this respect, the relationship between science and practice, knowledge-in-action and participation, change agents and their 'targets', rarely amounts to an equalization of participation.

While this twofold model conceives of research and practice as interpenetrating, it amounts to an essentially methodological model of reflexivity. For Lewin could not conceive of an insecure epistemology of knowledge or a decentring of agency within practice as a form of discourse. He simply believed that it is possible to develop knowledge and general laws that can be iteratively applied and tested as *theory into practice*. Just as the OD practitioner or action researcher as an autonomous agent can rationally explicate the relationship between knowledge and action on secure epistemological foundations, so the change agent as an autonomous feedback mechanism operating within functional systems of behaviour can facilitate the transition towards a desired end-state. Lewin had therefore no doubts about the objectivity and moral purpose of his enterprise and its social goals because he assumed that the rational presuppositions of science are given, and this self-certainty can be extended into objective self-reflection on practice. There is no need to purge science of its rationalist value presuppositions (i.e. objectivity) or practice of its moral ends (i.e. democracy) because these are both assumed as an unbounded and mutually reinforcing good.

What does this all mean for the scope of reflexivity? In the final analysis, Lewin's attempt to fuse a rationalist epistemological ideal of 'I think' with an epistemology of practice, 'I do', was unsuccessful. He gave reflexivity as rational self-reflection on knowledge a privileged role in knowledge production while he allowed the rational persuasion of the change agent as expert a pivotal role in legitimating knowledge through engagement with practice. In both cases, Lewin was reproducing a classical modernist notion of centred agency without leaving a space for self-reflective doubt regarding the presuppositions of knowledge and action, science and practice. This failure continues to haunt the organization development tradition in its search for a *modus operandus* to bridge the theory–practice divide (Bunker *et al.* 2004: 404).

Since Lewin's time the concept of reflexivity in the OD tradition has assumed many forms, but it still tends to be fundamentally Janus-faced: pointing in opposite directions towards epistemologies of knowledge and epistemologies of practice. If the link between knowledge and action, theory and practice is defined by scientific presuppositions, then the nature of reflection on change processes tends to follow the logic of 'instrumental problem solving made rigorous by the application of scientific theory and technique' (Schön 1995: 22). The change agent is primarily an expert providing reflexivity as knowledge in the form of feedback (Weick 2001: 400). If, however, the main focus is on practice or 'reflection in action', as in some models of action research, then the nature of change agency is conceived within an experimental methodology, iteratively moving back and forth between theory and practice. In this formulation the change agent is essentially a reflexive practical theorist committed to the service of theory to professional practice (Schön 1983).

Most OD practitioners, including some action researchers, tend to vacillate between these two invariably contradictory positions, although some have sought a fusion between science and practice in the notion of 'action science' that yields causal propositions and highly formalized techniques of reflexive practice – a hard position that harks back to Lewin's positivist reading of science (Argyris 1982: 14). In this instrumental formulation, the central goal of reflexivity is simply to reveal the causal nature of action and harness the capacity of human agents to make conscious rational choices to change their behaviour. Argyris (2003) is probably the most forceful representative of this tendency; although he argues strongly against the defensive reasoning embedded in normal science models of rigorous experimental research he remains a committed, if reluctant, positivist. But more paradoxically, while Argyris envisages the virtuous cycle of double-loop learning he does not extend this as a form of double-loop reflexivity to the nature of action science.

The absence of double-loop reflexivity reappears in various forms within the OD tradition. Even the apparently weaker or softer intervention techniques of the 'process consultant' proposed by Schein (1987) tend to involve a strongly rationalistic bias in that the practitioner is the scientist in action involved in and yet detached from both his subject and the diagnostics of practice. Schein may make the processes of intervention 'objects of diagnosis', and he may wish to diffuse expertise to the client, but his model strictly limits the scope of reflexivity. Essentially, the process consultant is still offering expert knowledge in both the objective-neutral manner of the interventions and the diagnostic tools applied (Schein 1988: 17).

Schön's classic work, *The Reflective Practitioner* (1983) appears to mark an important break with these ideas and the imprint of positivism, although this is rarely mentioned in the historiography of the OD tradition (Cummings and Worley 2005; Greiner and Cummings 2004). Schön (1995) claims that his enlightened model of the 'reflective practitioner' falls outside positivist methodologies of 'technical rationality', because it avoids universal generalizations, emphasizes the uniqueness of problems, and focuses on the enormous diversity of problem-solving practices. In this respect Schön shifts the focus of reflexivity towards epistemologies of practice and the more inclusive participative ideals of action research (Dickens 1998; Reason and Bradbury 2001). Yet Schön's focus on 'practice' tends to be developed as an epistemological critique of 'professional practice' in relation to the objectivity of 'normal' science, rather than a broader exploration of 'practice' as a relationship between knowledge and action, knowing and doing, that involves both the researcher and the researched.

> Professionals are in transaction with their practice worlds, framing the problems that arise, framing their roles and constructing practice situations to make their role frames operational. They hold reflexive conversations with the materials of

their situations and thus remake part of their practice world, revealing the
usually tacit processes of world-making that underlie all their practice.

(Schön 1983: 30)

While this amounts to a partial attempt to create a bridge between the
epistemological asymmetry of the individual or group as an object of
research set apart from the investigator, Schön is still operating with a
limited participant–observer concept of reflexivity as feedback from
practice that is fundamentally rationalistic in its understanding of the 'logic
of practice' (Bourdieu 1990). Wenger (1998) and other OD practitioners
have gone some way to address this practice deficit. But like Schön they
rarely go far enough in asking how reflexivity is created through practices
– practices which include the '*doxa*' or taken-for-granted discourses,
paradigmatic concepts and methodologies of professional practitioners.

If practice is to be adequately theorized then reflexivity has to go
beyond the methodological and professional protocols that will clarify
or enhance good practice. By focusing only on the reflexivity of the
reflective practitioner the ideal of an active self-reflective observer is
reinforced, while the ideal of the participants involved in knowledge
creation is pacified or marginalized. But the idea that the professional
practitioner can exercise autonomous rationality neutrally to scrutinize
the relationship between research practice and knowledge without
including the objects of the research is simply no longer tenable (Weick
1999; Johnson and Duberley 2003). Just as researchers are part of their
own data, so are the 'objects' of OD and action research: the
participants in the research process are reciprocally involved in the
constitution of what knowledge is as discourse. In this sense,
'knowledge/power' in the form of expertise presupposes knowledge of
the underlying practices and discourses through which it is produced
and reproduced (Foucault 1977). If the OD tradition continues to insist
on a Lewinian inspired model of action research that goes beyond
epistemologies of knowledge to embrace self-reflection on 'practice' in
the broadest sense, then it has to find a way to mediate the tensions
between researchers and researched.

Conclusion: after Lewin, after modernism

Lewin's unifying ambition to fuse science and reason, social change and
human agency was evident in almost all his work. He wanted to create a
practice-based science of group life that was going to further the

realization of a rational and democratic social world. For Lewin (1999), an integrated science that fused theory and practice and the goal of social integration were inseparable.

The underlying unitary ambition of Lewin's intellectual enterprise was perhaps most forcefully crystallized in his emergent, if under-theorized concept of change agency. Yet, surprisingly, there have been virtually no serious attempts to explore the rationalist and moral assumptions that underpin the key idea of change agency – and those that have tend to be dismissive or superficial. This neglect does not do justice to Lewin's legacy, nor its critical appreciation. For Lewin change agency as a model of intentional action was central to his belief in rationalism, the role of expert knowledge in managing change, the possibilities of extending freedom and autonomy in a democratic society, and his idealism regarding the self-reflective mediation of theory and practice, knowing and doing, science and action. Lewin like the other great architects of the OD tradition was a child of modernist science and rationalism.

While organizational development and action research traditions have continued to canonize, extend or reinterpret Lewin's legacy, they have rarely critically engaged with his core idea of change agency. This critical neglect is no longer sustainable, especially in a context of growing self-doubt and impending crisis over the future of the OD field. OD and action research interventions also face increasing challenges to their modernist models of organizational change and change agency (Reason 2003). These challenges not only come form 'emergent', and 'processual' concepts of organizational change, but also from relativist, constructionist and postmodernist attacks on intentional concepts of agency and change in organizations (Gergen 2003; Tsoukas and Chia 2002; Hardy 2004). If these challenges are not faced up to then the OD field may lose not only its claims to rationally and consciously designed or planned change, but its moral and ethical claims to transfer or diffuse change expertise through a participative ideal of reflective professional practice.

These challenges can be briefly highlighted under four headings: *rationality, expertise, autonomy and reflexivity.*

Rationality. Challenges to rationalism within the OD tradition are, of course, long standing. They first emerged from moderating explorations of 'bounded rationality', organizational contingency theories and the 'contextualist' exploration of processual change (Pettigrew 1997). These attacks have gradually broadened over the last decade into more wide-ranging postmodernist and constructionist critiques of the very notions of agency and change. There is, however, a thematic continuity to these various criticisms. They persistently challenge the models of agency and change envisaged by OD because it appears more suited to planned change, conceived as a rational and linear process within relatively stable or functional organizational systems that have the resources and time to implement incremental change. Increasingly, this is an unreal model of real world organizations, in which system complexity, non-linearity and ongoing 'becoming' of organizational changes are endemic (Tsoukos and Chia 2002). In addition, organization development models are antithetical to new process-based ontologies of organizing/changing that treat agency as discourse, talk, text or conversation (Hardy 2004). In the face of these criticisms OD models of change agency have lost much of their practical efficacy and promise, not only because of their theoretical deficit but also because it has proven almost impossible to operationalize a notion of episodic change interventions as discrete events that can be assessed in terms of predictable outcomes or measures of effectiveness (Robertson *et al.* 1992; Greiner and Cummings 2004).

Expertise. Attacks on expertise have also reinforced the questioning of rationalism, and these attacks have perhaps been even more corrosive of the change agent concept (Weick 2001). Certainly, the normative assumption that the change agent can facilitate consensus or agreement on change and that these apparently participative modes of change are 'best', tends to underplay the expert rhetoric, rational coercion and vested interests that underpin consultancy interventions, as well as the manipulative dynamics at work in group processes and the broader coercive and political aspect of power relations in processes of organizational change (Pettigrew 1997). Organizational development practitioners have, of course, partly addressed some of these issues by broadening the scope of practice to embrace larger issues of power and culture, as well as reflexivity. But unfortunately the expert-centred intervention techniques of the OD process consultant and change agent can often be comfortably complicit with power. Change agency as a professional practice is still firmly located in expert intervention techniques rather than the participative diffusion of expert knowledge through a truly inclusive mode of practice that includes an exploration of agency as dialogue or discourse.

Autonomy. Limits to the diffusion of expertise also highlight the intrinsic ambiguities and oblique concept of 'autonomy' that partly sustains the apparently unbiased neutrality of the change agent role, both as an expert intervention and a potentially participative mode of involvement. Yet, paradoxically, after Lewin and after modernism the OD tradition says very little that is really new about the goal of knowledge in the expansion of the possibilities of rational autonomy and freedom in organizations (Bradford and Burke 2005). What is encouraging, however, is that autonomy as an issue will simply not go away, even in the face of professional complacency. As originally conceived, the change agent role mixed rhetoric and reality, power and expertise (Lewin 1999: 334). It was an expression of the core democratic mission of the OD movement to further equality, empowerment and consensus building within the workplace, as well as being a practical action-centred mechanism for successfully implementing change. This mission still remains as an ideal among the missionary 'holdouts' within the OD field, but it is under enormous threat (Greiner and Cummings 2004: 384). The increasing shift of OD practitioners towards management-driven interventions that can deliver 'productive added value' or 'competitiveness' has led to a greater emphasis on more instrumental, mechanistic and product models of consultancy that place the 'change practitioner' primarily in the role of expert selling change tools or professional solutions (Worley and Feyerherm 2003). Given this convergence, it is increasingly difficult to differentiate the collaborative process role of the change agent as a facilitator of autonomy or empowerment in the workplace from other managerialist or consultancy conceptions of professional practice (Kipping and Engwell 2002).

Reflexivity. Finally, the OD concept of reflexivity looks increasingly problematic, not only because its prescriptive claims to rationalism fail to address issues of interest or power, but because it appears outmoded in the face of competing discourses on the temporal and embedded nature of practice and the idea of discourse as practice (Bourdieu 1990; Wenger 1998). Astoundingly, the OD tradition still does not have a theory of practice; it has instead a rational-cognitive conception of theory *into* practice that identifies reflexivity with self-reflection on professional practice. In contrast, theories of discourse as practice tend to emphasize the socially constituted, contextual, improvisational, and semiconscious nature of knowledge creation models (Hardy 2004). This represents a shift from epistemologies of *knowing* to epistemologies of *doing,* from ontologies of thinking to ontologies of discourse, text and talk. Interestingly, this shift is partly anticipated in Lewin's work. But because the OD tradition in general remains tied to rational and cognitive models of knowing, it invariably focuses more attention on how things are learned through explicit knowledge and learning, rather than how action and learning emerges from 'talk' or conversational experiences that are tacit, unreflective or practice-based. Certainly, most of the leading first generation of OD architects had no systematic conception of practice as the outcome of tacit, unreflective or practical knowledge, and they were equally reluctant to stretch participative involvement into a conception of discourse or dialogue as practice.

These omissions have enormous consequences. When Argyris (2003) expresses his exasperation at the defensive reasoning mindsets of single-loop learning he gives more emphasis to 'skilled incompetence' rather than how competencies may emerge from talk, dialogue or reasoned deliberation. One can interpret Argyris as saying that although actors may understand their behaviours as wilfully unpredictable, or the pursuit of goals that have had unintended consequences, the action researcher and change agent knows better – they can see through apparently reasoned self-deceptions. What Argyris does not appear to realize is that his distinction between single-loop and double-loop learning prevents him from submitting his own self-reflective practices to the same diagnostic analysis he applies to his 'object'. This would perhaps lead him to discover that what he describes as self-deception, the unpredictable and the irrational are nothing other than the same enactments of practice implicit in his own theorizing and human actions. Similarly, when Schein (1988) claims to transfer expertise to the client through 'process consultation', practice appears as a set of process consulting techniques, professional protocols and feedback mechanisms of rational persuasion rather than any exploration of how knowledge is enacted through practice-based modes of participative involvement and dialogue. Even Schön's (1995) reflective practitioner appears unable to see beyond the shadow of his own practice. When he identifies practice with the epistemological critique of professional practice he highlights the limits of expertise, but does not redefine the relationship between knowledge and action, knowing and doing as ontologically inseparable. If the goal of reflexivity is really to make epistemologies of practice self-referential then the reflective practitioner has to embrace ontological insecurity by including participants and discourse in knowledge creation practices. By refusing to fully engage with this disconcerting possibility Schön provides yet another 'native account' of reflexive practice. Ultimately, the OD tradition does not resolve or mediate the intractable theory and practice divide, it simply restates the old dichotomy as epistemologies of knowledge and epistemologies of practice that retain the false security of objective knowledge and the comforting self-identity of professional practice.

Perhaps the only way out of the epistemological and ontological dilemmas of the reflective practitioner is to contextualize the temporal and embedded meanings within practice by *decentring* them from a subject–object *episteme* of knowledge creation and participative involvement, thereby extending the possibilities of reflexivity beyond rationalism. With this postmodern dethroning of rationalism the change agent role would lose its privileged expertise, along with the naïve functionalist and psychological presuppositions of the OD tradition, and the idea of reflexivity as a system feedback mechanism. By burning these bridges OD would be unable to 'go all the way back home again and rely solely on group methods, personal feedback, re-education, and a singular focus on process' (Greiner and Cummings 2004: 385). In addition, if the relationship between the change agent and the client is no longer founded on a notion of expertise then the process techniques and tools of change interventions become problematic. But perhaps most importantly, the loss of expertise would dissolve the conventional consultant–client, change agent–group dyad by allowing agency and change to emerge within and between various forms of organizational discourse, knowledge creation and reflexivity. Participative involvement as a form of practice-based knowledge creation would then hold out the possibility of an equalization of autonomy founded on an ideal of open dialogue. Similarly, reflexivity would become less of a self-reflection on professional practice and more a constantly shifting reinterpretation of ongoing discourses/practices that constantly create new combinations of knowledge–action. In effect, *knowing* and *doing*, knowledge and action, practice and discourse would be treated as ontologically inseparable rather than epistemologically unequal; they would become essentially self-referential – you cannot have one without the other.

This rethinking of the 'function' and meaning of change agency outside the confines of modernist rationalism raises all kinds of perplexing issues for the OD tradition, both as a research field and a form of professional practice. Most obvious are the conventional dangers of relativism and fragmentation (Rorty 1995). But are they overstated, and are they really that disconcerting? The OD tradition is characterized by continued value-conflict and confusion over goals, and some have suggested the field is moving in the wrong direction: 'There has been a clear movement away from focus, agreement, and clarity to confusion, bickering, and fragmentation' (Worley and Feyerherm 2003: 111). Similarly, there is little agreement as to what a coordinated and potentially cumulative research programme for the OD field should be:

> Without coordination and the continued acceptance of 'old wine in new bottles' as truly innovative approaches, the field will continue to be fragmented by forces focused on the promulgation of separate and distinct interventions. At best, OD will be defined as 'tool kit'.
>
> (Worley and Feyerherm 2003: 113).

The prospect of more 'fads', new techniques and an increasing focus on formalizing instrumental models of professional competence threatens to take the OD tradition perhaps even further away from its theoretical and programmatic ambitions (Schein 1990b; Bradford and Burke 2005). It is no surprise then that the OD field is currently gripped by an emergent sense of crisis.

What then has the OD tradition got to lose by critically rethinking one of its central concepts? A further erosion of a precarious professional identity and the denting of claims to expertise? Perhaps. The answer is that it may have much more to gain as an academic research field. Coordinated theory and research around a re-conceptualization of change agency is enormously promising. By asking the OD tradition to question change agency as a mode of *centred agency* the most probing questions can be asked regarding the efficacy of its central presuppositions regarding *rationality, expertise, autonomy and reflexivity*. If Lewin bequeathed a legacy of reasoned hope, but also theoretical confusion regarding these ideas, it was partly because he explored the most challenging requirement for any form of applied behavioural science: the fusion of theory and practice. A re-conceptualization of change agency suggests the need for a more comprehensive and inclusive conception of organizational development theory and practice that goes beyond process interventions, reflection on practice or, worst of all, the reduction of OD to a tool kit of instrumental techniques. Ultimately, what a rethinking of change agency promises above all is the possibility of a new and more challenging theory of practice that reinvigorates and restores the moral mission and practical ambitions of a once powerful tradition of organizational inquiry.

4 Pettigrew and contextualism: organizational change and strategic choice

- Introduction
- Process and processual analysis
- In search of contexts
- Strategic change and strategic choice: leading change
- Theory, practice and engaged scholarship
- Discussion: the legacy of contextualism
- Conclusion: contextualizing contextualism

Introduction

Andrew Pettigrew's pioneering scholarly work over the past three decades has often been seen as offering a distinctively 'contextualist' approach to the study of organizational change and strategic choice (1985, 1997, 2003a). Against a background in which the orthodoxy of functionalist theories of organizations had collapsed, contingency models were in empirical disarray, and strategic change theory was increasingly synonymous with normative or recipes-driven prescriptions of managerial voluntarism, Pettigrew offered an apparently new and richly textured form of intensive case-based inquiry focused on the 'process, content and context of change' (Pettigrew 2002). From his highly influential case study of ICI, *The Awaking Giant* (1985) to his many wide-ranging reflections on the 'processual' nature of organizational change, Pettigrew has consistently championed the scholarly virtues of a contextualist perspective founded on rigour and relevance (2001). As organizational change theories and models of the strategy process have proliferated and become even more confusing and fragmented, contextualism would appear to offer a justification for intellectual pluralism while keeping alive the prospect that both theory and practice can be 'bridged', and that engaged academic scholarship can *make a difference* (Pettigrew 2001: 66, 2002: 25).

Although Pettigrew's formulation of contextualism has distinctive features its intellectual origins are complex, crossing a range of disciplinary fields. Simon's (1947, 1991) critique of the 'objective rationality' of decision processes in complex organizations, Lindblom (1959) on 'the science of muddling through', Cyert and March (1963) on 'bounded rationality', Child's (1972) focus on the importance of 'strategic choice', and Quinn (1980) on the 'logical incrementalism' of the strategy process are all forerunners or proponents of contextualist ideas, as is the work of Mintzberg (1994) on 'strategy as craft'. While many of these ideas have their origins in challenges to rational choice models of organizational decision-making, they also reflect a broader drift towards radical contextualism within strategic management research and a corresponding rejection of evolutionary models of economic behaviour and strategic change (Gavetti and Levinthal 2004: 1310).

Despite this prestigious lineage there have been few serious attempts to explore Pettigrew's contextualist position, and those that have tend to be overly referential or unduly critical. An attitude of respectful admiration is perhaps understandable (Pettigrew 1998; Van de Ven 2002). Pettigrew has struggled with some of the most perplexing questions and dilemmas posed by theories of organizational and strategic change. When he states the requirements for a robust theory of organizational change one begins to sense the difficulty and immensity of the task. Such a theory should in his view simultaneously 'explain forces of stability and change, including exogenous and endogenous sources of change. Link phenomena at macro and micro levels of analysis and deal with issues about the rate, pace and direction of change' (1987: 6). In addition, Pettigrew insists that such a theory should be practical: 'We all know that it is much easier to go for scholarly quality on its own, or for relevance on its own, but it is much more difficult to try and achieve this simultaneously' (Pettigrew 2002: 25). Clearly a scholar who embarks on such an arduous enterprise is to be both admired and respected, and Pettigrew has certainly gained recognition for his academic achievements. He is the first European scholar to be honoured as a Distinguished Scholar by the American Academy of Management.

Perhaps because of his ambitious scholarly goals, practical intent, and the international recognition of his work, Pettigrew has numerous critics, and they tend to be unforgiving. Willmott (1997: 1330) has argued that Pettigrew's exploration of organizational change and development at ICI 'is largely decoupled from an appreciation of the politico-economic conditions and consequences of change'. He suggests that this limitation derives from Pettigrew's definition of context which does not offer a reading of the macro–micro conditions of action; 'In effect, the micro is identified with group behavior while the macro is equated with untheorized shifts in politico-economic policymaking and ideologies' (Willmott 1997: 1330).

Pettigrew has also been consistently attacked from a practice-based reading of change management theory. Buchanan and Boddy (1992) argued that Pettigrew addresses academic validity more than practical efficacy: 'The social and interpersonal dynamics of the processes Pettigrew addresses are not explored in a manner that facilitates the easy identification of practical advice' (1992: 62). Certainly, Pettigrew offers little in the way of prescriptive advice on change agency as a form of instrumental intervention. In a similar vein, Dawson (2003) has attacked Pettigrew's contextual model from a practice and outcome viewpoint while endorsing its 'processual' counterpoint to system models of planned organizational change.

More recently, Chia (1999, 2002) has characterized Pettigrew's contextualist position as an emergent and processual counterweight to evolutionary and 'punctuated equilibrium' models of organizational change, but criticizes it because it is not sufficiently 'process-based'. For Chia, Pettigrew is still seduced by the idea that we can uncover the dynamic interplay between the context, content and process of change without embracing an ontological awareness of the essentially temporal nature of change: 'Expressed in this manner … change context and process take on thing-like characteristics rather than as dynamic flux and transformation' (Chia 1999: 212). Chia then poses an alternative 'Rhizomic model' of organizational change which he claims 'affords a better understanding of the inherently dynamic complexities and intrinsic indeterminacy of organizational transformation processes' (1999: 209).

While many of these critical readings illuminate particular aspects of Pettigrew's position they rarely address the broader scope of his work and the meaning and significance of contextualism. What precisely defines Pettigrew's *strategic change–strategic choice* version of contextualism? How does it differ from other approaches to organizational analysis and strategic change? Can it challenge system equilibrium models of evolutionary organizational change or purely rationalist concepts of agency, change and strategic choice (Pettigrew 2002)? Does it offer a new approach to understanding the 'embeddedness' of strategic change that goes beyond leader-centric models of 'strategic agency' (Giddens 1984; Granovetter 1985)? If so, is it consistent, coherent or theoretically integrated; and what implications, if any, does it have for practice?

Although Pettigrew's contextualist position on organizational change and strategic choice is complex and has evolved (and is still evolving) in various directions, it can be summed up in two programmatic goals.

First, Pettigrew's overall intent is to create 'theoretically sound and practically useful research on change', that explores the 'contexts, content, and processes of change together with their interconnectedness through time' (Pettigrew 1987: 268). Context encompasses the 'outer and inner' contexts of the firm or organization. Content refers to the specific empirical arena of transformation, whether it is technology, products or organizational culture. Process refers to 'actions, reactions and interactions' of human actors as they produce and reproduce change (Pettigrew 2003a). This tripartite division of context–content–process was conceived as a direct challenge to 'ahistorical, aprocessual and acontextual' approaches to organizational change; especially planned change approaches, managerial ideals of control, and the variable-centred paradigms of organizational contingency theories (Pettigrew *et al.* 1992).

Second, Pettigrew's focus on the iterative, non-linear or processual nature of change over time was designed to emphasize the contextual influence of micro-politics and conflicts between organizational actors over the direction, rationality and outcomes of change (Pettigrew and Whipp 1991). For Pettigrew the unintended consequences, unpredictability and paradoxical nature of all rational action, management planning and strategic decision-making are not only a confirmation of the limits of human action but a reaffirmation of the possibility of human agency and strategic choice.

While some of these ideas are interesting on their own, what makes Pettigrew's work of broader significance is his synthetic intent with regard to organizational change and strategic choice. Against a background of planned or instrumental strategic change theories and their counter-images of emergent change models, Pettigrew's original contribution was to transform case histories of change into context-rich case studies of organizational and strategic change processes that illuminate the *embeddedness* of agency and change (2003b: 336). For Pettigrew, understanding 'process in action' is a way of capturing the 'action, reactions and interaction' of human agency as change processes unfold over time (2003a). Similarly, 'context' is not a substitute structural category, defining the heavy hand of historical context; rather it is an affirmation of bounded choice. This 'process-context' duality with the empirical mediation of 'content' is ultimately the methodological and political rationale of his 'return to embeddedness as a principle of method' (Pettigrew 2003b: 336).

If embeddedness is the defining principle of Pettigrew's methodology, his overall mission for contextualism is more than simply a historicist return of organizational theory and strategy management research to case histories (Pettigrew 1987). What Pettigrew appears to promise instead is not just a reworking of the old dichotomies of action and structural mechanisms, but their synthetic and holistic socio-historical analysis and interpretation. It is no surprise then that Pettigrew (1997) sees his work as partly a parallel reworking of Giddens' agency and structure distinction, by reformulating it as a duality between process and context. Just as for Giddens the notion of the 'duality of structure' or 'structuration' theory is the core of his process-based view of human agency, so the idea of redefining agency and change is at the core of Pettigrew's mission for contextualism.

But does Pettigrew's contextualist position really succeed in redefining the nature of organizational and strategic change processes? And what role does agency and strategic choice play in these processes? Here it will be argued that contextualism fails as a project of synthesis because it leaves too many hard questions unresolved. Four main criticisms will be offered.

First, contextualism as 'processual analysis' does not adequately explore the reciprocal relationship between organizational structure and organizational change (Pettigrew 2003a). If one stretches the concept of *structure as system* too far one ends up with classic dilemma of substance and stasis (Luhmann 1995). Conversely, if one stretches the concept of *structure as process* (e.g. structuration) too far one ends up with becoming and temporality (Giddens 1984). Pettigrew scrupulously separates the processes of organizational change from any system reference points to organizational structure, effectively turning structure and organizing into temporal processes of micro-behaviour that point towards organizational change as a theory of *incrementalism with transitional breaks*. This idea takes various forms, including the identification of change as 'subtle processes of additively building up a momentum of support for change' followed by a vigorous phase of implementation (1985: xviii). While this idea may have considerable case-specific validity it also undermines a reciprocal understanding of order and continuity in organizational change processes as well as their counter-images: discontinuity and transformational change. Ultimately, Pettigrew (1997, 2003b) wants organizational and strategic change as *organizing/strategizing* defined by the interconnectedness of processual contexts and incrementalism, rather than organizational change that may be a temporal interplay of systems and processes, continuity and discontinuity.

Second, just as Pettigrew's analysis of process is theoretically limited so too is his exploration of 'context'. If processual analysis is a method for turning organizational structure as organizational change into the temporality of 'process', contextualism is a methodology for embedding human agency and choice in the particularity of historical contexts. For Pettigrew *context* is fundamentally a holistic idea that cannot be disaggregated into specific conceptual meanings, and so he offers no consistent systemic, functional or network concept of the 'outer and inner context' of organizations and their environments (1997, 2002). As a consequence Pettigrew has no adequate concepts that theorize the environmental boundaries of organizations or the possible efficacy of organizational structures as system entities with emergent properties. Correspondingly in most of his work he has limited interest in the possible predictive or causal 'fit' between structure and environment – despite valiant claims to the contrary (Pettigrew 1997, 2003b). Instead, the narrative interpretation of the uniqueness of historical contexts performs an explanatory role, replacing any structural, institutional or variable-centred analysis of hypothetical patterns of causality (Pettigrew 1985, 1997). Ultimately, this leads to a conception of context as a realm of *strategic choice*, rather than a powerful arena of constraint and possible determinism.

Third, the central importance Pettigrew places on organizational politics or competing interests has two key functions in his work: it clarifies modes of 'bounded rationality' in decision-making while affirming the possibility of strategic choice (Miller *et al.* 1999). In this respect, contextual analysis is explicitly anti-deterministic; it retains a strong affinity to the virtues of choice and, by implication, liberal individualism (Pettigrew 1985). Yet paradoxically, by emphasizing the rich narrative of decision contexts as a dynamic of choice rather than constraint or closure, strategic agency appears to lose any decisiveness in defining goals or bringing about outcomes. It is simply a micro manifestation of competing interest group behaviour within contexts that appear to have no structural efficacy or environmental trajectories. In this respect, processual analysis as a narrative of competing interests and micro-power sidelines a systematic exploration of organizations as broader economic, cultural or institutional entities involved in larger patterns of resource allocations, social reproduction, normative regulation or the mediation of professional expertise (Pettigrew 1987: 659).

Fourth, Pettigrew has insisted that contextualism as an analytical framework is designed to be rigorous and practically useful. However, his focus on the unintended consequences of action and the lack of predictability of change processes allows few possibilities to define the directionality of strategic change and therefore to prescribe any practical advice on how strategic change can be managed (Dawson 2003). In this respect, contextualist discourse appears to reject the apparent reductionism of 'causal process theories' of organizational change and prescriptive concepts of strategy, both of which still retain instrumental models of expertise or archetypes of strategic agency that partly bridge the gaps between theory and practice (Ansoff 1991; Van de Ven and Poole 1995). Naturally, this criticism can lead to a rejection of contextualism as a form of academism impotent in the face of practice, or, at best, a methodology emasculated by the immense evidential complexities it uncovers. These judgements may be harsh, but if contextualism wishes to achieve both scholarly rigour and practical relevance as a body of knowledge it has to clarify its model of practice, including an ideal of practice that goes beyond reflection on the professional practice or method of 'processual analysis'. In other words, contextualism as an academic discourse has to include within the 'logic of practice' an attempt to self-reflexively contextualize contextualism – however daunting this task may appear (Bourdieu 1985, 1990).

Each of these criticisms will be examined in turn. The overall goal will be to examine critically the limits of contextualism as an exploration of organizational change and strategic choice. It will then be argued that contextualism as an object of contested empirical, theoretical, cultural and political value, ends in a paradoxical outcome. Rather than providing a potentially powerful rationale for the understanding of organizational and strategic change that translates empirical research into practice, it leads to a reaffirmation of choice as an expression of the virtues of engaged scholarship and liberal individualist values. As such, contextualism needs to be contextualized as the rhetorical discourse of *Homo Academicus* (Bourdieu 1988).

Process and processual analysis

Pettigrew's research commitment to the 'longitudinal processual study of organizations' is evident in much of his early work (1979). In a clearly synthetic paper on the study of organizational cultures during the early stage of his academic career, he affirmed his programmatic intent and the underlying presuppositions of process analysis:

> A longitudinal processual analysis is more likely to be interested in language
> systems of becoming than of being, of processes of structural elaboration rather
> than the precise description of structure forms, of mechanisms that create,
> maintain, and dissolve systems of power, rather than just attempt to codify
> distributions of power at one point in time
>
> (1979: 570)

One detects a note of passion in these comments and a sense of political
ends. But this embryonic definition of processual analysis, with 'system'
as an oppositional term, only really begins to take on the methodological
form of contextualism in Pettigrew's later study of ICI:

> Out of this study came the two key precepts of my theory of method. First of all
> the need to study changes in their context, a return to embeddedness as a
> principle of method. Second the need to catch reality in flight, to study changes
> over long periods of time
>
> (2002: 21)

And Pettigrew adds:

> Of course these two precepts needed one another. It is impossible to connect up
> firm level, with sector level, and with social and economic contexts without
> seeing those phenomena over quite long periods of time. So the contextual
> analysis needed the temporal analysis and vice versa.
>
> (2002: 21)

If the study of ICI crystallized processual analysis as case-based research
on the historically embedded nature of change processes, Pettigrew was
still amplifying and clarifying his position a decade later. In one of his
most self-reflective essays on his method and practice, he asked: 'what is
process, and what is processual analysis'? (1997: 337). While he partly
clarifies what these terms mean his central focus tends to be on his
'theory of method', or the process of processual analysis, rather than
epistemological issues or an ontological clarification of 'process' in
understanding organizational or strategic change. To gain a little more
clarity it is worth briefly exploring the concept of 'process' in more detail.

The idea of 'process' in the study of organizational and strategic change
covers a multiplicity of meanings, many of which overlap (Van de Ven
1987; Garud and Van de Ven 2002). At least four meanings can be
differentiated.

Process can refer to the explanatory logic of a causal relationship between
variables in a variance theory (Van de Ven and Poole 1995: 512). This
may take the form of 'casual process theories' referring to the diagnostic
logic used to explain causal events within a time series, which may range

from the periodic to the random or chaotic. The presuppositions of causal process theories of change therefore involve a systems ontology and a corresponding model of organizations as structural or system entities that can be unravelled in terms of their 'underlying generative mechanism' (Dooley and Van de Ven 1999). This does not mean, however, that organizations are in a single state, or that change unfolds in a linear or predictable path or single pattern: 'Rather, measured attributes of organizational processes can indicate the state of certain organizational processes and/or subsystems, as seen through a particular theoretical and observational lens' (Dooley and Van de Ven 1999: 359).

Process can encompass categories used to describe activities of individuals, groups or organizations (e.g. decision-making processes, the strategy processes, communication processes, etc.). For some theorists of organizational change these processes may 'explain an organization result', but not how the 'mechanisms of change unfold over time' (Van de Ven and Poole 1995: 512).

Process can be identified with 'how' an organization changes and develops. Van de Ven and Poole (1995) are perhaps the most forceful advocates of this position when they refer to 'process as progression (the order and sequence) of events in an organizational entity's existence over time' (p. 512). Using this definition they provide a typology of four 'change process' theories: *life cycle, teleology, dialectical* and *evolutionary theories*. Life cycle theories operate with linear or developmental constructs of birth, growth, maturity and decline. Evolutionary theories operate with biological analogies of competitive selection or system survival; and within this category the most influential theories are 'punctuated equilibrium' models. Dialectical theories operate with the idea of an antithesis or conflict between social forces, interests or group behaviour which often generates discontinuous change. Teleological theories operate with purposeful or goal-oriented models of functional differentiation or system adaptation. Van de Ven and Poole (1995) claim that these theories 'provide four internally consistent accounts of change processes in organizational entities' (p. 519). The classification tends, however, to be somewhat mechanistic and this is reinforced by the virtual absence of any reference to agency. This undermines the efficacy of the models in theorizing the relationship between agency and structure, and hence the relationship between strategic choice and organizational change.

Finally, an alternative process theory of change can be derived by counterpoising an ontology of 'being', substance and persistence with an ontology of 'becoming' in which change is constant and indivisible (Chia 2002). This conception of process can capture the ongoing nature of change, but it also creates major analytical problems. If constant movement characterizes reality then it is almost impossible to capture the nature of this emergent reality, its sources or effects, by using static system concepts or categories. Nor is it possible to intervene to change reality from one relatively stable state to another or to measure outcomes. While a process ontology of change as becoming highlights why the phenomenon of *organizations, systems and structures* is deeply problematic and in need of explanation, it can be potentially analytically and empirically vacuous in that it may offer few analytical categories to differentiate change, analyse practice or explain the impact or efficacy of specific forms of organizational change (Chia 2002). Paradoxically, a process ontology emphasizes that everything is constantly changing, but there are no specific things, states, processes or events that change.

Pettigrew's usage of 'process' tends to slip, sometimes imperceptibly, between these various and sometimes confusing meanings. This occurs partly because he defines process in such a comprehensive manner as 'a sequence of individual and collective events, actions, and activities unfolding over time in context' (1997: 338). Clearly this definition encompasses process as sequence as well as categories of human activities, and it includes the ubiquitous catchall of 'context'. Pettigrew also appears to identify process with a process ontology of becoming: 'Human conduct is perpetually in a process of becoming. The overriding aim of processual analysis therefore is to catch this reality in flight' (1997: 338). However, he does not clarify the scope of this potentially process-based ontology and it tends to be essentially a methodological injunction to study change by exploring large blocks of historical time.

The only apparently missing component in Pettigrew's definition of process is the focus of 'causal process theories' on explaining the 'generative mechanisms' of organizational change, and potentially their predictive patterns. Pettigrew appears to reject the overtly positivistic connotations of explanation–prediction, although he remains an epistemological realist when he suggests that process analysis can find the 'underlying mechanisms, which shape any patterning in the observed processes' (1997: 337). This is, however, an enormously difficult 'induction challenge' for process analysis because: 'The mechanisms may also be elements in the interactive field occasioned by links between levels of process and context around the primary process stream under analysis' (Pettigrew 1997: 339). Moreover, Pettigrew is deeply sceptical about a causal analysis of change, not just because of the limits of induction and deductive analysis, but because processual analysis challenges assumptions about 'path dependent' or evolutionary change processes: 'With time series analysis there is always the literal comfort of fixed or predetermined phases and stages. With the agreeable structuring of phases or models should also come the discomfiting recognition that shifting contexts may mean that social processes are inherently discontinuous and open-ended' (Pettigrew 1997: 339). From this viewpoint, Pettigrew suggests that change processes can be 'linear, directional or cumulative and perhaps reversible, while others may be non-linear, radical and transformational' (1997: 339). In practice, however, Pettigrew rarely consistently applies this dual focus on continuity and discontinuity.

One of the central issues raised by Pettigrew's multifarious use of process and processual analysis is how these ideas theorize potentially realist notions of organizational *structure* and organizational *change*. There are broadly two ways to conceptualize structure and change in organizational theory. One can begin with a systems ontology or a process ontology, and either of these positions has implications for epistemology as well as research practice and method. If the starting point for structural analysis is a systems ontology (e.g. functionalism) then 'structure' as systems can be conceived as relatively stable entities overlaid with predictive patterns or stages of evolutionary change (Luhmann 1995). But the major danger with this systems view of structure is that order and stability can take precedence over instability, discontinuity or any exploration of non-linear or non-evolutionary change (Parsons 1951). If, however, the starting point for an analysis of structure is a process ontology of change, then systems, order and predictive patterns can become lost in patterns of temporality and continuous change (Giddens 1984). Adequate theories of organizational change must by definition be adequate theories of organizational structure (Luhmann 1995: 347). You cannot have one without the other (March 1981).

Pettigrew's work is interesting because sometimes he appears implicitly to recognize this reciprocal relationship between 'structure' as *system* and structuring as *process*. For example, he claims that: 'Change and continuity, process and structure, are inextricably linked' (Pettigrew 1985: 1). However, his historical location of organizational change processes within 'processual dynamics of changing' undermines the analytical clarification of *structure* as a 'continuing system' or entity with potentially enduring or relatively coherent micro-macro properties. Instead, structure or structuring is diffused within the holistic analysis of 'outer and inner context' and the processual analysis of the ongoing action or interaction of human agents – and this is compounded by the absence of any clear definitions or classifications of contexts. For Pettigrew, the couplet of process–context is the antithesis of structural categories; process and context are holistically as one because they appear to form processes of emergence that are always temporal and indeterminate (1997: 338).

This holistic and ontological affirmation of temporality is, however, contradictory. Not just because Pettigrew does not explicate a process ontology beyond an idea of 'processual analysis' as a method, but because he rejects the need to combine it with a systems ontology in developing any adequate theory of organizational change. Organizational change as an apparent counterpoint to systemic ideas of order, stability or structure is therefore identified primarily with *processual* change, rather than both continuities and discontinuities that may be both predetermined or open-ended. As a result processual change, despite Pettigrew's (1987, 1997) claims to the contrary, becomes synonymous with incrementalism or its sub-variant, emergent incremental transitions, rather than structural, environmental trajectories or other 'path dependent processes'. Processual analysis is concerned with change that is by definition unintended, unplanned, unstructured and indeterminate (Donaldson 1997). Even the idea of process as 'sequence' is rarely linked directly to connected 'stages'. Rather, sequence unfolds as improvisational 'dramas' of action and events that are unpredictable with respect to outcomes (Pettigrew 1985). In this way, Pettigrew turns the 'processual analysis' of 'process' into a methodological tool that counteracts all system-based models of organizational change, and in particular punctuated equilibrium models. While this represents an important corrective counterblast against 'causal process theories' of change, it is essentially almost as one-sided: the possibility of continuity as order and stability and discontinuity as radical transformational change are seriously underplayed. Ultimately, what Pettigrew wants is organizational change defined by the perpetual temporality of processual contexts, rather than organizational change that is a temporal interplay of continuity and discontinuity, incrementalism and transformation, systems and processes.

In search of contexts

If the goal of processual analysis as a method is essentially to redefine 'structures' as *processes in action*, and therefore change as unpredictability, the broader ambition of contextual analysis is to transform the idea of fixed boundaries between organizational entities and their environments. This involves a rejection of static, variable-centred paradigms or any deterministic models of causality in favour of a new 'holistic' principle of 'the context–process cycle of change' that is fundamentally indeterminate. This overall ambitious partly explains why the meaning of 'context' in Pettigrew's work covers a multiplicity of meanings that overlap with the idea of 'process', rendering both ideas intrinsically complex and often deeply confusing:

> If process is a river, replete with interrelating steams, flows, eddies and swirls, the context is the bank and the river bed: that which directs the flow of the process. *Context is therefore anything that may be seen to shape a process.*
>
> (2003a: 309, emphasis in original)

Despite this sweeping 'dual analogy' of context, Pettigrew tends to group context into two broad categories:

> Outer context includes the economic, social political, competitive and sectorial environments in which the firm is located. Inner context refers to the inner mosaic of the firm; the structural, cultural and political environments which, in consort with the outer context, shape features of the process.
>
> (1997)

Broadly, this is the definition of context that Pettigrew first used in his study of ICI, and it is repeated in much of his later work (2003a: 312).

Ostensively, the reference points of outer and inner context allow Pettigrew to explore 'levels of analysis' while remaining cautious about any systemic or overly rigid distinction between internal and external environments of the firm. But the idea also performs other more messy functions. Outer and inner context operate as substitute or surrogate terms for the broader historical exploration of 'structure' as a systemic category. More broadly, context also acts as a 'holistic' framework (i.e. contextualism), which justifies the research practice of processual analysis. Finally, all of these meanings are convergent with 'process' as realm of action and choice rather than macro-determinism or predictive causal analysis.

It is worth trying to briefly unravel some of these meanings and their significance by exploring Pettigrew's distinction between outer and inner context.

Outer context

Organizational theories are constantly beset by problems of defining what constitutes the 'environment'. This issue particularly perplexed early contingency theorists, because they sought to define the appropriate 'fit' between specific internal organizational factors and external or macro-environmental contingencies. This led to system-based and variable paradigms of organizational–environmental fit that were essentially static, and therefore open to critical attack. By the beginning of the 1980s contingency theories were in retreat, and organization studies as a disciplinary sub-field began to fragment (Whitley 2003: 486). However, the recent revival of neo-contingency theories suggests that the apparent rout of contingency theory may have been wishful thinking (Donaldson 2001). This revival has been fuelled by a more dynamic and change-oriented view of organizations as systems of reinforcing 'complementarities' or bundles of flexible manufacturing policies and HR practices which together can improve performance. In this reformulation, 'performance' is taken as a shifting goal of proactive change interventions (Pettigrew et al. 2003: 126).

Pettigrew's early work emerged during a period when contingency theories appeared to be exhausted as a viable paradigm, and so he was deeply sceptical about the notion of 'fit', or ideas of a causal relation between environment and organizational structure. He was particularly loath to draw any dividing line between organizations and their 'external' environments. That is why the outer and inner context of firms or organizations are rarely explored using a strong internal versus external dichotomy (Pettigrew 1987, 1997). Instead boundaries are virtual and constantly subject to redefinition as the overall environmental contexts of firms or organizations change. Moreover, if one cannot define what constitutes the environment and organizational 'structure' then the idea of system-wide, planned or evolutionary change toward a new structure or predictable performance outcome becomes empirically problematic.

Nevertheless, Pettigrew wanted to keep some sense of the 'environment' as a strategic concept involving multiple 'levels of analysis', otherwise it would dissolve into a diffuse exploration of historical particularity. For example, he warns in his study of ICI that it is not sufficient to treat the macro 'context' as 'either just a descriptive background, or an eclectic list of antecedents' (1985: 36–37). This would turn context into 'just a stimulus environment' rather than an 'arrangement of structures and processes' (1997: 341). In this respect, Pettigrew often advocates the systemic exploration of environments using 'industry structure analysis' and benchmarking models of national competitiveness (1990: 129; 2003a: 309). Similarly, he also warns of the dangers of not capturing the linkage of 'process and outcome', because process analysis would be 'pragmatically endangered by this omission'; it would have no implication for practice: 'The irreducible purpose of a processual analysis remains to account for and explain the what, why and how of the links between context, process and outcomes' (Pettigrew 1997: 340).

Yet with some notable exceptions Pettigrew often appears to ignore his own advice on these crucial matters (Pettigrew and Whipp 1991). Part of the problem is that the holistic ambition of contextualism sets up an almost impossible theoretical and empirical challenge. Outer contexts or environments and the organizations within them are merged in an all-encompassing contextual landscape of flows and dependencies that never appear to come to rest because they have unclear beginnings or end points, and certainly few clearly defined outcomes (Pettigrew 1997: 340). It is no surprise then that Pettigrew (1987, 1997) has always tended to prefer relational models of contextual influence that are intrinsically problematic with regard to outcomes or practice. Only in his more recent work is there an engagement with more integrative neo-contingency models of 'complementarities', although this is treated in a characteristically cautious manner: 'Integration is both a source of strength and a source of weakness. There is potential for internal synergy, but without the right context, good initiatives can easily turn bad' (Pettigrew et al. 2003: 132).

Is the root cause of this caution again Pettigrew's continued reluctance to theorize systems ideas? If so, this is in some respects surprising. Even with the use of the contextual landscape metaphor there is still the possibility of conceiving environment–structure relations as one of 'outer' and 'inner' contexts: sets of external institutional arrangements, internal structuring forces or even a hypothetical aggregation of complementary organizational competencies that define performance. But Pettigrew's strong scepticism towards systems ideas or causal models leads him to downplay or sidestep these various possibilities. No systemic, functional, structural or network concept of the potential inter-relationships of internal–external environmental or organization contexts is offered in his work.

The consequences of this omission are far-reaching. Pettigrew wants outer context as environment to have some macro-efficacy as continuity or embeddedness, yet he wants context as a holistic category to be open-ended, indeterminate and always emergent. Context–process is in this sense essentially inseparable: 'processes are embedded in contexts that produce and are produced by them' (Pettigrew 1997: 340). This appears to lead at some points to an implicit argument for 'contextual circularity' (Pettigrew 2003a). Certainly, it is often unclear from Pettigrew's work where outer and inner context, process and context, begin and end. Processes are embedded in contexts, which produce processes and are reproduced by processes, which are in turn context-dependent. Ultimately, the rationale behind this contextual circularity is not just to diffuse any hint of determinism in context–process relationships, it is also to reaffirm choice. Context as a possible arena of constraint, causality or determinism, does not produce–reproduce the outcomes and unintended consequences of change, actors do.

Inner context

If Pettigrew's use of outer context as a substitute for 'environment' is often unclear because it simultaneously encompasses internal–external meanings, his use of inner context as a surrogate for 'structure' is equally confusing. Inner context appears to have no coherent meaning beyond how it is defined and operationalized within a particular case study or time frame of historical analysis. In this respect, structure appears as purely an inductive evidence-based construct that has no substantive meaning or existence within processual analysis – or outside of it. In effect, structure is a processual concept that is chosen within a specific mode of research practice. Nevertheless, Pettigrew argues that process analysis must search for 'structures and underlying logics' and how they constrain action over time. How does Pettigrew somehow reconcile these different meanings of structure, as an open-ended definitional construct and structure as constraint over time?

In searching for answers Pettigrew often turns to Giddens' (1984) attempt to overcome the dualism of structure and agency by establishing a 'duality' of structure:

> This duality provides two crucial analytical building blocks for the process scholar. First of all, structure and context are conceptualized not as barriers to action but as essentially involved in its production, and, second, there is scope to demonstrate empirically how aspects of context (such as deteriorating industrial and economic scene) can be mobilized by actors as they seek strategic outcomes important to them.

(Pettigrew 1997: 341)

While this restatement of Giddens provides Pettigrew with a rationale for the empirical focus of contextual analysis it does not really resolve the structure as context problematic (Reed 1997). The problem of structure is simply restated as another question: *How can structure be formulated as an aspect of outer or inner context?* Pettigrew does not fully address the more awkward question: if structure or structuring/organizing refers to patterns of social relations that stretch over long periods of historical time, then how is this institutional continuity or embeddedness of structures and human agency in contexts sustained?

Giddens (1984) tried to resolve this problem by distinguishing between 'structure' as 'rules and resources' and 'system' as reproduced social relations. Unfortunately, this distinction underplayed the distributive or institutional dimensions of economic and political power within societies and organizations while allowing 'agency' as a theoretical concept to become an abstract principle of autonomy and choice. When Giddens therefore tries to explore structuration as a theory of change he is constantly constrained by the need to supplement his notion of structure as rules and resources that empower agency with a systems-based notion of power that constrains agency. This results in both a weak notion of structure as process and an under-theorized and highly abstract notion of agency that sometimes verges on old-style voluntarism with liberal individualism tacked on (Giddens 1984). Giddens' theoretical-political position is therefore anti-deterministic and anti-positivistic. Moreover, because Giddens identifies the reproduction of social life with continuous processes of incremental social change that have no potentially structural or emergent macro-properties, he tends to offer few ideas about the directionality of change processes (1990b: 303).

Pettigrew appears to end up in a similar position. He follows Giddens in treating structure as the medium and outcome of human agency and choice. But because his primary focus is on change rather than organizational structuring or structuration he goes even further than Giddens in affirming the openness of organizational change:

> The past is alive in the present and may shape the emerging future. Beneath the surface events and chronology, the process scholar searches for recurrent pattern in the process, for structure and underlying logics. But there is no assumption of predetermined timetables, of ordered and inevitability sequences or stages. Trajectories of strategy processes are probabilistic and uncertain because of changing contexts and human action.
>
> (Pettigrew 1997: 341)

Despite the references to 'recurrent pattern', 'structure and underlying logics', Pettigrew does not give these ideas any real analytical weight or explanatory power in understanding organizational change. Inner context is a weak reference point to patterns of organizational continuity and it diffuses 'structure and underlying logics' into the efficacy of agency. In this way Pettigrew emulates Giddens in flattening out structure as an analytical category (Layder 1987). Yet paradoxically, Pettigrew's emphasis on context as a realm of constraint and action does not lead to a broader exploration of agency in organizational change, whether in the form of leadership or managerial agency. Just as Giddens' theory of structuration is weak as an exploration of both structure and agency, similarly Pettigrew's contextualism is weak in defining context and action. The sources of this paradox lie in Pettigrew's shared intellectual affinity with liberal individualistic traditions of social and political theory that seeks simultaneously to undermine determinism and emphasize constraint, while also moderating voluntarism and affirming choice. The dilemmas of reconciling these apparently contradictory positions are most evident when Pettigrew's work turns to the contextual issue of 'leading change' as a counterpoint to instrumental notions of strategic choice.

Strategic change and strategic choice: leading change

Pettigrew's contextualism decisively influenced his views on the limits of leadership and strategic choice in organizational change processes. There are four major components to Pettigrew's conception of leading change.

First, he argues that leading change is unique to context: 'Leadership requires action appropriate to its context' (Pettigrew and Whipp 1991: 165). This idea is more than a reworking of conventional 'situational' models of leadership. For Pettigrew leadership is not simply a set of individual attributes or styles of leadership that can be adjusted to suit situational contingencies. Nor is contextualism a restatement of a sophisticated version of contingency theory: different leaders are needed for different contexts. Instead, Pettigrew appears to be offering a much more particularistic and context specific position: *each leader is different and each context is different.*

Second, leading change is a long-term, complex and incremental process of shaping how change unfolds over time: 'The art of leadership in the management field would seem to lie in the ability to shape the process in the long term rather than direct a single episode' (Pettigrew and Whipp

1991: 143). In this sense leading change is rarely a single pragmatic or unified intervention by a transformational leader, but is rather a series of disparate and fragmented activities at various levels: 'Leading change calls for the resolution of not so much great single issues but rather a pattern of interwoven problems' (Pettigrew and Whipp 1991: 165).

Third, leading change is a deeply political process. Unlike the OD tradition and rationalist models of the strategy process that both significantly underplay politics and conflict over ends while overstating the role of leadership, expert knowledge and change agency, Pettigrew places politics at the centre of his image of organizations: 'Because the past can be interpreted in many different ways and future outcomes are contested, the system in the present is subject to the 'filtering' of information brought about by relations of power and politics' (2003a: 302). This interest in politics as a counter-image to expertise and consensual ideals of action is strongly evident in Pettigrew's early exploration of 'information control as a power resource' and his later studies of the 'veneer of rationality' in policy formulation and corporate decision-making processes (1972). In these respects, his work is a continuation of long-standing micro-political views of organizations as entities consisting of coalitions of individuals and groups who do not follow optimal goals or rational choice processes, but rather pursue their own personal objectives or interests (Miller *et al.* 1999). For Pettigrew, the rationalist notion of intentional action, whether in the form of instrumental economic action, rational choice theory or archetypes of strategic actors, is simply unable to explain political behaviour and hence organizational change.

Fourth, leading change is envisaged as an enormously complex process requiring distributed leadership, rather than a single transformational leader (Pettigrew and Whipp 1991: 145). The main reason for this, Pettigrew argues, is that linking strategic and operational change consistently highlight the role of distributed leadership at all levels: 'If people at the lower and middle levels do not have the confidence and capability to lead then the strategic goals of those at the top are bound to be frustrated' (2002: 23). In this sense, Pettigrew (2002) prefers the idea of 'teams of leaders' or the more inclusive notion of 'change leaders', rather than conventional models of leadership or, worse still, 'heroic transformational leadership'.

Paradoxically, one consequence of Pettigrew's contextualist focus on leading change as a unique, incremental political and distributed activity is that it leaves the role of 'agency' in organizational change and strategic choice poorly defined. If leaders, managers or other potential strategic actors cannot plan and execute strategy as a rational, instrumental or transformational process of action, then how do they exercise choice? Pettigrew does not really try to answer this question directly. Instead, he seeks to steer an empirical course between voluntarism and determinism, between the duality of process and context, between human agency and the competitive and institutional forces of economic, political and technological contexts.

Is this mediation successful? Yes and no. Pettigrew appears to partly avoid both voluntarism and determinism, but with the result that we have neither a clear theory of the micro-contexts of action or agency nor a convincing macro-contextualism of systems, structures or institutions. In effect, Pettigrew avoids a reconceptualization of the micro-macro distinction. If the question is therefore asked, 'can leaders or managers plan and execute strategy?', Pettigrew's answer is that this is essentially an empirical, inductive and atheoretical issue of observing 'process' in action. Similarly, if the question is asked, 'does structure follow strategy or does structure determine strategy?', the answer is that context is always processual and open-ended. In both cases, Pettigrew avoids offering an explanatory account of 'managerial agency', or a systematic analysis of the constitutive influence of context over action (Hales 1999).

Yet, paradoxically, despite this apparently neutral stance, Pettigrew is offering within the narrative of contextualism an implicit explanatory account of agency that affirms choice while downplaying structure. Leading change as a unique, incremental, political and distributed activity that unfolds over time allows choice to emerge from context (Child 1972). But context in this sense is not primarily an arena of constraint, but rather a constantly shifting construct that allows new emergent possibilities of action. Essentially what Pettigrew wants contextualism to affirm are the possibilities for choice as a counterforce to constraint or determinism, without necessarily succumbing to voluntarism, although the danger is that he can be seen as affirming both positions: a voluntarist in terms of an abstract principle of choice, but sociologically conventional in his emphasis on context.

This dualistic, mildly anti-voluntaristic and strongly anti-deterministic idea of the notion of agency and choice partly explains why Pettigrew sidesteps leadership theory and research as a possible conceptual component of his process–content–context exploration of organizational change. Leadership theory is simply too leader-centric and voluntaristic to explain change. Similarly, rationalist models of strategic agency and strategic choice are unacceptable. Pettigrew therefore shows little interest in planned change models of organizational development or the tools and techniques of strategy analysis, both of which place a major emphasis on archetypes of rational strategic action and change agency. For Pettigrew leaders or managers rarely have efficacy over the shaping of events or planning of outcomes, although they have context-dependent choices. But does this dualistic emphasis on the embeddedness of agency as choice amount to writing leadership, strategic action and change agency as problematics out of contextualism?

Pettigrew is aware of this potential criticism and understandably sensitive to it. He argues that all his major case studies examined 'how key people within a company led change' – and this is to some extent true. For example, he notes that his study of ICI did not undervalue the role of individual leadership: 'After all, *The Awakening Giant* had clearly shown the tremendous influence of ICI's Chairman John Harvey-Jones in initiating and driving through change processes even when he was not in the very top power position of the firm' (2002: 22). Pettigrew also insists that his focus on linking strategic and operational change highlights the role of distributed leadership and broader forms of strategic action (2002: 23).

Despite this insistence, Pettigrew's contextualist focus on leading change does not lead to a 'contextual theory of leadership' (Osborn *et al.* 2002). If leadership is a contextual construct this raises difficult issues of how one distinguishes leadership and context in any coherent sense, and certainly in a manner that avoids the circularity of a process–context duality: 'The context alters leadership as leadership alters context to the point that, over time a clear-cut separation along conventional lines becomes extremely difficult' (Osborn *et al.* 2002: 809). Pettigrew highlights this problem but he does not explore context as a realm of practice within which leadership is enacted (1990: 144). Nor, more importantly, does contextualism offer a broader exploration of the forms or types of distributed leadership or change agency in organizations. The micro-politics of change explored by Pettigrew (1992) are about issues of decision-making and choice by managerial élites constrained by context, not distributed modes of agency. Just as the macro-context of systems as a potentially explanatory model is dissolved into processes of change that are defined by continuity with the past, yet paradoxically, have no path-dependent directionality, so strategic agency and change is dissolved into conflicts between actors over ends, values and ideals that are ultimately matters of choice.

While Pettigrew's dualistic formulations may have enormous analytical validity within an empirical case-based framework, they are also potentially one-sided. By definition, Pettigrew allows 'leading change' as a processual category and a contextual construct to define both continuity with the past and the embedding of strategic agency and choice in the present. He thereby effectively undermines the possibility of radical, transformation or discontinuous change, emerging either from 'process in action' or overpowering contextual forces that would imply determinism. His message for leaders, change agents and strategic actors appears to be: concentrate on iterative processes of incremental change, because the emergent context of change is so complex that it will only allow for possibilities of action and choice that are gradual continuations of the past.

If contextualism wants to fill the theoretical and practice gaps implied by this vision of change then it will have to create a more rounded processual model of agency and a more credible notion of context that goes beyond a bias toward incrementalism. The challenge of rounding out agency is essential because contextualism has eroded conventional notions of strategic agency, while offering a notion of leading change that is not adequate to the task of exploring leadership or the distributed or dispersed forms of decentred agency that characterize the increasingly more complex and flexible forms of organizing and strategy-making within organizations. Without a rounded concept of agency and more synthetic process-systems models of organizational structure, including potentially path-dependent models of organizational change, contextualism would appear to have few direct implications for practice.

Theory, practice and engaged scholarship

Pettigrew often makes a very strong case for 'practically useful' research on organizational change and the inspirational virtues of 'engaged' scholarship (1985, 2001). Echoing Giddens' (1984) belief that the link between agency and change in the social sciences is founded on an ideal that our actions should *make a difference*, Pettigrew affirms a similar injunction: 'The duty of the intellectual in society is to make a difference' (2001: 68). Pettigrew recognizes, of course, that this is no easy task. He is deeply aware, as Van de Ven (2002) notes, that academics have no monopoly on knowledge creation and that engagement with practitioners and other stakeholders involves negotiation, mutual respect and collaboration. But Pettigrew also wants to defend the integrity of the scholar against a pro-practice bias. Management research on organizational change is therefore not simply to be identified as an applied field of practice. Equally, he is perplexed by the increasing fragmentation of the various fields of management research and their increasing disengagement from the disciplinary streams of the social sciences that have traditionally nourished them: a process reinforced by the turn of some management researchers away from 'conscious pluralism' towards epistemological perspectivism. The overall remit of contextualism therefore involves not only building bridges between theory and practice, but also a holistic ambition to counteract disengagement and any postmodern turn towards even more fragmentation: 'After modernism there are new possibilities to widen and deepen our concept and practice of scholarship. A more contextualist and dynamic view of knowing will open doors to all the other potential stakeholders of management research' (2001: 69).

Despite this synthetic ambition and Pettigrew's overall note of liberal optimism regarding contextualism his work tends to be overwhelmingly strong on scholarship and relatively weak on practice (Dawson 2003). This takes various forms. The idea of *theory into practice*, whether in the form of applied theory, hypothesis testing or iterative models of action research, is rarely addressed (Pettigrew 1987, 1997). Ideas of 'best practice', 'core competencies' and other generic models of competitiveness are also treated with deep scepticism – and sometimes justly so (Pettigrew and Whipp 1991). Similarly, ideas of a successful 'fit' between organizations and their environments appear unsustainable in a contextual focus on the relational particularity of historical contexts: everything interacts but no set of factors is decisive (Donaldson 1997). Finally, as regards more mundane prescriptive ideals of planned change, one can find virtually no recipes or programmatic advice on 'how to manage change' in Pettigrew's work. More often, Pettigrew laments how complex change really is, and this partly explains why his work continues to have little appeal for practitioners. In all these respects, contextualism is not inclusive of practice or pro-practice, but sometimes stubbornly anti-practice.

Pettigrew would probably despair at this characterization, but it highlights an intrinsic problem for contextual analysis and the broader agenda of engaged scholarship: the absence of a rationale for practice. Indeed, one sometimes senses that Pettigrew may secretly wish this were not the case. Perhaps he may be revealing his sensitivity on this issue when he notes the remarkable similarity between the nine factor model of 'successfully managing change' he developed with Whipp in *Managing*

Change for Competitive Success (1991) and the eight steps model proposed by Kotter four years later (Pettigrew 2003a: 317–318). Kotter's (1996) model has been influential in change implementation practice and it is everything that Pettigrew and Whipp's model is not: it tends to be strongly linear, prescriptive and directly relevant to leading change as an episodic process with a beginning and an end. Such a model appears to bridge the theory–practice divide not because it is analytically rigorous, but because it is pro-practice.

This raises, of course, the broader question of what is the purpose of understanding organizational change (Sturdy and Grey 2003). Is it to achieve a greater knowledge of the complex, confusing and indeterminate nature of change? Or is it to define the causes, directionality, outcomes or 'how to' of successfully managing change? Unfortunately, without convincing synthetic answers to both questions there is very little possibility of reconciling theory and practice.

While Pettigrew recognizes the dangerous split between theory and practice, in the opposition between planned versus emergent change, managerial instrumentalism versus contextual complexity, his work as a whole remains firmly in the territory of academic values and scholarship, rather than the frustrating dilemmas of practice. When he therefore criticizes planned change models and by implication action research traditions, it is on the basis of their evidential paucity and lack of rigour, not their claims to relevance or practice. But does this realistic, if harsh, judgement miss the point? What really matters for these practice-based approaches is not that evidential knowledge is primarily 'objectively' validated before action is taken, but that practice *makes a difference* – or at least that it appears to work as an expert intervention or iterative mode of 'sensemaking' agency (Weick 1995).

Pettigrew sets up the problematic of practice in his work not only because he wants to *make a difference* through 'practically useful research', but because the holistic ambitions of contextualism are designed to provide an alterative interpretation of organizational change that fuses engaged scholarship and conscious pluralism as countervailing forces against naïve managerialism and the fragmentation of postmodern discourses. Yet curiously, Pettigrew does not provide a theory of practice – and this has fateful consequences.

Without a theory of practice, contextualism cannot create a credible theory of agency, organizational change or strategic choice. In this respect, Pettigrew's continued focus on the all-enveloping complexity of 'context' poses a broader research challenge in making good his practice claims. It may be useful to state a principled opposition to instrumental tools, prescriptive recipes of practice or programmatic action as a cautionary starting point, but this does not amount to providing alternative conceptions of practice. Nor is an anti-practice defence against the mounting threat of instrumental managerialism really convincing. One must therefore ask whether embeddedness as the guiding methodological principle of 'contextual realism' is a safe haven against the perceived ills of postmodernism (Pettigrew 2001). In the long run these defences are not really sustainable in a context where knowledge creation is itself increasingly problematic. Until contextualism seriously confronts the issue of practice it will remain a conventional liberal defence of scholarship and academic virtues in the face of the practice-bias of managerial action and the apparently corrosive logic of postmodern discourses.

Discussion: the legacy of contextualism

Four major criticisms of contextualism have been made as an overall approach to the understanding of the nature of organizational change and human agency. First, contextualism does not provide a coherent understanding of organizational structure–organizational change as a dynamic interplay between systems and processes, continuity and change. Instead, contextual analysis highlights the processual nature of organizational change, while underplaying the broader system characteristics of organizational structures. A truly coherent theory must incorporate both: organizing/changing are an inseparable couplet. Second, Pettigrew uses the idea of 'outer and inner' context to undermine structural concepts of organizations or their environments, effectively turning context into a holistic image of organizational change processes that are primarily incremental, open-ended and indeterminate. Organizational change therefore invariably appears as *incrementalism with transitions*. Third, Pettigrew's focus on the micro-dynamics of organizational politics and power is designed to emphasize constraint while simultaneously undermining determinism and emphasizing choice. Yet, paradoxically, it also underplays the exploration of leadership and strategic action in organizations. Essentially the model of action in contextualism is thin while the model of context is thick. In this respect, contextualism, despite its emphasis on agency and strategic choice, does not offer a 'contextual theory of leadership', or an understanding of the processes of leading change. Fourth, contextualism does not provide a theory of practice, and so its claims to provide 'practically useful knowledge' and a model of engaged scholarship are difficult to sustain. Ultimately, contextualism is a reaffirmation of scholarly rigour and academic practice, founded on the methodological injunction of 'embeddedness' and a liberal individualist concept of choice, rather than a convincing theory of organizational change and human agency.

Together these criticisms undermine the holistic intent of contextualism and raise broader issues of the origins, development and future of a distinctively contextualist approach to the study of organizational change. Should we dismiss contextualism as a failed approach to organizational change and strategic choice? Or, should we seek to engage contextualism with its limitations and its counterpoints?

Early versions of contextualism grew out of an opposition to instrumental models of rationality and strategic action, and this was often reinforced by the limited remit of theory versus empirical research. Pettigrew's case-based research methodology reproduces this ambivalence: 'While a contextualist methodology perhaps naturally points towards the adoption of an intensive, longitudinal, case study based form of analysis, it does not by itself supply an adequate theoretical underpinning' (Pettigrew *et al.* 1992: 23). The reasons for this theoretical deficit are intrinsic to the particularity of case-based analysis, but they also derive from what it excludes. Pettigrew's version of contextualism was constructed as a series of counterpoints against rationality, order, planned change, deliberate strategies, managerial agency, and systems thinking. But as a series of competing methodological contentions, contextualism has been unable to develop ideas that can really challenge or replace the theoretical edifices of competing discourses. Paradoxically, by emphasizing difference, contextualism is always in danger of becoming simply anti-system, anti-structure, anti-planning and therefore the antithesis of both systematic theoretical analysis and strategic action.

The other intrinsic danger with the legacy of contextualism is its intrinsic eclecticism. Because Pettigrew extends and reworks the disparate legacy of contextualism his work tends to result in a theoretical hybrid that empirically mixes ideas and crosses disciplinary demarcations. As a consequence his work does not fit into the neat sub-divisions of management theory, organizational analysis or strategic management research. Without a disciplinary home contextualism can therefore appear marginal to more mainstream disciplinary debates.

Because of these theoretical and disciplinary limitations Pettigrew's ambition for contextualism has always been frustrated. He is not, however, a lone contextualist (Johns 2001; Whittington 2003). There are other individual contextualists and multifarious 'process scholars' out there, as well as the institutional legacy of a 'Warwick tradition of process research' – although there is no evidence of a coherent school in the sense of the once formidable 'Aston School' (Pettigrew *et al.* 2003: 334). There is also a discernible intellectual genealogy to Pettigrew's work that stretches back to Simon (1947) and is reinvented and reinvigorated in the work of Child (1972) and others. But again one has to be cautious in reading too much into these connections. For example, it is not possible to easily place Pettigrew within the traditions of a 'strategic choice school' emanating from Child (1972). Child certainly influenced Pettigrew's principled opposition to any deterministic view of organization structure and organizational change: 'the "strategic choice" perspective was originally advanced as a corrective to the view that the way in which organizations are designed and structured is determined by their operational contingencies' (Child 1997: 43). But Pettigrew's work marks a broader shift towards the exploration of the problematic relationship of strategic change and strategic choice. Fortunately or unfortunately, this problematic is never fully clarified. In this respect, it is perhaps appropriate that Pettigrew's ambition for contextualism is perhaps more celebrated as an academic and methodological stance towards scholarly research on strategic change and strategic choice, rather than a coherent research programme with followers.

Yet even without the affirmative foundation of a unifying research programme or a school, Pettigrew's version of contextualism still deserves our attention. In particular, there is a need to engage with other competing schools and specialist research programmes, such as neo-institutionalism in organizational theory (DiMaggio and Powell 1983; Whitley 2003). Curiously, Pettigrew's links to institutional theory have rarely been explored, even though there are some strong affinities as well as major differences. If institutionalism reconnects organizational theory with society and its economic and political institutions, contextualism appears to reconnect 'organizing' as an emergent process with agency and strategic choice (Lounsbury and Ventresca 2003). As neo-institutional theory has begun to include models of strategic agency and collective action within homogenizing archetypes of organizational fields, there are, however, new possibilities of a long overdue engagement between structural analysis and contextualist ideas of strategic change and strategic choice (Hensmans 2003).

The possibility of a positive dialogue between contextualism and conventional organizational development models of organizational change looks, however, much more problematic. Contextualism is essentially a counter-image to the concept of planned change. Pettigrew's tripartite *context–content–process* formulation of contextualism is virtually the antithesis of organizational development models of *context* as system, *content* as what to change and *process* as how to bring about change (Burke 2002: 143). In this respect, the contextualist and organizational development approaches appear to be mutually incomprehensible to each other, although their continuing counterpoints suggest the possibility of a dialogue of disagreement.

Another area of more positive reciprocal engagement is the growing 'practice turn' of organizational theory and strategy management research (Orlikowski 1997; Whittington 2003). Despite the glaring absence of a 'theory of practice' within contextualism, Pettigrew partly endorses this focus when he questions the dichotomy between strategy formulation and implementation, as well as the separation of strategy content and strategy process research (2002: 21). For Pettigrew both distinctions are redundant: 'The link between formulation and implementation is not unilinear or straightforward: they form interrelated parts of the strategy process' (2003a: 301). More recently, Pettigrew and some of his colleagues have gone further down this route by conceiving 'organizing/strategizing' as inextricably linked in a 'single duality' rather than forming two separate activities (Pettigrew 2003b). But paradoxically the shift towards a 'practice perspective' involves an attempt to distinguish its analytical remit from the 'process tradition' associated with contextualism (Whittington 2003). This has some uncomfortable implications, in that a fully developed practice perspective would redefine, absorb or even transcend contextualism.

Finally, there are some interesting connections between Pettigrew's desire to avoid the instrumentalism and hubris of 'managerialist discourses' of strategic change and more recent innovations in organizational discourse (Alvesson and Karreman 2000). By 'embedding' agency in context Pettigrew implicitly decentres the familiar 'subjects' of management discourse: the multifarious models of 'strategic agency'. In general, the underlying assumptions of strategic agency models are fourfold. First, strategy is a centralized planning function that can be controlled and coordinated from the top of organizations (Ansoff 1991). Second, there is a clear distinction between strategy formulation and implementation, or between planning and execution (Mintzberg 1994). Third, strategic change and innovation is a planned process of diffusion and technology transfer. Fourth, strategy implementation is a cascade of means–ends decision processes that can be subject to supervision and monitoring. Once agency is embedded in context it is difficult to sustain any of these assumptions, and this is further exacerbated if 'agency and structure' are completely submerged within organizational discourse. Pettigrew rarely articulates these issues except for some broad endorsements of Giddens' work. Nevertheless, there are some interesting parallels between Pettigrew's contextualist reading of agency and more recent attempts to fuse 'discourse analysis' and Giddens' ideas on agency and structure with a focus on the 'socially embedded' nature of power in contexts of action (Heracleous and Hendry 2000; Heracleous and Barrett 2001). Unfortunately, as we have seen, Pettigrew never manages to escape the liberal individualist undercurrent in agent-centred discourse of strategic choice, but neither of course did Giddens (1984).

By clarifying the scope and implications of contextualism one can hopefully begin to break down some of the intrinsic disciplinary barriers between neo-institutionalism, organizational development theory, organizing/strategizing concepts of practice, and the more recent innovations in organizational discourse. In this respect, Pettigrew's work deserves serious engagement as a discursive act of self-clarification by any scholar who claims to study organizational and strategic change or by those practitioners involved in change management practice. To simply dismiss the legacy of contextualism because of its methodological limitations, practice deficit and programmatic failure as a school, is to forget that organizational theory and management research is still in search of theories and practices of organizational transformation and change. Pettigrew's work and contextualism remain an important chapter in this ongoing quest.

Conclusion: contextualizing contextualism

No overall critical appreciation of Pettigrew's work and the legacy of contextualism would be complete without raising one final issue: the cultural origins and significance of Pettigrew's intellectual commitment to forms of contextual discourse. If the concept or idea of contextualism is itself a cultural and historical artefact, then contextualism has to be contextualized. Pettigrew (2002) partly recognizes this issue, and he is clearly sensitive to the academic and political context out of which his work grew. But he invariably conceives this critical task as a reflection on professional practice or methodological issues, rather than a self-reflexive exploration of the taken-for-granted assumptions or underlying presuppositions of contextualism. How can a more probing idea of self-reflexivity be explored?

One possibility is to explore contextualism as a construct of Homo Academicus (Bourdieu 1988). In this respect, contextualism as an academic construct partly represents what Bourdieu describes as an intellectual 'field' of practices that never form a homogenous social space. Rather, intellectual fields are a constantly shifting interplay between orthodoxy and heterodoxy as participants seek to affirm the truth and objectivity of their own partial and partisan views (Bourdieu 1988: xiv). Intellectual fields are therefore not a world of 'conscious pluralism', but of dissonant pluralism, an idea that if pushed too far may eventuate in epistemological and moral relativism – a position that Bourdieu deliberately avoids. Academic discourses within intellectual fields also articulate political values, although there is rarely a simple homology between academic and political discourses: 'it is not political stances which determine people's stances on things academic, but their positions in the academic field which informs the stances that they adopt on political issues in general as well as on academic problems' (Bourdieu 1988: xvii–xviii).

If one avoids the hidden traces of reductionism implicit in Bourdieu's work, this dual characterization can be partly applied to contextualism. Pettigrew's academic oeuvre grew out of critical dissatisfaction with the relative absence of empirical research on how change occurs, and a deep antipathy to planned change, managerial voluntarism and the recipe-driven normativism of change management theory. This partly defines his perceived challenge to orthodoxy as a dichotomy between system-based versus process-based theory. More broadly, Pettigrew also appears to have conceived his work as a counterforce against the prevailing static system-based orthodoxies of structural-functionalism and contingency theories and the more dynamic, if old, heterodoxies of Marxist ideals of change as radical discontinuity. Against the stasis of system orthodoxy and the radical illusion of historical discontinuity, Pettigrew (1987, 1997) invariably presents a process-based vision of incrementalism: change as a gradual context-dependent transition process that is essentially unpredictable and indeterminate.

One also finds this oppositional image mirrored, if obscurely, in the political context out of which contextualism grew. Pettigrew partly captures this context when he observes:

> In the early 1980s the dominating policy issues in all aspects of organizational life was change. In Margaret Thatcher, Britain had a right-wing conservative

leader with a revolutionary agenda and who looked like she was going to
maintain power long enough to drive through a programme of transformation in
both the public and private sectors.

(2003b: 315)

Thatcherism was in many senses the ideological antithesis of a process-based and incremental view of contextual change, because it attacked institutions directly and conceived its mission as a radical break with the past; although it was in many respects a counter-revolutionary return to market values through *deliberate* policies of non-intervention, privatization, outsourcing, internal markets and the ubiquitous emphasis on efficacy and effectiveness in the public services.

This dual reading of contextualism as an intellectual field with an academic practice and contra-ideological image is illuminating because it highlights what is missing from contextualism as an objectivistic discourse on organizational change. Pettigrew tends to see contextualism as essentially a methodological practice that somehow ensures academic rigour and justifies scholarly engagement on the basis of objective knowledge. In this sense, the broader moral and political goal of academic practice is therefore to educate managers and other stakeholders to become more reflexive by recognizing the contextual complexity of change. Allied to this the aim of contextualism it is to ensure the professionalism of management research by affirming the necessity of re-engaging with the social sciences, rather than succumbing to the instrumentalism of practice.

But are these formulations sufficient to explain what is being produced by contextualism, and whom it is for? Pettigrew never sufficiently historicizes his embrace of contextualism to ask more pointedly self-referential questions: why did I become a contextualist? What extra-academic values or larger institutional forces shaped my commitment to processual analysis? Who is the 'subject' of contextualist discourse – the engaged scholar? Can the engaged scholar really become a reflexive practitioner? Can the engaged scholar make a difference?

These disconcerting questions have to be asked because the process–context duality of contextualism is essentially a reworking of agency and structure, voluntarism and determinism, mediated through the 'content' of Pettigrew's embedded methodology of case-based empirical research. This allows him enormous scope to defend scholarship and the holistic ambitions of contextual analysis against its perceived enemies, from managerialism to postmodern discourses. But does this stance afford the opportunity to contextualize contextualism as an academic practice with a potentially political intent? At the heart of Pettigrew's contextualism is not just a vision of scholarship but a politics of liberal individualism: it is inspired by the belief that choice as a principle of autonomy matters more than rational plans, predictive models or future strategic visions. When he quotes Loasby's (1976: 5) elegant affirmation of choice he perhaps reveals his true inner self-image and the moral centre of gravity of contextualism: 'If choice is real, the future cannot be certain; if the future is certain, there can be no choice' (Pettigrew 1997: 341). Ultimately, Pettigrew wants choice as the opposite of cause, determinism or future outcomes, rather than choice as the outcome or effect of a cause. Paradoxically, contextualism ends not in an epistemological or ontological justification of objective knowledge or the efficacy of practice, but in a moral and political reaffirmation of choice.

5 The edge of chaos: complexity theory and organizational change

- Introduction
- Complexity theories: four core concepts
- Beyond order: from systems to processes of change
- Evolution and adaptiveness
- Systems and agent-based interaction
- Decentred agency
- Discussion
- Conclusion

Introduction

Chaos and complexity theories, with their origins in physics, mathematical biology, meteorology, computer science and systems thinking have had a profound impact on recent discussions of organizational change, and their influence appears to be growing (Brown and Eisenhardt 1997; Chia 1998; Cilliers 1998; Tsoukas 1998; Anderson 1999; Carley and Hill 2001; Fitzgerald and Van Eijnatten 2002; Levinthal 2002; Smith 2003; Stacey 2003; Van Eijnatten and Putnik 2004; Houchin and Maclean 2005). The central idea of 'complexity science' is that natural systems are characterized by dynamism, non-linearity and unpredictability, rather than simply equilibrium, order and predictability. In this respect, chaos and order are simultaneous attributes of complex non-linear systems: for underlying chaos and randomness is an emergent or hidden order of orderly instability (Hayles 1991; Kauffman 1993; Flake 1998).

Applied to organizational change theory these ideas suggest that conventional complex systems models of organizations are outmoded because they only conceive of change as linear or cyclical, while conceiving any random patterns of change as disorderly or 'dysfunctional': deviations from a norm of functional order or equilibrium (Parsons 1951; Luhmann 1995). Chaos and complexity theories of organizations offer alternative and more positive explanations of disorder, irregularity and non-linear change (Brown and Eisenhardt 1997; Styhre

2002). Unlike early cybernetic and general system models of stable equilibrium within dynamic systems, complexity theories of chaotic systems shift the focus to the positive forces of 'non-equilibrium', combining stability and instability. If reducing complexity (i.e. finding order and maintaining stability in the midst of chaos) was once the higher order reference point of systems self-regulation or environmental adaptation, chaos now becomes the central defining feature of the emergent hyper-complexity of systems (Luhmann 1995). Chaos is the norm, and this is positively interpreted. Organizational systems poised at the 'edge of chaos', or 'far-from-equilibrium', are therefore viewed as optimal in generating innovation, transformation and change.

The 'edge of chaos' phenomenon is one of the most synthetic expressions of the order–disorder viewpoint, and it encompasses many of the central ideas of complexity theories. The edge of chaos refers to narrow intermediate zones of 'bounded instability' between order and chaos that allow new patterns of transformation and change to emerge. When organizations as systems drift from stable equilibrium founded on negative feedback towards unstable equilibrium founded on positive feedback they do not disintegrate. Instead, at their system boundaries the contradictory forces of negative and positive feedback operate simultaneously to create self-organizing processes that are neither stable nor unstable, but rather a combination of both, thereby ensuring that organizations retain flexibility in adapting to their environments (Thietart and Forgues 1995). Sustaining this edge of chaos is increasingly viewed as essential in managing the 'hyper-complexity' of network organizations and economies, and the growing challenges of 'informational capitalism' and 'global complexity' (Castells 2000; Urry 2003).

Despite the enormous intuitive appeal of chaos theories for understanding the constantly evolving and emergent nature of organizational change at a system level, there is growing concern that recent innovations in complexity theory do not provide adequate concepts for understanding agency and change in organizations (Caldwell 2005a). Early chaos theory was essentially a mathematical 'theory' that constructed macro-system models of low dimensional phenomena, and there was very little focus on agential interaction at a systems level. This has disadvantages when applied to organization analysis. For change within organizations is not just a naturalistic property of non-linear dynamic systems or network interaction, it also appears to be the outcome of various forms of human agency and group behaviour (Lane 2004). In chaos theory, systems do not have intentionality, but neither do actors.

Recent attempts to rework chaos-and-complexity theories of organizations as process, interactional or actor network versions of 'complex adaptive systems' are partly attempts to reconnect the system effects of complexity with an idea of agency. Rather than conventional macro-structural models of system change, complex adaptive systems attempt to theorize models of 'decentred agency' as modes of self-organization within actor networks or group processes of interaction (Arrow *et al.* 2000; Blackler *et al.* 2000; Macy and Willer 2002; Stacey 2003). This requires a shift from the generative rules of chaotic systemic entities to the lower-level self-organizing rules and 'schemata' of interaction between agents: a precarious move from systems as structural entities at the edge of chaos to systems as network 'processes' of information, communication and change founded on the interaction of 'complex adaptive agents'.

This shift has also led to an increasing fusion (some would say conflation) of chaos theory and 'complex adaptive systems' (CAS) of agent interaction and other varieties of actor network theorizing. Certainly, chaos-and-complexity theories and actor network theories (ANT) are mutually reinforcing, even if the theoretical objects are somewhat different (Latour 1999, 2005). Actors in networks and 'complex adaptive agents' are treated as 'actants' or automata as agency is attributed to objects or patterns of interaction. This emphasis on bottom-up emergence, interaction and networks marks a shift in chaos-and-complexity theories of organizations towards a redefinition of chaos and the role of intentional agency. Increasingly the overall emphasis of complexity theories of organizations is on the 'social morphology' of decentred agency in local networks rather than the pre-eminence of structural wholes. In this reformulation, agency and change appear to be decentred as the contingent artefacts of complexity or local actor network interaction.

Is this apparent shift in the organizational focus of chaos-and-complexity theory credible or convincing? Can complexity theories offer new models of organizational change and agential dispersal while keeping at bay the spectre of chaos – the collapse of the virtuous system coupling of chaos–order? To partly address these overarching questions two overlapping sets of questions will be examined.

First, can complexity theories of organizations reconcile the conventional concept of 'system' as a functional entity with a new 'process' overview of organizational change? What happens if one takes away the functionalist and evolutionary assumptions of system concepts and replaces them with a processual ontology of change (Tsoukas 1998)? Without functionalism can the systems focus of complexity theories really hold together? More broadly, if one takes away conventional evolutionary notions of 'survival' and 'fitness', does complexity theory have any hope of constructing 'causal process theories' of organizational change (Dooley and Van de Ven 1999; Garud and Van de Ven 2002)?

Second, is the concept of 'agency' in complexity theory simply the outcome of self-organizing rules of micro interaction? Does this decentring of agency mean that we do not need concepts of intentional agency? Then how can human actors exercise rationality, autonomy or reflexivity in the choice of ends (Lane 2004)? More importantly, if agents as network actors or teams are free to follow their own self-organizing rules, how is order and change possible? Will self-organization lead to a reinstatement of chaos as the antithesis of order?

Complexity theories of organizations have been slow to address these perplexing questions, partly because of their intrinsic systems bias, their latent scientism, and their related inability to explore the duality of 'agency and structure' in any kind of synthetic manner (Giddens 1984). In virtually all systems theories, including many varieties of organizational complexity theory, 'structure' as an implicit functionalist or system ordering principle referring to real or 'observed objects' is given priority over agency as an explanatory category (Luhmann 1995). As a consequence there is always a danger of treating 'change' as an evolutionary appendage to functionalist assumptions, and agency as an epiphenomenona of complex systems. This is the powerful message that has come out of sociological explorations of agency and structure over the past three decades, although it appears to have had little impact on the burgeoning field of complexity theories of organizational change, innovation and learning (Smith 2003).

Some complexity theorists believe, of course, that they can 'subvert' or dispense with the agency and structure distinction altogether (Urry 2003: 47). Because complexity analysis assumes a state of 'in-betweenness' in which neither order nor disorder predominate there appears to be no need for a distinction between organizational structure and organizational change; stability and discontinuity are always implicated. Similarly, because 'agency' is neither free nor predetermined there is no need for a theory of casual determinism nor free will: agency is 'decentred' as a relational property of iterative systems of interaction that cannot be subject to predictive models of rationality, control or strategic choice.

Change in complex systems cannot therefore be explained by the planned change of structures or the actions of intentional agents. Rather change appears to stem from the emergent system effects of complexity over time and the unpredictable patterns of non-intentional interaction.

While these ideas appear to carry considerable logical force, escaping the agency and structure duality is not as straightforward as it appears. Agency gets attached to structure (i.e. systems) in new forms: the complexity theory couplet of 'complex adaptive agents' and 'complex adaptive systems' is essentially a reworking of agency and structure. Even Giddens' (1984) famous process-based and change-oriented model of 'structuration', conceived as a manifestation of agency, still retains 'system' as the unintended consequence of the recursive actions of knowledgeable agents. If the complexity turn of organizational theory is to gain credibility it has to face up to the classic ontological dilemma of theorizing systems and action together while keeping them epistemologically distinct (Archer 1983, 2003). To do this, complexity theory would somehow have to fuse systems and process ontologies of organizational structure and organizational change – an enormously challenging task.

One possibility in facing up to this challenge is to build bridges between complexity theory and postmodernist and construction ideas of change as 'becoming' and agency as 'discourse' or 'text' (Chia 1998: Bouchikihi 1998; Cilliers 1998: Stacey 2003). But this too raises many awkward issues. Postmodern and constructionist discourses seek to deconstruct notions of system, agency, change and they reject all foundational claims to knowledge (Hardy 2004). Knowledge is discourse and truth is temporal. In contrast, chaos and complexity theories seek to redefine the nature of system dynamics and agential interaction by reconstructing a 'new science' of complex systems. These projects may have some methodological affinities in their underlying emphasis on temporality and change, but they appear to be ontologically and epistemologically incompatible (Price 1997; Midgley 2003). This tension creates the preconditions for paradigm wars. For some the goal of complexity theory is to give postmodernism scientific status as a 'postpositivist' science, while for others the new science of complexity will finally 'eradicate' postmodernism (Morcol 2002).

This chapter begins by briefly outlining four of the core concepts of complexity theory: *ordered unpredictability*, *strange attractors*, *small change/large effects*, and the overarching concept of *self-organization*.

This outline is primarily for the benefit of readers unfamiliar with complexity theory. Next, the linkages between complex 'systems' and 'process' concepts of organizational change are examined. Self-organization and evolutionary 'adaptiveness' are then explored in relation to the teleological notion of organizations as 'complex adaptive systems'. The focus then shifts to a brief exploration of the untheorized agency–structure linkages between 'complex adaptive agents' and 'complex adaptive systems'. This is followed by an examination of the problems of linking systems of self-organization to concepts of decentred agency, *broadly conceived as emergent modes of relational interaction that are non-intentional.* It is then concluded that some complexity theories of agential dispersal and change in organizations are in serious danger of falling apart as they stray into the territory of postmodern and constructionist discourses of decentred agency and processual ontologies of change (Chia 1998: Cilliers 1998; Stacey 2003).

Finally, it should be emphasized that this critical review is not conceived as a commentary on the validity or otherwise of 'complexity science' – assuming that such a science has emerged (Thrift 1999). Rather, the review is limited to an exploration of the theoretical and practical implications of complexity theories for an understanding of organizational change and human agency.

Complexity theories: four core concepts

The theoretical implications of complexity theories for organizational analysis invariably derive from four of the core concepts of complexity science (McKelvey 1999): *ordered unpredictability, strange attractors, small change/large effects,* and the overarching concept of *self-organization.*

Ordered unpredictability. The idea that organizations are systems characterized by emergent patterns of unpredictability or dynamic chaos while also retaining structural patterns of stability and order has enormous intuitive appeal, although it is not an easy idea to grasp, either theoretically or practically. Some of the most powerful analogies of the simultaneous order–disorder phenomena within dynamic systems have come from considerations of time series analysis (Kiel and Elliott 1997). The graph of a time series may appear to be affected by considerable stochastic error when in fact the series is very structured: a generating equation for the series with no stochastic components can be produced. This appears paradoxical. The chaotic series is determined but also undetermined: we know the generating equation but we cannot make any predictable forecasts based on this equation or knowledge of the time series.

This paradox of 'deterministic chaos' is central to most varieties of chaos-and-complexity theory, and it has two broad implications. First, non-linear dynamic systems appear to be in constantly emergent processes of change or adaptation and so they do not reach either a fixed endpoint or a state of cyclical equilibrium. Second, although these processes rule out linear cause–effect models of forecasting, chaotic systems appear to revolve around orderly patterns that are deterministic (Anderson 1999: 217). Contrary to the common usage of the term 'chaos' to mean 'disorder', complex dynamic systems therefore imply a causality that is orderly and determined, yet unpredictable.

Strange attractors. A central problem in understanding non-linear complex chaotic systems is the idea that although they are unpredictable, they somehow are in shifting equilibrium around 'strange' or 'chaotic attractors', self-referential points or states that create order while allowing new patterns of non-linear change to emerge. Strange attractors therefore share the same tension-inducing properties of chaotic systems, they are determined and unpredictable, stable and unstable at the same time: 'A new form of order is found out of chaos. The apparent random behaviour gets "attracted" to a given space and remains within its limits' (Thietart and Forgues 1995: 21). How then do strange attractors ensure that relative order emerges?

Strange attractors appear to have two order reinforcing characteristics. First, they keep the overall trajectory followed by an unpredictable system within a particular coherent pattern, creating self-organizing order, although the pattern will never repeat itself exactly (Anderson 1999: 217). Second, the attractor patterns that govern complex systems appear to be recursive at different levels or scales of a system through a process of 'self-similarity': attractors as 'fractual' parts or objects of a system are similar in form to the 'fractual wholes' of the system (Flake 1998).

Because of the potentially order-generating properties of strange attractors they appear to act as substitutes for conventional macro-equilibrium or central feedback mechanisms, tight system connectedness or integration, as well as influencing the emergence of new micro patterns of order (Baker 1993). Similarly, although they give inherently chaotic non-linear systems coherence once they are in 'motion', they can be reconfigured through small changes that can send a system towards the pull of a new attractor pattern. It is in this sense that one can perhaps understand Kauffman's claim that 'attractors literally are most of what a system does' (1993: 174).

Small changes, large effects. Most complexity theories are informed by the principle that small changes in interactively complex systems can alter the long-term behaviour of systems – the famous 'butterfly effect'. Computer simulations of long-range weather forecasts revealed the classic example of this effect, where small changes to data parameters generated enormously divergent weather patterns over time. Although the relevance of this modelling is incidental to the incremental use of constantly updated data in short-range weather forecasting, the discovery reinforced a focus on non-linear relations within complex systems as a way of understanding the nature of chaotic patterns underlying long-term unpredictability (Holland 1998: 44).

Applications of this concept to organizational analysis and change theory have so far not been very encouraging, and there have been almost no solid empirical studies. Sometimes the 'small change–large effects' principle has been simply used to justify conventional system dynamic ideas that there are crucial strategic leverage points of system change, while in other cases it is used to support the diffusion or dispersal of change through self-organizing processes of interaction or participation: a micro-process formulation of 'loosely coupled systems' (Weick 2001). More broadly, the small change–large effects principle can also be cast in a more paradoxical form: large-scale failures in changing organizational systems can result from the interactions of small failures – complex organizational systems collapse because of a thousand small failures rather than one single systemic event (Perrow 1999 [1984]).

Self-organization. Systems driven to the edge of chaos appear to exhibit spontaneous processes of self-organization. This idea has some similarities to conventional system-cybernetic notions of *homeostasis*, in which systems maintain self-regulation in the face of unexpected disturbances or perturbations. Self-organization appears, however, to be a more sophisticated form of homeostasis, in which autonomous *autopoietic* processes of self-production and reproduction are mutually reinforcing. It is in this sense that Luhmann defines 'autopoietic reproduction' as: 'everything that is used as a unit by a system is produced as a unit by the system itself. This applies to elements, processes, boundaries, and other structures and, last but not least, to the unity of the system itself' (1990: 3). If the underlying system presupposition of homeostasis is that self-regulation is a form of system maintenance, the underlying system presupposition of self-organization is that self-production and reproduction exist as a principle of order/disorder and ongoing change.

With this shift from self-maintenance to self-production and reproduction complexity conceptions of self-organization at the edge of chaos are partly decoupled from equilibrium models of systems stability. Physicists had first begun to explore this idea when they asked why physical systems far from conventional patterns of equilibrium did not disintegrate. Their answer was that systems could pass through phases of randomness before achieving new levels of order as 'dissipative structures' that acquire new energy and survive (Prigogine and Nicolis 1989). This insight marked a shift from mechanist to non-equilibrium thermodynamics as an analogue for self-organization in complex systems.

Transposed into organizational change theory, 'dissipative structures' of energy are reframed as order-generating rules within systems and networks of information and communication, which allow the unfolding of relative chaos while providing new forms of order. This 'living' self-organization explains why complex systems can maintain themselves in the face of constant environmental uncertainty. Effectively, order is free since it appears to emerge from simple bottom-up rules and iterative interaction processes that create non-linear dynamics of bounded instability (Kauffman 1993; Boal *et al.* 2003).

The four reciprocal ideas of chaotic determinism, strange attractors, small change/large effects, and self-organization as an overarching concept are central to most complexity theories of organizations. We now need to explore how these ideas are applied to system change, evolution or development over time, as well as concepts of agency.

Beyond order: from systems to processes of change

The potentially enormous advantage of complexity theories for the understanding of organizational change is that they shift the focus from stability within systems to 'processes' of change and development. Organizations are not just 'structures', either stable or unstable, but ongoing processes of emergence and self-organization that are simultaneously ordered and disordered. An apparently curious mix of negative and positive feedback, self-organization and competitive survival, randomness and predictability, system interaction and dispersed control, somehow ensures the simultaneity of order and chaos, stability and change.

Combining order and chaos has far-reaching implications for one of the central questions of organizational theory: how does one account for the reciprocal relations between perceived order and ongoing change? Or more precisely, how can the apparent analytical asymmetry between organizational structures (systems) be reconnected with organizational changes (processes)?

As argued in Chapter 2, most attempts to capture the nature of organizational structure have used atemporal or static categories allied to system ontologies and realist epistemologies (Luhmann 1995). In contrast, many attempts to explore organizational change tend to use temporal categories allied to process ontologies and 'interpretative' models of action (Giddens 1984). Atemporal structural categories are often very misleading because they can lead to essentialist ideas of societies or organizations as purely mechanistic, systemic or functional entities outside of time or history (Parsons 1951). Systems are external structures 'out there'. Introducing change into this reading of structure usually becomes a mechanistic exercise at overlaying change onto structure. Change inevitably becomes identified with linear, multi-linear or broader evolutionary patterns of change defined by causal events, predictive movements or teleological processes leading from one stable stage or state to another (Van de Ven and Poole 1995). Parsons' (1951) structural-functional theory is a classic sociological exploration of structure as a system entity and change as 'moving equilibrium'.

Attempts to avoid a realist notion of structure as a system entity with hypothetical properties usually gravitate towards an ontological view of structuring or 'structuration' as a temporal process: as the activity of organizing (Giddens 1984). Giddens' 'structuration theory' is a powerful expression of this position and it is animated by a consistent hostility to the atemporal nature of systems ideas. For Giddens the ontological relationship between agency and structure is one of identity or synthetic 'duality'. Structuration refers to both the temporal processes of producing–reproducing structures and the epistemological identification of agency and structure. This viewpoint makes sense in capturing the processual nature of organizational change, but Giddens gives too much efficacy to agency over structure, and so structure appears to have no analytical status as an ontological category. In effect agency appears to subsume structures as systems into temporal processes of agential interaction, an issue that still poses major challenges for structuration theory (Heracleous and Hendry 2000).

Within the field of organizational change theory there have been few attempts synthetically to explore 'process' and 'system' concepts or organizational structure and change, and even fewer attempts to incorporate agency into this exploration (Chia 1999). Instead, the major tendency has been to identify 'how' organizations as structural entities change and develop. As already noted in the discussion of Pettigrew's work, Van de Ven and Poole (1995) are advocates of this position when they refer to 'process as progression (the order and sequence) of events in an organizational entity's existence over time' (p. 512). Using this definition they provide a typology of four 'change process' theories: *life cycle, teleology, dialectical* and *evolutionary theories*.

Life cycle theories conceive of organizations as organic entities and they treat organizational change as 'a single sequence of stages or phases' of growth, maturity and decline (Van de Ven and Poole 1995: 513). Evolutionary theories also operate with biological metaphors of organizational development, but change is conceived as a constant of competitive selection or system survival punctuated by periods of relative order/stability or 'punctuated equilibrium'. Dialectical theories assume that organizations operate in a 'pluralist world of colliding events, forces, or contradictory values that compete with each other for domination and control' (Van de Ven and Poole 1995: 517). These antithetical forces or conflicts can potentially lead to a new creative synthesis of discontinuous change or organizational collapse. Teleological theories assume that organizations are purposeful entities with goals that reflect the organizational requirements of functional differentiation or system adaptation.

Van de Ven and Poole (1995) claim that these theories 'provide four internally consistent accounts of change processes in organizational entities', and they also hint that complexity theory may provide a more unified meta-theory (p. 519, p. 536). Their classification tends, however, to be too rigid and mechanistic, partly because it narrows the definition of 'process' (Tsoukas and Chia 2002). For example, evolutionary and teleological theories are often mutually reinforcing because they feed off system and process interpretations of change. In addition, the virtual absence of any reference to 'agency' in these models undermines their efficacy in theorizing the relationship between agency and structure, and hence the relationship between process and system concepts.

Alternative 'process' theories of change can be derived by counterpoising an ontology of 'being', substance and persistence with an ontology of 'becoming' in which change is constant and indivisible (Chia 2002). However, the analysis of organizational change using temporal categories can also be misleading because they define change as a seamless and continuous process of interaction that situates the past and present, the before and after, in ongoing processes of becoming (Chia 1999; Tsoukas and Chia 2002). Pushed to its logical conclusion, process-based ideas of temporality can lead to concepts of social and organizational change as always-emergent processes created by perpetual change and always open to the future (Giddens 1984). Ontologically this understanding of temporality is sound, but epistemologically it can potentially be analytically vacuous; it invariably defines change as constant and indivisible, but it does not explain when, how or why change occurs. Recent attempts within organizational theory to define change as 'becoming' have therefore ended in attempts to replace a systems ontology of structure with a process ontology of change (Chia 1999). Taken to its extreme the ontological opposition of systems and processes can create a recipe for paradigm warfare (Abbott 2001).

One way out of this dilemma is to argue that static and temporal categories are not either/or choices. Ontologically systems and processes are inseparable, but epistemologically they can be analytically differentiated in developing a temporal theorizing of 'structure' that can accommodate both continuity and discontinuity (Archer 1983). Luhmann's (1995) social systems theory appears to come close to this position when he proposes a theory of self-reproducing social systems that can accommodate change: 'structural change presupposes self-maintenance; this much has always been clear. It follows that change and preservation cannot be explained by different theories [...] but that *every theory must always deal with both* (p. 347, emphasis added). Despite this insight, Luhmann proceeds to outline an evolutionary model of social change (organizational and societal) in which the self-reproduction of systems generates random mutations that allow the 'natural selection' of changes (Hendry and Seidl 2003). This amounts to a conventional attempt to conjoin systems concepts and evolutionary theory rather than an attempt to reconcile system and process ontologies of change.

Complexity theories of organizations confront similar synthetic issues in reconciling systems and processes, continuity and discontinuity, stasis and change. But the issues appear much more intractable, partly because of the focus on system complexity and non-linear change. In a complex

system the components of the system cannot be clearly identified and
their patterns of interaction cannot be explicated (Cilliers 1998: 109). Nor
can 'process' and 'system' concepts be easily conjoined. Complex systems
are *recursive* and so they follow processes of development that exhibit
interdependent, multiple and non-linear dynamics that may emerge from
different feedback loops. Moreover, because complex systems are in a
constant state of motion or flux the probability of such systems ever
returning to the same state is remote. In effect, complex systems never
find themselves in the same place twice and as a consequence: 'Similar
actions taken by organizations in a chaotic state will never lead to the
same result' (Thietart and Forgues 1995: 27). Nevertheless, complexity
theories appear to operate with system presuppositions that appear to
promise a scientific insight into order/chaos as a state that is both
unpredictable and determined. By definition complex chaotic systems
therefore require a process ontology of change and discontinuity, not just
a systems ontology of stability and predictability.

But can complexity theories really handle system and process concepts
in a synthetic manner? Is there any realistic prospect of conjoining
systems concepts of organizational structure and organizational change
with a 'process' understanding of organizational change (Garud and Van
de Ven 2002)?

At present there are few positive answers to these questions. Complexity
theories have as yet been unable to explicate theoretically the dynamics
of chaotic system change in organizations, and there is a massive deficit
of empirical evidence (Houchin and MacLean 2005). This criticism
applies with almost equal force to each of the four core ideas of
complexity science that have been transposed into organizational
analysis.

For example, the idea of chaotic time-series analysis seems to imply that
order and disorder are not opposite or fixed states, but rather forms of
non-linear determinism. In this formulation 'causal process theories' can
refer to the explanatory logic of a causal relationship between variables
(Van de Ven and Poole 1995: 512). The presuppositions of causal process
theories of change therefore appear to involve a systems ontology and a
corresponding model of organizations as structural or system entities that
can be unravelled in terms of their 'underlying generative mechanism'
(Dooley and Van de Ven 1999). This does not mean, of course, that
organizations are in a single state, or that change unfolds along linear or
predictable evolutionary pathways (Dooley and Van de Ven 1999: 359).

But despite this caution regarding deterministic chaos many complexity theories of organizations allow for predictable evolutionary stages or patterns of adaptiveness – a mix of ideas that appear deeply contradictory. Alternatively, chaotic systems can be viewed as the emergent manifestation of continuous and temporal processes of *becoming* that are never repeated – a postmodern reading of complexity as temporality that appears incompatible with system presuppositions of evolutionism and the concept of 'complex adaptive systems' (Kauffman 1993).

Similarly, the notion of strange, chaos-absorbing attractors appears best suited to continually changing systems, but this raises questions of how new attractor patterns emerge in the first place and how they facilitate, limit or stabilize system changes. We are never precisely sure what attractors are in organizational settings, how they are measured and how they provide coherence to complex organizational systems if they never repeat over time (Anderson 1999: 217). It is no surprise then that attempts to apply the analysis of 'attractor patterns' within natural systems to organizations as system entities have usually ended in rather abstract and banal propositions (Thietart and Forgues 1995: 26).

One has also to question the idea of small change–large effects. This idea may be useful as an analogy and as a computational exponent in computer simulation data sets, but its empirical and theoretical formulation in any practical organizational sense is unclear. How can small change be explored as larger system shifts if complex systems interact in non-linear ways? Can small changes be somehow linearized and made marginally more predictable in the mathematical equivalent of the 'disjointed incrementalism' of strategic change processes (Thietart and Forgues 1995: 26)? Are small changes a logic of intra-system interactions within tightly and loosely coupled systems, or a process dynamic of systems as a whole (Perrow 1999 [1984], Weick 2001)? Should we concentrate on understanding micro-changes within complex systems of group behaviour or the interaction of micro-macro changes (Arrow *et al.* 2000)? Is there any realistic prospect of empirically tackling any of these kinds of processes?

A similar range of criticisms applies to the ubiquitous concept of self-organization which has multiple meanings in terms of how chaos–order is sustained and how the organizational change process unfolds. At one level the positive reading of chaos/order in complexity theories of organizations is partly achieved because autopoiesis is extended beyond system self-production and self-regulation to *self-reproduction* and evolution over time. It is assumed that organizations as autopoietic entities are capable of self-regulation and evolutionary adaptiveness (Kauffmann 1993). While this may be a useful hypothesis in examining the survival of 'living' natural systems it is highly problematic to consider organizations or societies as entities that evolve toward some higher-level goal or purpose.

In sum, trying to translate the core system concepts of complexity science into process theories of organizational transformation and change is a perplexing and often frustrating task.

Despite these difficulties there have been some notable synthetic attempts to explore chaotic system change as a coherent 'process theory' of organizational development. Applying 'chaotic' time series analysis to organizations is only one of a variety of ways of understanding different 'generative mechanisms' of change and transformation. Dooley and Van de Ven (1999) have proposed an illuminating clarification of four different types of time series analysis: 'Periodic and white noise dynamics stem from systems where causal factors act independently, or in a linear fashion, while chaotic and pink noise systems stem from systems where causal factors act interdependently, in a non-linear fashion' (p. 358). This classification of time series is useful because it suggests how researchers may identify different mechanisms at work 'behind' an 'observed-process' of system dynamics.

This system-based classification does, however, have its downside. Dooley and Van de Ven (1999) tend to identify the analysis of organizational change with the 'objective' exploration of 'process theories' of development and change that are dependent on an epistemological ideal of instrumental knowledge concerned with the causal dynamics of system change: 'Such knowledge can help us explain the past, predict the future, and develop intervention strategies' (p. 358). Organizational change is essentially an 'object' with system properties that can be uncovered and a 'process' with temporal patterns and pathways that can be charted and strategically controlled (Van de Ven 1987: 331). This amounts to a 'hard' or strongly 'reductionist' reading of 'process' that identifies organizational change within systems or sub-systems as constituted by interacting causal variables. Moreover, this modelling of the causality of systems virtually dispenses with any notion of agency in formulating theories of organizational change (Van de Ven and Poole 1995). It is only variables that appear to do things, not human actors.

There are, however, other critical issues at stake in the system complexity focus on 'organizational dynamics'. The alternative ontological reading of 'change' as a process of 'becoming' is lost in the observer–process classification of change as processes of development within systems (Chia 1998; Tsoukas and Chia 2002). Conceived positivistically, systems are presumed to consist of the causal interaction between variables that define the sources, mechanism and outcomes of change. Complexity theory therefore appears to be simply an alternative methodology for capturing patterns of change and development that may appear to be completely random. This excludes serious consideration of the ontological possibility that organizational change, as a temporal 'process', may be both unpredictable *and* indeterminate, rather than unpredictable but determined. Ultimately, the realist system presuppositions of an organizational complexity theory of 'deterministic chaos' limit the definition and exploration of 'structure' to a systems ontology. An adequate theory of structure or structuring must include both systems and processes.

Evolution and adaptiveness

The more one probes into the systems assumptions of complexity theories the more fundamental the questions become. What is a functional system? Can one distinguish function from purpose? How do systems with functions become systems that evolve? Can complex self-organizing systems become more adaptive?

These questions point to two of the central problems that have always plagued systems models of society and organizations that combine function and purpose: the reciprocal dangers of *teleology* and *tautology* (Parsons 1951). Teleological arguments go wrong when it is assumed, for example, that organizations need power structures, career systems, profit-making or some other set of 'functions', because these activities, structures, sub-systems or practices serve the needs of the system as a whole – alternative structures could perhaps meet these needs. Similarly, systems thinking can become tautological when a conclusion merely restates a premise: the whole is defined in terms of its parts and the parts are defined in terms of the whole. Complexity theories that combine function and purpose are often guilty of both these entrapments (Kauffman 1993: 235).

Avoiding these theoretical entrapments is not easy (White *et al.* 1997; Anderson 1999; Stacey 2003). The exploration of complexity in natural systems is concerned with both the emergent relational properties of systems and their evolution over time. Non-linear changes in the properties of functional systems are therefore somehow conjoined with evolution towards some end, purpose or goal (e.g. adaptiveness). *'Adaptive evolution achieves the kinds of complex systems which are able to adapt'* (Kauffman 1993: 235, emphasis in original). But by assuming that systems are inherently evolutionary, complexity theories rarely seriously explore the links between systems as dynamic functional entities and change as a process. This has serious implications in organizational change theories, for the move from systems to processes can conflate functionalism and evolutionary theory in the highly problematic teleological and tautological notion of organizations as 'complex *adaptive* systems'.

Most attempts to go beyond dynamic systems as functionally integrated entities towards a reconceptualization of complex systems as interactional processes usually amount to attempts to overlay self-organizing processes with grander evolutionary assumptions: the apparently dynamic *functionality* of complex systems is capable of 'adaptiveness'. Kauffman's (1993) influential application of 'NK modelling' of nodes within networks to the exploration of 'fitness landscapes' is just one example of how system complexity, functionality and evolutionary theory can be combined.

In Kauffman's reinterpretation of complex self-organizing systems, 'fitness' is an evolutionary form of 'natural selection' incorporating system functionality and goals. 'Complex adaptive systems' are viewed as co-evolving within their environments that contain other co-evolutionary systems. In this respect, the overall environment can be envisaged as having a 'fitness landscape', the behaviour of which is unpredictable from the viewpoint of any one system. Just as landscapes have features causing variations in their number of peaks or valleys, so systems may vary in the way they navigate their rugged fitness landscapes (Levinthal 1997, 2002). Some systems effectively ascend high peaks and cross fitness valleys while others do not. Superior evolutionary systems are apparently those capable of iteratively probing their unknown landscapes, looking for ever higher peaks and elevations.

Applying the fitness landscape analogy to the co-evolution of various self-organizing natural systems is plausible. Unfortunately, it can become enormously diffuse and confusing when applied to internal functional measures of 'fit' within organizations or external measures of environmental fitness. Traditionally, 'fitness' has been conceived as the functional attributes of fit in the form of structure, technology and production processes (e.g. the more 'complex' the technology the more extended are chains of command). In complexity theories of organizations, however, fitness appears to take on a much broader range of meanings. Fitness is the overall fit between organizational systems or sub-systems and their environments. It may therefore relate to competitive measures of market survival in terms of profits, market share or growth cycles. Alternatively, a fitness landscape may reflect the way in which institutional environments 'select' and modify organizational fields in terms of higher-order 'organizational capabilities' (Levinthal 2002).

With such a potentially wide-ranging and disparate array of concepts and measures the question arises of what 'fitness' is and how self-organizing systems can achieve it (Maguire and McKelvey 1999: 23–24). Could one have complexity without fitness, a complex pattern that has no adaptive function? Similarly can one have change that is neither functionally helpful nor harmful to an organization? Or, to reformulate these questions in the broader context of evolutionary theory: how effective is self-organization as the 'natural selection' mechanism of evolutionary change? Must all aspects of self-organizing behaviour within natural or social systems be viewed as adaptations or manifestations of selection (Gould 2002)? By raising such awkward questions one realizes that the fitness concept is not simply a reformulation of complex system dynamics: complexity as functionality. Rather, the evolutionary 'goal' of self-organization is to make self-organizing systems more adaptive (Kauffman 1993).

The incorporation of goals within systems is central to Kauffman's interpretation of complex adaptive systems. Fitness as an evolutionary form of 'adaptiveness' appears to conjoin 'self-organization' and Darwinian 'natural selection' by going beyond conventional notions of system functions or goals. Organisms as functionally integrated systems are not just 'mixtures of contraptions and design under the aegis of natural selection' (Kauffman 1993: 3). Rather, they are structural and functional wholes that evolve through both 'self-organization' and 'selection'. Kauffman is deeply ambivalent, however, about Darwin's attempt to exclude purpose from nature by taking teleology out of biology, the analogy of the 'blind watchmaker' leaves nature as a mindless creator of contraptions rather than purposeful systems. If the Darwinian notion of natural selection dispenses with the illusions of teleology (nature as god's creation), it also fractures the idea of organisms as functional self-generating wholes driven by the logic of adaptiveness: 'Since Darwin we have come to view selection as the overwhelming, even the sole, source of order in organisms. Natural selection operating on gratuitous random mutations is the sieve that retains order and lets chaos pass into oblivion' (Kauffman 1993: 11). If evolutionary theory is to be more than just an understanding of the disparate mechanisms and history of natural selection, then it needs to account for the genesis of complex self-organizing wholes, or the 'origins of order' in nature. For 'origins of order' read *design in nature* and one has the programmatic intent of Kauffman's project to put teleology back into evolutionary theory (Ruse 2004). Ultimately, what Kauffman wants is evolution with order, systems with purposes, mechanisms with ends, laws with universal foundations, order within chaos.

The combining of functional and evolutionary ideas in the notions of adaptiveness or fitness partly explains why attempts to apply the edge of chaos concept to social and organizational change invariably take the form of prescriptive developmental typologies. Again, Kauffman (1993) sets a powerful precedent for this theorization when he classifies random 'Boolean networks' into three broad evolutionary regimes of behaviour: *ordered, chaotic* and *complex*. Ordered regimes consist of many frozen elements, while in chaotic regimes there are no frozen elements: 'Instead, a connected cluster of unfrozen elements, free to fluctuate in activities, percolates across the system, leaving behind isolated frozen islands' (p. 174). It is, however, the transition region between ordered and chaotic regimes that is most dynamic: 'Boolean networks near the edge of chaos have fitness landscapes whose ruggedness optimises the capacity of networks to evolve by accumulating useful variation' (p. 174).

Parallel typologies of evolving fitness landscapes appear in organizational theory. Thietart and Forgues (1995) classify organizations into various self-contained stages of development: 'An organization will be in one of the following states: stable equilibrium, periodic equilibrium, or chaos' (p. 25). Similarly, Stacey (1995, 2003) uses the edge of chaos concept to identify three types of order–disorder in which organizations as 'complex adaptive systems' operate: an arena of stable equilibrium, an unstable state of instability and a zone of bounded instability at the edge of chaos. In the stable state organizations may ossify and die, while in the unstable state they are likely to explode or disintegrate. Only at the edge of chaos do organizations have the ability spontaneously to self-generate processes of transformation and innovation in order to survive. While this final state is apparently the most desirable one, it is not an inevitable evolutionary outcome. The edge of chaos is enormously difficult to achieve because it requires a balance between the forces promoting organizational stability and those challenging stasis.

The most obvious criticism of these ideas is that organizations do not exist in self-contained states: 'different observed states of organization will display different temporal dynamics, demanding different (but hopefully consistent) process theories' (Dooley and Van de Ven 1999: 359). The more serious criticism, however, is that the 'process theories' implicit in complex system dynamic models of organizations are essentially a conflation of functionalism and evolutionary theory. By conceiving the edge of chaos as the most desirable stage for organizations, complexity theorists impute an evolutionary superiority to those organizations that can hypothetically evolve to master non-linear and unpredictable dynamics of change.

How this process unfolds, however, is unclear (Houchin and MacLean 2005). Is it the product of the evolution of self-organizing systems or intentional agency? If evolutionary change happens as a fortuitous consequence of fitness or though the unfolding of an organizational change 'process' that is unpredictable then agency seems to operate as a backstage activity:

> Managers of complex systems can only dimly foresee what specific behaviours will emerge when an organization's architecture is changed. Instead of relying on foresight, *they rely on evolution*, changes that produce positive cascades of change are retained, while those that do not are altered.
>
> (Anderson 1999: 229, emphasis added)

Evolutionary change appears to emerge spontaneously without prediction, control of planned interventions, and yet human actors can somehow select out its negative effects.

The paradoxes of system-evolutionary formulations of change highlight one of the central problematics of complexity theories. Complexity as an idea of *systems with functions* is overlaid with *complexity as adaptiveness*: the processes of development of a system towards an ever-higher evolutionary stage. How this function versus process, or system-dynamic versus evolutionary understanding of complexity is synthesized without a teleological residue is unclear.

Some complexity theorists appear to see a curious mixture of virtuous intelligence and inner system dynamics at work within processes of non-linear change. For example, negative feedback loops appear to keep a system stable within predefined functional parameters while positive feedback somehow produces unstable equilibrium. Only when these two contradictory forces operate simultaneously, however, do they somehow push or propel the system forward towards goals or a higher-level order.

Alternatively, the virtuous intelligence of self-organization operating within fitness landscapes may remain inexplicable in terms of any functional structure or overall design principle. The self-organization of complex systems is inexplicable in terms of their functional components, how they interact or an overall pattern of system development. Hillis (1998), for example, in recounting his pioneering reformation of number-sorting programmes into thousands of intelligent or self-learning mini-programmes that could 'evolve', freely admitted that he did not understand how they worked. Self-organization somehow arrives at self-selection through evolution without any functional unity or teleological principle of intelligent design.

The perplexing issues of how self-organizing systems hold together and 'evolve' are even more difficult to unravel in real world organizations where both functionality and goals are equally problematic (Perrow 1961). The functional components of organizations as integrated-differentiated systems cannot be understood by generic references to the importance of structured randomness, strange attractors or decentralized control (Cilliers 1998: 2). Similarly, adaptiveness or evolutionary fitness cannot be presumed to emerge unwittingly from bottom-up rules creating a higher-level order and purpose. In particular, we are never really sure what the goal of self-organization as a panacea for organizational change is: the avoidance of too much order or too little order? Nor can it be presumed that 'purpose' is a property residing in a complex adaptive system, rather than an ideological phenomenon created by those who can set goals or predefine the evolutionary mission of the organization. Until complexity theories critically explore their functionalist presuppositions and the evolutionism implicit in the idea of 'complex adaptive systems' they are unlikely to offer credible theories or models of organizational change.

Systems and agent-based interaction

If complexity theories have difficulties in exploring organizational change as non-linear processes of emergence within systems, they have even more difficulties in linking ideas of self-organization to concepts of agency. This is a persistent problem in social systems theory in which action and intention is often under-theorized, or subordinated as a micro category: the assumption being that the apparently macro reality of systems as structural objects or causal entities cannot be derived from the interaction of individuals (Parsons 1951; Luhmann 1995). Instead, 'a supra-human, self-generating, and self-maintaining social system is ontologically and methodologically prior to its participants' (Dawe 1978: 366). The recent reformulations of chaos theories as models of complex adaptive systems with 'complex adaptive agents' often exacerbate these issues because they gravitate towards self-organizing concepts of 'decentred agency', rather than conventional models of intentional agency founded on rational choice, economic behaviour or instrumental action. Essentially agency is decentred into simple lower-level rules of interaction that can create complex and unexpected behaviours.

There are numerous versions of complexity theory which consider the understanding of the dynamic relations between 'agents' within systems as more important than understanding the overall dynamics of chaotic systems or structures (Macy and Willer 2002). 'Complex adaptive systems' (CAS) are, for example, often defined as systems with multiple agents interacting in a dynamic manner, following local self-organizing rules rather than higher-level directions. In this sense, complexity theory as a systems construct is becoming more 'relational' (interactional) rather than purely systemic or holistic:

> CAS models represent a genuine new way of simplifying the complex, of encoding natural systems into formal systems. Instead of making non-linear systems tractable by reducing them to a set of casual variables and error terms, CAS models typically show how complex outcomes flow from simple schemata and depend on the way in which agents are interconnected.
>
> (Anderson 1999: 220)

While this formulation captures the emergent nature of agent-based models of interaction, it is also clear that many forms of complexity theory rely on moving back and forth from micro-behaviour to macro-behaviour to capture the 'structural' logic of systems. Without this systemic 'swarm logic' or 'causal collectivity' of indirect control and order, interaction would result in anarchic micro-behaviours. Explicating the relationship between 'complex adaptive systems' and 'complex adaptive agents' is therefore essential in any adequate theorization of the agency–structure problematic of complexity theories.

Various intriguing, if disparate, examples of 'agent' interaction, whether in the form of cell aggregation patterns, ant colony behaviour or evolving programmes within computer simulation models, have all indicated how systems rely on random interactions to self-organize rather than reliance on predefined or higher-level goals or instructions (Flake 1998). The interactions may appear arbitrary or unpredictable because there are so many agents in a system, yet these interaction processes somehow allow the emergence of new macro-systems of behaviour.

Translating these ideas into organizational or social contexts at first appears very promising, but it also carries hidden dangers. It can all too easily become another way of replaying the old agency–structure and action–system dichotomies in various either/or formulas. Agency can be conceived as a planned mechanism for mediating the swarm logic of complex systems, or agency can become a heterogeneous mechanism of co-evolving forms of self-organization decoupled from macro-behaviours. If early cybernetic and system design models of 'complex organizations' gravitate towards the former, recent agent-based models of complex adaptive systems gravitate towards the latter:

> In environments far from equilibrium where cascades of change are constantly playing out and overlapping with one another, adaptation must be evolved, not planned. Adaptation is the passage of an organization through an endless series of organizational microstates that emerge from local interactions among agents trying to improve their payoffs.
>
> (Anderson 1999: 228)

Again, this formulation captures the processual and emergent nature of organizational change as an incremental and distributed activity among interacting agents. But it also appears to underplay the extent to which agential interaction in complexity theory is a modification of conventional linear-models of rational action and choice. Rational choice theories of individual self-interest are virtually synonymous with defences of economic and market behaviour under industrial capitalism, while notions of complex adaptive agents are increasingly identified with the 'new economy' of networks and 'informational capitalism' in which 'agency' as a concept is distributed or dispersed. It is perhaps no surprise then that some of the best work on complexity theory has come from experimental and computational economists who challenge 'the holy trinity of rationality, selfishness and equilibrium' (Colander et al. 2004: 485). But if complexity theories of organizations are not to be subsumed into a new rhetoric of market chaos and 'chaordic organizations' then it will have to clarify the extent to which the idea of complex adaptive agents as a mode of 'decentred agency' is not a reworking of the rhetoric of rational choice theory. If it is radically different then rational choice and complex adaptive action may have to be decoupled.

Decentred agency

As complexity theories struggle to address questions of organizational change, human agency and choice, the issue of 'decentred agency' (i.e. non-intentional action) increasingly appears to be of central importance. If agency is decentred then intentionality, rational action and expert models of practice become problematic. Certainly, without a theory of how complex adaptive systems with widely distributed complex adaptive agents interact to produce organizational change, complexity theory would lack a rationale for causal intervention and change management practice (Van de Ven and Poole 1995; Stacey 2003).

Until recently the dominant functionalist and instrumental views of systems theory and management practice were informed by an ideal of centred agency. As Stacey *et al.* observe: 'The dominant voice talks about the individual as autonomous, self-contained, masterful and at the center of an organization' (2000). Some complexity theorists claim to have thrown off this dominant voice, yet their system modelling techniques still use the language of regularities, rational design and management control. Stacey admits that his early work on complexity theory exemplified the dominant voice of systems thinking. He once believed that organizations were purposely adaptive functional systems in which human agents acted on the basis of instrumental action, expert knowledge and predefined roles (Stacey 1995). Against this view he now argues that there are a chorus of voices within various social science disciplines emphasizing a new more participative perspective on human agency: 'These voices emphasize the radically unpredictable aspects of self-organizing processes and their creative potential. These are the voices of decentred agency, which talk about agents and the social world in which they live as mutually created and sustained' (Stacey *et al.* 2000). Applied to organizational change theory these ideas have encouraged a rejection of conventional rationalist subject–object dichotomies of knowledge creation, concepts of centred agency and a reinterpretation of organizational change as an emergent, self-organizing and temporal process of communication and learning.

But how far can one push the notion of decentred agency before it implodes? Complexity theorists influenced by postmodernism are increasingly embracing 'sensemaking' and constructionist notions of 'agency as discourse'. With this shift emphasis is given to participative self-organization through temporal processes of communication, thus allowing agency and change to emerge in a nonlinear movement towards an unknown future: 'That movement is the participative self-organizing processes of bodily communicative interaction between people forming and being formed by itself at the same time in a circular, reflexive and self-referential causality' (Griffin 2002: 18). One can still detect the language of complexity theory in this formulation, but 'system' as an epistemological category and change agency as a form of expert intervention have become almost redundant.

More attempts to lead complexity theories away from system assumptions and concepts of intentional agency and towards processes of change and decentred agency are likely to occur, but it is unclear where they are leading. If the self-organizing process of 'interaction' between decentred agents becomes the central focus of attention this requires a reformulation of notions of autonomy and reflexivity, as well as a theory of how agency as modes of 'sensemaking' or 'discourse' are enacted in 'practice' (Weick 2001; Hardy 2004). It also raises the broader issue of whether the concept of 'system' at the structural or macro-behavioural level is still useful in understanding agency. Agency-based models of the micro-behaviour of self-organization appear to need both, despite claims to the contrary. Only if decentred agency becomes subsumed by the paradoxical logic of human practices does the micro–macro distinction appear to be redundant – at least in principle (Bourdieu 1990). But what would then be left of complexity theory if the efficacy of decentred agency in processes of interaction lost its higher-level centre of gravity in a systems concept? At this point complexity theory would have crossed over into postmodern organizational theory and constructionist discourse.

Discussion

In one of the classic works of organizational theory, *Normal Accidents* (published in 1984), Perrow posed a question that still resonates today: 'do complex systems threaten to bring us down?' (reissue 1999: vii). Perrow provided a deeply disturbing answer to this question. He demonstrated how interactively complex and tightly coupled organizations using dangerous high-risk technologies can fail catastrophically (Urry 2003: 35). For within tightly coupled systems 'normal accidents' are the inevitable consequence of system failures rather than individual error (Perrow 1999: 11).

Complexity theories appear to pose a new question for organizational analysis: do new modes of self-organization promise order within chaos?

Many complexity theorists answer this question positively. At the edge of chaos, systems within intermediate zones of instability will eventually find new patterns of order, rather than simply fall apart (Brown and Eisenhardt 1997: 29). Chaos is not abnormal, accidental or the outcome of malfunctions. Instead, order will somehow emerge through mechanisms of self-organization and decentred agency that generate change and innovation, rather than risk, uncertainty and organizational collapse.

But are these evaluations overly optimistic, are they theoretically sound, and are they supported by empirical evidence (Maguire and McKelvey 1999)? There are certainly many reasons to exercise caution in probing these questions.

Complexity theories of organizations are characterized by ever increasing diversity (Thrift 1999). Typically these theories diverge along a variety of major and minor research pathways, and there is little agreement on the convergent propositions of 'complexity science'. For some this state of paradigm emergence has been interpreted positively as a model of theoretical plurality: 'Complexity thinking should be conceded as a method for understanding diversity, rather than a unified meta-theory. Its epistemological value could come from acknowledging the self-organization of nature and society' (Castells 2000: 74). This assumes, of course, that the nature and society analogy holds and that the insights gained are not just theoretically compatible but are of some empirical or practical value: both positions are highly contestable (Stewart 2001). There are enormous problems in translating naturalistic assumptions to social behaviour and the practical implications of the insights can often be contradictory and confusing, especially when they are simply applied as analogies or metaphors of how organizational and strategic change actually occurs.

The more immediate issue, however, in defending a position of diversity or 'discordant pluralism' is its potentially negative counter-effects: fragmentation (Gregory 1996). As complexity theories are 'applied' to ever more areas of organizational behaviour they not only become more diverse, they also appear to be losing their centre of gravity in 'systems' concepts of macro-behaviours or aggregated patterns of agent-based interaction. This trend is already prevalent and its implications can be confusing: 'We end up with functionalist, interpretative, emancipatory and postmodern versions of complexity theory emphasising, respectively order beneath chaos, learning, self-organization and unpredictability' (Jackson 2003: 130). Even within the limited area of organizational change theory there is already a divergence between more top-down 'chaordic system' models of organizational learning and emergent ideas of 'chaos as a meta-praxis of organizational change' (Fitgerald and Van Eijnatten 2002). In this sense, the positive interpretation of plurality without the perceived need for a coherent paradigm creates fragmentation without the prospect of a rigorous or cumulative research programme: potentially anything goes.

The implications of plurality versus fragmentation are perhaps most apparent in the move to shift organizational complexity theories towards postmodernism and constructionist discourses (Cilliers 1998; Stacey *et al.* 2000). With this shift priority appears to be given to 'process' rather than 'system', decentred agency rather than the centred epistemological subject of rationalism and intentional agency. But if the self-organizing processes of interaction and decentred agency become the central focus of attention, do systems ideas become secondary or totally redundant? Certainly, if complexity theory embraces change as an ontological process category then the epistemological idea of systems as entities with developmental pathways begins to fracture (Chia 2002).

Without a strong systems concept would complexity theories become even more diffuse and potentially more theoretically incoherent? Probably. They would certainly lack a methodological rationale for practice or change interventions (Checkland 1981). How can one have a *modus operandi* for practice if one does not believe that underlying the randomness and indeterminacy of change 'there exists a relatively simple system of non-linear dynamic relations' among a few 'motors' or leverage points of change? (Van de Ven and Poole 1995: 536). It is the systems concept that provides complexity theories with a potential structural reference point for agency and path-dependent models of organizational change. Similarly, if one takes away systems the very notion of 'adaptiveness' begins to implode. It is through the interactions of the parts of a self-organizing system that the 'system effects' of adaptiveness emerge without intentional intervention. Moreover, if one hollows out the idea that systems exist as 'objective', realist or causal entities, the very notion of the rational scientific observer as the discoverer of order or law-like patterns within chaos begins to lose any binding claim to scientific knowledge or expertise.

Few complexity theorists appear to explore these perplexing possibilities. But once the underlying assumption of complexity theory is questioned the challenge of putting systems, agency and expert practice back together can be daunting. Certainly complexity theories have often operated with a naïve conception of practice and expertise, partly because they assume that agency is a function of 'system' decisions concerned with adaptiveness or lower-level self-generating rules designed to improve 'payoffs'. This is the dominant discourse of many complexity theorists and it needs to be challenged if the 'complexity' concept is not to become a neo-liberal repackaging of the rhetoric of rational choice theories. Equally, however, the move to embrace postmodernism and constructionist discourses of decentred agency can be flawed if it does not involve a re-conceptualization of practice that allows for the efficacy of expert knowledge. If practice is a self-organizing form of communication enacted in the present, essentially a form of self-referential insight – my practice is my theorizing is my knowledge – then practice dissolves into conversational patterns of interaction and communication: *practice is discourse*. This may allow complexity theory finally to affirm its affinities with postmodernism. But where do such temporal, iterative and narrative accounts of practice lead (Gergen 2001a)? Do they destroy the possibility of knowledge of or expert interventions within complex systems? Again, the interrogation of these questions would potentially take complexity theories of organizational analysis far from their roots in systems concepts.

But perhaps the central problem with complexity theories in exploring organizational change and human agency is that they appear to be continually seduced by the promises of self-organization (Kauffman 1993). When self-organization takes place in natural systems it is hypothetically an automatic process somewhere in between order and chaos that somehow engenders evolutionary development. Applied to organizational analysis, self-organizing processes are therefore identified with the spontaneous emergence of order and structure that will lead to positive evolutionary change without external intervention or the hidden hand of agency.

In real world organizations, however, agency and structure is always a curious mix of non-intentional and intentional actions – system behaviour and interaction – that is often unpredictable in the multiplicity of forms it takes and in its outcomes. This creates enormous ontological and epistemological dilemmas of how we interpret agency as an intentional category or interactional concept (Giddens 1984; Latour 1999). If self-organization occurs without agents exercising free will, how are we to have a viable concept of choice or the causal possibility that human actors can make a difference?

Self-organization also creates a parallel theoretical dilemma for how 'structure' is interpreted. If 'order is free', the result of bottom-up processes or self-generated rules, then how do we explain power, its sources, structural contingencies and more diffuse manifestations (Boal et al. 2003). The reality is that self-organization may not occur because the system obstacles to the process have not been made transparent, but because powerful individuals deliberately impede this self-fulfilling ideal. Order is free only if there is the possibility to self-organize. But even if this freedom and autonomy existed in real world organizations, it might still result in stasis: if chaos dominates change may fail, if order dominates change may never start. Confronted with such paradoxes, organizational actors choose power over autonomy not just because knowledge follows power, but also because the hidden benevolence of chaos as the counterbalancing force of order is always unpredictable. Ultimately, complex organizations poised at the edge of chaos are just as likely to fall apart as they are to adaptively embrace positive transformation and change.

Conclusion

Complexity theories promise enormous potential for understanding the nature of organizational change, but they also leave unresolved many of the classic issues of organizational theory and analysis. Four major criticisms of complexity theories of organizational change have been made, and they suggest four important areas of further theoretical clarification and future research.

First, complexity theories do not provide a synthetic approach to 'system' and 'process' concepts of organizational structure and organizational change. Without a synthetic approach there is a danger that complexity theories may follow well-worn paths and divide into two opposing camps: those who seek a system-based and interventionist science of deterministic chaos linked to 'causal process theories', versus those who believe that complexity theory offers a postmodern and post-positivistic understanding of non-linearity and the temporality of change. This divide must be bridged if complexity theories are not to degenerate into paradigm wars and an increasingly anarchic theoretical enterprise which lacks a coherent rationale for practice.

Second, complexity theories do not provide an adequate understanding of how organizations as complex adaptive systems evolve and develop over time. Instead, conventional teleological and tautological arguments are redeployed in the exploration of evolutionary system change, with the result that system concepts are conflated with ideas of fitness landscapes and abstract notions of adaptiveness: the process of development of organizations towards ever higher evolutionary states. To avoid this conflation, complexity theories of organizational change should clarify the underlying epistemological presuppositions of system and evolutionary concepts of organizational structure and organizational change.

Third, complexity theories have been unable to provide an adequate theorization of the relationship between complex adaptive agents and complex adaptive systems with the result that the dynamic between agency and structure, and micro and macro behaviours within organizations, remains profoundly obscure (Giddens 1984). Until complexity theorists re-engage with classic agency–structure debates they are unlikely to provide credible concepts of organizational change.

Fourth, as some complexity theories move ever closer to postmodern and constructionist discourses of decentred agency they are likely to lose their analytical centre of gravity in system concepts of organizational change and instrumental ideals of change management practice. Any attempt to push this process further, however, will require complexity theories of organizational change to clarify not only a postmodern process ontology of change, but also alternative concepts of practice and change management intervention.

All of these criticisms raise broader issues of whether complexity theories of organizations really provide new insights into the nature of organizational change and human agency. If complexity theories are to form a viable paradigm, metatheory or metapractice of organizational change then they will have increasingly to demonstrate their theoretical coherence, empirical validity and practical relevance.

6 From Foucault to constructionist discourses: change without agency?

- Introduction
- Discourse and the subject
- Power/knowledge and resistance
- Embodiment and identity
- Self-reflexivity and ethics
- Discussion: agency and change
- Conclusion

Introduction

The pervasive influence of Michel Foucault's work on postmodern organizational theory and social constructionist discourses of identity is often seen as an assault on the possibilities of agency and change in organizations (Reed 1997, 2000; Newton 1998). By decentring the epistemological and moral 'subject' of rationalism and humanist thought Foucault appears to remove human agents from centre stage (Carr 1997; Gergen 1999; Linstead 2004). We can no longer rely on the ontological security of subject–object dualisms that allowed us to believe we could gain objective scientific knowledge of the world and the mind. Instead, passive 'subjects' who are the conduits, bearers or sites of discourses of power/knowledge replace the individualist belief in agency as a universal manifestation of rationality, autonomy, choice and reflexivity (Giddens 1984). Nor are there class or gendered constructs of collective social subjects or actors to which we can refer the possibilities of action and change in the social world (McNay 2000).

With this apparent destruction of the epistemological and moral subject of science and rationalism and the eclipse of individual and collective social action the very idea of a link between agency and change becomes profoundly problematic. How can there be any possibility of agency, any hope of change, if human actors as moral agents and social subjects are unable and incapable of exercising choice, free will or autonomy?

Within the sociological tradition, Giddens (1982, 1984, 1993) was one of the first critics to suggest that Foucault's work was a sustained attack on the possibilities of agency and change because he had defaced the 'subject' and the human body. For Giddens agency had to be conceived as part of the 'duality of structure' if the intentionality of human action and the possibilities of change were to be preserved: 'A decentring of the subject must at the same time recover that subject as a reasoning, acting being' (Giddens, 1982: 8). Paradoxically, however, Giddens' 'structuration' theory created a duality between agency and structure that narrowed the scope for the exploration of agency and change (see Chapter 2). For Giddens the causal power of intentional choice and the possibilities of change are ontologically and epistemologically connected in a strongly individualistic and moral ideal of agency as choice (Barnes 2000).

Within organization theory, attempts to re-work Giddens' reading of agency are still influential, although the agency and structure duality has become almost completely exhausted within sociological theory (Lash 2003). The persistence of this interest in Giddens' structuration theory is perhaps related to the dismal legacy of the agency concept in organizational theory – the disciplinary focus has recurrently gravitated towards the primacy of structure (Reed 1997, 2000). In this respect, the reinstatement of Giddens' agency-centred view of structure as 'rules and resources' and a form of purposeful communicative action is to be welcomed; both because it rebalances the long-standing over-emphasis on 'structure' as a static entity with mechanism and fixed properties, and because it allows the analysis of 'agency' as discourse (Heracleous and Hendry 2000; McPhee 2004).

What is often forgotten, however, is that Giddens's agency-centred critique of Foucault has more negative than positive implications, and it sets the template for a dangerous interpretative orthodoxy. Among Foucault's critics and defenders the 'negative paradigm of subjectification' (McNay 2000) has increasingly become identified with the view that 'subjects are mere passive reflections of power/knowledge discourses' (Knight 2004: 24). Critics of Focauldian organizational theory and constructionism therefore argue that Foucault has no concept of agency because he allowed autonomous 'discursive practices' to become subjectless (Newton 1998). Similarly, Foucault's defenders argue that agency and realist ideas of self, truth and objectivity must be formally expunged from the exploration of discursive practices and the programmatic goals of postmodern organizational theory, organizational discourse analysis and social constructionism (Gergen 1999, 2001a).

But was Foucault's relentless rejection of humanism, rational self-certainly, and liberal individualistic faith in the power of reflexivity and a coherent moral self, really a wholesale abandonment of any notion of agency (Hayward 2000)? Surely this would contradict the other overarching ambition of Foucault's intellectual *oeuvre* to disclose 'new possibilities for change' (1991). Could the relentless 'decentring of the subject' therefore really mean the death of agency and change? Or, is it possible to have change without an intentional concept of agency?

This chapter will argue that Foucault's work is an original and often powerful attempt to break with subjective and humanistic notions of intentionality or centred agency founded on *rationality*, *knowledge/expertise, autonomy* and *reflexivity*. Foucault's rejection of ontological dualism and a realist epistemology of the self lead to his attempt to decentre the subject in discourse and somehow theorize without a notion of the self. While this has often been interpreted as a 'defacing' of the subject and a rejection of agency, I will argue that Foucault's attempt to dispense with the counterpoints to intentional notions of centred agency can be re-conceptualized as a theorization of *decentred agency* consisting of four key components: *discourse, power/knowledge, embodiment and self-reflexivity.* Far from destroying intentional agency, decentred agency allows new possibilities for resistance and the dispersal of agency and change in organizations and societies. Foucault's apparent destruction of the 'subject' is not the postmodern end of agency but its partial reinvention.

Yet it will also be argued that Foucault is partly responsible for the confused interpretative reductions of his concept of agency. In his constant search for alternative forms of resistance and empowerment directed against intentional agency, Foucault appears to hold out the paradoxical possibility of *change without agency*; an idea that has been assimilated into the programmatic intent of postmodernism and constructionist discourses (Gergen 1999: 49). Gergen is perhaps the most forceful advocate of 'clearing away the self' when he claims that it is pointless to ask questions about the nature of human agency: 'Whether mental concepts are true – whether experience or agency are real ... are simply questions that do not require answers' (1999: 225). With this rejection of epistemological realism, agency can be conceived as a nominalist category that is talked or written into being as discourse or text (Hardy 2004).

Despite this apparent rejection of realism many postmodernist organizational theorists and constructionists are often perplexed by how far one can push the implications of nominalism without losing a sense of individual agency. Gergen may argue against intentional agency, yet he wants to retain 'moral adjudication' and the possibilities of social and personal change, as well as the virtues of democratic politics (1999: 118; 2001: 419). Here it will be argued that questions of agency and change still deserve serious interrogation, whether we search for answers in realist hypothetical cause–effect models of rational action, the rhetoric of subjectless discourses, or the confused grammar that we use to describe moral action and behaviour (Davidson 2001).

By questioning the apparently surface-thin rationalist ontology of the self, Foucault opened up a potentially deeper and darker exploration of what subjectivity, personality, intention and agency are – especially in relation to the possession and exercise of power (2000: 12). Instead of the conventional ontological dualities of individual and society, agency and structure, Foucault shifts the focus towards the possibilities of *agency and change* – but without the liberal individualist conception of agency as choice. This innovation was, however, doubled edged. If one takes away notional concepts of 'self', 'personality' or 'agency' and situates them in self-reflexive modes of discourse, then what possibilities are there for intentionality and choice? If our 'identity' is an ever-changing construction in a sea of competing rhetorics of self, or the self-divided expression of our polyvocal voices, then identity is constantly in flux, constantly unknown to itself, and we are therefore constantly in a state of self-doubt as to why or how we can change ourselves or the world (Gergen 1999: 80). Ultimately, without a synthetic concept of agency one cannot have a credible conception of change.

By clarifying Foucault's concept of decentred agency the broader limitations of his theorization of the 'subject' become apparent. In particular, Foucault leaves us with few answers on how to reconnect decentred agency with change agendas derived from its apparent conceptual opposite: the activist, politically engaged and potentially autonomous epistemological and moral subject of rationalist and humanist discourses. Until Focauldian organizational theory and constructionist discourses re-engage with concepts of intentionality, autonomy and reflexivity they will remain fundamentally flawed in their under-theorization of the relationship between agency and change in organizations and societies.

The chapter begins by exploring each of the four key components of *decentred agency*: 1) discourse as a counterpoint to rationalist or intentional ideals of the knowing 'subject' of knowledge; 2) power/knowledge and 'disciplinary power' as a critique of scientific and expert knowledge that leads to a reformulation of agency as transgression and resistance to power; 3) embodiment or 'embodied agency' as a partial critique of notions of intentional agency, autonomy and individual choice; 4) self-reflexivity as a mode of self-formation and identity that provides an alternative to the limited reflexivity of rationalist models of agency. This leads to a broader discussion of the unresolved ontological and epistemological issues raised by Foucault's conception of agency and change. Finally, the major limitations of Foucault's conception of agency are summarized and the case is made for a critical re-engagement of postmodern organization theory and constructionist discourses with forms of intentional agency.

Discourse and the subject

Discourse has an enormous and often confusing range of meanings in Foucault's work and it is often impossible to separate them. At least four meanings can be partly differentiated: discourse as rule-bound systems of statements, discourse as 'discursive practices', discourse as 'power/knowledge' and discourse as *Discourse,* as a grand meta-narrative against Enlightenment rationalism (Foucault 1972, 1981). All of these meanings allow Foucault (1991) to explore both how the knowing 'subject' appears in discourse, and how any form of subject entity (e.g. the self, the rational individual, the moral actor, the author) can be removed from the exploration of discourse.

For Foucault discourses are primarily structured, grouped and regulated by rules which state who can say what, where and how. Discourses therefore define the conditions or hidden rules through which subjects appear in discourse as intentional actors, moral beings or the more abstract epistemological and thinking subject of knowledge. These discourses are structured in such a way that they determine who the 'subject' is as well as defining, limiting and controlling the relation between how subjects perceive themselves in their relation with the world. This allows Foucault to ask how statements are possible within a specific discourse and how subjects are defined: 'What are the modes of existence of this discourse?' 'Where does it come from; how is it circulated; who controls it?' 'What placements are determined for possible subjects?' 'Who can fulfill these diverse functions of the subject?' (Foucault 1977: 138). As these statements indicate, Foucault often assumes an objectivistic stance towards discourse, so much so that he appears to conceive the exploration of the hidden rules of discourse as a discourse-neutral activity.

Discourses are not simple autonomous free-floating rules regulating systems of statements defining what a particular subject can say about an object. Discourses are also embedded in 'discursive practices', in the way the natural world is understood and social relations and human institutions are organized. Foucault therefore refers to discourse as 'practices, which form the objects of which they speak' (1972: 49). Discourse is nominal and material, a self-referential representation of meaning and a transformative instrument: words and things are inseparable because they have effects in the 'real world' of human practices.

Despite this notion of the embeddedness of discourse, Foucault tends to absorb practice as discursive practices into discourse, rather than relating discursive practices to the 'materiality' of reality, the 'structural' properties of social institutions or the agency of human subjects (Newton 1998; Reed 2000). This partly explains why Foucault appears to have no need for an 'objective' scientific theory of 'society', a concept of social structure or a notion of intentional agency: these are all constructs embedded in discursive practices that are discursively constituted. Similarly, he has no need for a theory of 'practice' or a concept of theory *into* practice because *discourse is practice*: 'theory does not express, translate or serve to apply practice: it is practice' (Foucault [cited in Kritzman] 1988: xix).

Because discourse appears to structure and regulate what statements it is possible to say and the conditions under which they are considered true or false, discourse is also a form of 'power/knowledge' (Foucault 2000). Discourse 'transmits and produces power' while simultaneously producing knowledge. For Foucault to classify and define things and objects is to exercise power by producing a particular form of knowledge. To define what is objective and subjective, what constitutes sane and insane behaviour, justice and injustice is to produce knowledge and exercise power over others (Foucault 1979). In Foucault's vision of things, it is impossible to separate expert knowledge from power, knowledge and power always occur together. But because knowledge/power is an 'effect' of discourse it is not a possession that some people have and others do not. As discourse, power and knowledge is everywhere; it forms networks of social relations and discursive practices that disperse and circulate power both within the 'social body' and within the self.

Finally, discourse can refer to the 'general domain' of all statements, to almost every activity through which meaning, the self and objects of knowledge are constituted. In this sense Foucault uses discourses as an alternative category to question the self-construction of the world as an object of study (ontology) and the way we as potentially rational or intentional subjects know or explain it to ourselves (epistemology). It is in this sense that discourses and discursive practices can be characterized as a 'delimitation of a field of objects, the definition of a legitimate perspective for the agent and of knowledge and the fixing of norms for the elaboration of concepts and theories' (Foucault 1977: 199). If everything, including our self-conception, is constructed or produced within discourse then there appears to be no non-discursive realm outside of the *order of discourse*: 'we must not imagine that the world turns towards us a legible face which we would only have to decipher; the world is not the accomplice of our knowledge; there is no prediscursive providence which disposes the world to our favour' (Foucault 1981: 67). This defacing of the world 'out there' also becomes the de-naturalizing of the self as a fixed physical or biological entity or a form of self-consciousness or mind to which we can refer our sense experience. The body and the self are experienced through discourse.

Overall, these four overlapping meanings of discourse suggest that Foucault appears to conceive D/discourse/s as self-referential systems of meaning that *cannot* disclose the relationship between subject and object, discourse and 'reality'. Discourse analysis simply replaces any analysis of how discourse (language, symbols or signs) represents or corresponds to the world (Deetz 2003). Discourse is therefore the antithesis of Enlightenment rationalism or any attempt at the empirical materialization of the mind as an object of knowledge. This does not mean, however, that 'objects' or 'things' do not exist independently of thought, consciousness or mind. Rather, Foucault appears to assume a certain 'materiality' to the world, to words and things, although he insists that we cannot refer objects to sense experience, facts or causes that exist outside of discourse. In this sense, Foucault (1972) claims that his 'archaeology' of the material conditions of knowledge is not reducible to ideas of consciousness or mind. It is never clear, however, whether discourse and 'the world', word and thing are analytically separated in the creation of knowledge, or whether they are identical. This equivocal position creates enormously perplexing questions. How do you distinguish discourse from the 'materiality' of the non-discursive, appearance from reality? Does discourse itself define what is 'real' and what it is possible to say?

What counts as knowledge within discourse? Can one separate discourse from power? If so, is it then possible to reconnect agency and change?

Foucault never answers these philosophical questions with any degree of rigour or consistency and this partly explains why his work ends up in a series of confusing and often self-contradictory positions. For example, he does not offer an exploration of the nature of consciousness or mind, and this is reinforced by his rejection of virtually any hint of naturalism. Without a philosophical clarification of what consciousness, mind or thought is we are never really sure what discourse is or how it is *produced* through discursive practices, and this is compounded by Foucault's confusion over how one can draw any useful distinction between what is 'prediscursive', 'discursive' and 'non-discursive' (Foucault 1972).

Power/knowledge and resistance

Foucault's exploration of power/knowledge is an historical examination of the transformations of the self, subjectivity and human agency in the emergence of modern Western social and political institutions. One of the most momentous transformations occurs, according to Foucault, with the shift away from 'sovereign power' of kings manifest in grotesque ceremonial rituals of torture and public executions to the 'disciplinary power' of modernity manifest in the insidious disciplinary regimes of the prison, the factory, the school, the hospital and all the institutions of the modern democratic state (1994: 3–7). These new forms of power reach into subjects through a web of regimes of power and knowledge that regulate the body and mind, including our most intimate behaviour and inner thoughts. What interests Foucault, however, is not the ubiquity of these new forms of power, or the apparently humane shift from regimes of brutal 'torture' to regimes of behavioural 'correction', but their relation to human subjects: how they impact on how we think, feel and act as 'subjects' of power and knowledge.

The exploration of the 'subject' of power/knowledge takes four forms.

Power is knowledge. Foucault argues that power and knowledge are inseparable. Power as knowledge operates through discourses in which subjects form the sites where knowledge is produced: 'the subject who knows, the object to be known and the modalities of knowledge must be regarded as so many effects of the fundamental implications of power/knowledge and their historical transformations' (Foucault 1991: 27).

For Foucault power/knowledge as 'truth' 'expertise' or 'facts' is decentred from any ontological or epistemological concept of the human subject as an autonomous or rational agent with access to objective knowledge, and therefore from any notion of specific individual 'causal powers'. By blurring any distinction between power and knowledge, subject and object, Foucault seeks to destroy the optimism of Enlightenment reason; its faith in individual autonomy and self-identity through rational knowledge of the self and the world: 'Knowledge and power are integrated with one another, and there is no point in dreaming of a time when knowledge will cease to depend on power; this is just a way of reviving humanism in a utopian guise. It is not possible for power to be exercised without knowledge, it is impossible for knowledge not to engender power' (Foucault 1979: 52). For Foucault this complicity of power and knowledge appears to rule out the possibility of any future emancipation from power.

Power is everywhere. Unlike mainstream theories of power which focus on what power is, who exercises it, how it is distributed and who gains and loses from the use of power, Foucault conceives power as a nominal construct: 'power is not a thing, an institution, an aptitude or an object' (Foucault 1979: 93). Correspondingly, it is not a substance or property of structures or an attribute of individuals. With no realist notion of the ontological and epistemological location of power, power appears to be intrinsically disparate and diffuse; it is everywhere because it appears to be everywhere: 'Power has its principle not so much in a person as in a certain concerted distribution of bodies, surfaces, lights, gazes; in an arrangement whose internal mechanisms produce the relations in which individuals are caught up' (Foucault 1994: 202). For Foucault 'power' cannot be ontologically grounded or epistemologically explained because there is no subject–object standpoint outside power/knowledge, rather power must be explored as a shifting nominalist construction within the particularity of historical discourses of power and knowledge.

Power is relational. Power is everywhere not because it is hegemonic, monolithic or all-embracing, but because it 'circulates' or flows though the entire 'social body' by a multiplicity of mechanisms and archipelagos of localized power relations, each of which exercises its own relational forms of power:

> I am not referring to power with a capital P, dominant and imposing its
> rationality upon the totality of a social body. In fact there are power relations.
> They are multiple: they have different forms, they can be in the family relations,
> or within an institution, or an administration.

(Foucault 1988: 38)

Because power is something that is relational, something that circulates within and through discourse, Foucault (2000) argues that it must be explored as chains, networks or capillary connections in which individuals are the localized carriers or sites of power, not its 'points of application'.

Power is embodied. Power as 'disciplinary power' is so deeply submerged in human subjectivity that it is the embodiment of self-subjugation through self-discipline. This power is productive and positive, not simply repressive and negative. For Foucault subjects as willing selves and 'docile bodies' give themselves up to existing forms of power/knowledge not because they are oppressed or repressed, but because they are capable of exercising power over themselves. As a consequence it is almost impossible to search for the sources of a 'true self' with a fixed identity within discourses of knowledge/power or to separate or absolve the self from the 'exercise' of power. 'If I feel the truth about myself it is in part that I am constituted as a subject across a number of power relations which are exercised over me and which I exercise over others' (Foucault 1988: 39). The self is possessed by power, not its possessor, yet it can exercise power over the self and others. For Foucault power somehow retains an inner intentional core, an act of agency and autonomy in its exercise over the self and others, but subjects do not possess power.

At first reading Foucault's four overlapping domains of power/knowledge and disciplinary power appear to create a bleak image of the human subject and its possibilities. There is no scope for separating power and knowledge, or power and agency. The multifarious forms of disciplinary power arise within discourses of knowledge/power which create insidious modes of subjugation by expertise (e.g. the regulation and surveillance of behaviour) and self-subjugation through self-discipline. These discourses of power/knowledge are dispersed throughout the entire social body. They are not only organizationally decentralized, they are also decentred from any ontological or epistemological concept of the human subject as an autonomous or rational agent with 'causal powers' (Giddens 1984). In effect, Foucault decouples agency and power. The subject is therefore a diffused historically constituted entity, a site of power within discourse, always subsumed or determined by power and apparently unable to step outside itself to unmask or deface this power (Hayward 2000).

Despite Foucault's (2000) intensive focus on power his work holds out possibilities of agency in the form of resistance: 'where there is power there is resistance'. Like power, resistance appears to be everywhere: it transverses all power relations, it flows through its networks and it assumes a multiplicity of localized and distributed forms. Foucault also conceives resistance as a positive or 'productive' force, rather than simply a negative counter-reaction against rationality or expert knowledge. Processes of resistance are, however, deeply problematic because resistance is situated within power, is itself a form of power and can reproduce relations of power. Moreover, resistance as agency can have no recourse to self-certainty founded on rational knowledge or an ethical stance towards what is 'good' for others. Resistance is ultimately an act of refusal; it allows those who are 'subjects' of power to reject their confinement and self-subjugation within predetermined discourses of power/knowledge.

By redefining the limitations of conventional concepts of agency founded on notions of reason, intention, knowledge and power, Foucault appears to create alternative possibilities of resistance. Resistance is always emergent because discourse is never completely instrumental, self-enclosed or unified; it is surrounded by uncertainty and constantly at the mercy of the discontinuities and localized tensions it seek to suppress:

> discourses are not once and for all subservient to power or raised up against it, any more than silences are. We must make allowances for the complex and unstable process whereby discourse can be both an instrument and effect of power, but also a hindrance, a stumbling block, a point of resistance and a starting point for an opposing strategy. Discourse transmits and produces power; it reinforces it, but it also undermines it, renders it fragile and makes it possible to thwart it.
>
> (Foucault 1979: 100–101)

For Foucault, multiple subject positions are possible within discourses, and so discourses can be subverted by alternative subject discourses. A discourse therefore begins to unravel once we begin to question claims to self-certainty, truth, power or knowledge. For example, because power is diffused and fragmented rather than integrated and centrally controlled, there is no formally unified discourse of power (Foucault 2000). This allows considerable possibilities for groups and individuals to challenge power. Similarly, because power is dispersed through a multiplicity of networks and 'nodal points' there are localized or diverse contexts in which the discursive practices of power can be challenged. In this sense any search for universal notions of self or subjects is replaced by a 'polyphony of voices', each of which may construct its own discursive identity (Gergen 2001a). Moreover, as power assumes an increasingly symbolic efficacy separated from the instrumental exercise of power by institutions or persons, it is vulnerable to fragmentation. This allows new possibilities for exercising resistance/power and agency through the everyday micro-contexts of disciplinary power and the 'bio-power' that incorporates the biological existence of the person, the self or the body (Foucault 2000). If the self and the body are symbolically inscribed with sexual or gendered self-images that only allow the acting out of the power discourses of others, these can be counter-posed with alternative self-images: with a refusal to embrace the disembodiment of the self (McNay 2000).

Embodiment and identity

Most theories of agency, whether in the form of rational action, intentional behaviour or moral principles of conduct, ignore the 'body'; it forms the invisible shadow of the self. The origins of this mind–body split have a complex genealogy, but its division is most forcefully stated by Descartes: 'The concept of the body includes nothing at all which belongs to the mind, and the concept of the mind includes nothing at all which belongs to the body' (Descartes 1984: 158). Foucault (2000: 12–13) appears to challenge this separation. The body is not simply the outside or receptacle of an activistic inner self or mind, but the form that embodies who we are as historical, cultural and gender-specific beings defined by discourse of power and knowledge.

For Foucault (1979) the body is the major site for the insidious discourses of 'disciplinary power' and 'bio-power' that enact and inscribe who we are as subjects. Disciplinary power works on the body by regimes of subjugation through self-discipline. In contrast, bio-power operates at the macro-level of regulation by diffuse networks of institutional authority which seek to exercise control of populations by regimes of expert knowledge which measure, monitor, normalize bodily behaviours from individual sexual conduct to one's inner desires (Foucault 1979: 25). These processes of normalizing sexual behaviours and moral conduct are inseparable from acts of self-scrutiny and confessional self-definition which seek to disclose the 'true nature' of the self or our sexuality. In this way the self as a construct is 'psychologized' and we conspire in becoming objects for intervention and control by experts (Burrell 1988: 223).

At times Foucault's reading of the 'disciplining of the body' by discourses of power and expert knowledge appears to be so all-enveloping that agency becomes invisible (1994: 304). This explains why Giddens accuses

Foucault of defacing the body: 'Foucault's bodies do not have faces' (Giddens 1984: 157). Giddens (1992) also argues that Foucault's focus on the body as an effect of bio-power underplays the cognitive and affectual dimensions of self-identity, gender and sexuality. While these criticisms have considerable force, Giddens' notions of intentional agency and identity are equally problematic because they seriously underplay the pre-reflexive and embodied aspects of self-identity by conflating identity and agency with the possibilities of choice (Barnes 2000). Agency is not the endogenous effect of discourses of embodiment, but the intentional ability of individuals to 'make a difference' (Giddens 1984).

Foucault's reading of the body is certainly at odds with the cognitive thrust of Enlightenment rationalism and the scientific objectification of the body. He rejects a dualistic Cartesian view of the world along with a belief in an abstract moral subject, and he has a deep antipathy to any naturalistic foundations of the self (Foucault 2000: 10–11). But Foucault's focus on the body rather than the self, agency or the individual subject is designed primarily to counteract the disembodied self of liberal humanist thought by re-embodying the self. The self or thinking subject of rationalism is no longer conceived as a bodily organism joined to a self, but a body with the possibility of a face or a multiplicity of faces.

In re-embodying the self as a corporal being, however, Foucault calls into question the 'body' and the 'self' as entities that define a coherent identity and the possibilities of human agency. Just as the self has no inner self-certainty that somehow discloses 'true self', so the 'body' is a shifting nominal construct within discourses of power and knowledge. Foucault therefore argues that:

> the individual is not to be conceived as a sort of elementary nucleus ... on which power comes to fasten ... In fact, it is already one of the prime effects of power that certain bodies, certain gestures, certain discourses, certain desires, come to be identified and constituted as individuals.

(Foucault 2000: 98)

Individuals are not fixed entities, nor are our bodies. For Foucault (1991) the body is the 'inscribed surface of events' within discourses, and the genealogical task of examining these shifting discourses is to de-face power and 'expose a body totally imprinted by history and the processes of history's destruction of the body' (p. 83).

Foucault's exploration of how the body is constituted and reconstituted within discourse is perhaps most dramatically apparent in his three-volume study of the *History of Sexuality* (1978–1986). These studies do not constitute a systematic attempt to 'write a history of sexual behaviours and practices, tracing their successive forms, their evolution, and their dissemination' (Foucault 1986: 3). Rather, Foucault wishes to bracket the banal familiarity of our modern notions of sexuality in order to explore the polymorphous forms and unintended consequences of different discourses of sexuality, from our preconceptions of the sexual taboos of the Victorian era to the delimitations of the sexual and moral self in ancient Greece.

Foucault often excels at this genealogical project. He demonstrates how attempts during the eighteenth and nineteenth centuries at the repression of sexuality have unintended consequences: they intensify the pleasures gained from violating taboos, and they set a precedent for imagining that modern forms of sexual freedom are a route to self-fulfilment or individual freedom. For Foucault putting sex into the disciplinary discourse of the body, of what is permitted, has not subdued the desire for the forbidden, instead it has constituted an unending search for ever new and more permissive forms of sexuality: 'the techniques of power over sex have not obeyed a principle of rigorous selection, but rather one of dissemination and implantation of polymorphous sexualities ... the will to knowledge has not come to a halt in the face of a taboo ...' (1986: 300). In an equally provocative formulation, Foucault's exploration of sexual conduct in ancient Greece suggests how the practice of sexual acts by men with women, men or boys were not in themselves acts that define one's identity, rather identity is related to acts that express the moderation and control of sexual desire: 'what differentiates men from one another ... is not so much the type of objects toward which they are oriented, nor the mode of sexual practice they prefer; above all, it is the intensity of that practice' (Foucault 1986: 44). Again, Foucault challenges the link between fixed concepts of the body and desire, forms of sexual behaviour and moral conduct, repressive prohibitions of desires and their intensified expression in new forms.

Some feminists and constructionists who wish to affirm an ideal of embodied agency as a counterforce to the sources of oppression and/or repression of women have been attracted to Foucault's (1979, 1986) subversive challenge to the idea of the body as a fixed entity. Certainly, the 'temporalization inherent in the idea of embodiment' allows escape from essentialist notions that sexual differences and gendered behaviours are primarily biologically founded, as well as providing a refuge from scientific naturalism – the idea that behaviours have a causal substrate (McNay 2000: 25). If perceptions of the body are always changing, and our behaviours cannot be classified as 'natural', then they can be changed by changing the forms of discourse through which they are expressed (Knight 1997). Foucault's account of the body is therefore potentially powerful because it re-embodies agency, yet allows for change in terms of new discourses of the body.

Other feminists are, however, much more cautious in their critical assimilation of Foucault's work, precisely because it limits the possibilities of agency. Foucault's new insights into the potential for discursively redefining embodied agency and gendered identity are often undermined by his tendency to nominalize the body within discourses of power: 'There is a tendency to conceive of the body as essentially a passive, blank surface upon which power relations are inscribed' (McNay 2000: 166). The disciplinary regimes of femininity as power/knowledge can therefore appear everywhere and nowhere. This leads to an over-emphasis on the symbolic or discursive construction of the body and a corresponding neglect of the social, material and institutional dimensions of gendered norms (Newton 1998; Reed 2000). There is also the danger of emphasizing the peripheral counter-norms or 'ex-centric' forms of sexuality at the expense of a theorization of the mundane forms of heterosexuality (McNay 2000).

More importantly, however, the focus on how bodily inscription and self-subjugation occurs within discourse does not clarify how the self can become autonomous. Autonomy as a concept is treated as a rationalist abstraction within which the disembodied self is imprisoned (Foucault 1994). Yet Foucault argues that the bodily subjugation of the self can be challenged by voluntary acts of resistance. The body may appear determined, but it is only determined within discourses that could be otherwise, although we are never told how or why this should occur. Foucault can therefore be accused of exaggerating bodily inscription through discourse and in turn exaggerating the unending possibilities of redefining the self within discourse. Paradoxically, Foucault appears to avoid the disembodied self of rationalism by re-embodying the self, yet he de-naturalizes and de-humanizes the body by removing any sense of its living materiality, substantive properties and socially constituted boundaries (McNay 2000). For Foucault there is no fixed knowledge of the body or the self, only what is historically imposed and what is voluntarily resisted.

This oscillation between determinism and counteraction, between bodily inscription and embodied agency as resistance, partly arises because

Foucault refuses fully to theorize subjectivity and agency in relation to the body. Instead, notions of autonomy and self-reflexivity are subsumed into the self-subjugation of disciplinary power that is the opposite of ideals of self-constitution and intentional agency. It is only in his later work that the regimes of control over docile bodies are opened up with a more normative notion of self-reflexivity (Foucault 1991: 351). This allows an ethical consideration of a positive aesthetic ideal of autonomy and self-formation through 'technologies' of self-discipline, and a broader reconsideration of the connection between agency and change (Foucault 1986). But this again raises more perplexing questions: can one have an active notion of the self or self-creation without rebuilding an intentional or centred notion of autonomy and agency within discourse (Giddens 1984)? How can self-knowledge become self-liberation unless there is a clear separation between power and knowledge? Can self-discipline as a moral and ethical form of self-reflexivity lead to a model of ethical conduct? Can Foucault really find a way of re-centring agency and change by re-working the virtues of self-discipline beyond regimes of disciplinary power?

Self-reflexivity and ethics

Foucault's early work on disciplinary power and discourse dissembles a unified notion of reflexivity by abandoning the epistemological and moral subject of rationalism. By situating reflexivity within discourses of knowledge/power Foucault calls into question the idea of an objective or neutral observer and challenges rationalist epistemologies to justify their ideal of reflexivity. Moreover, because Foucault wants to theorize without any notion of a subject he not only undermines rationalism but also the possibility of critically scrutinizing the relationship between the self and discourse by invoking any subject–object, mind–body dichotomies.

By refusing a modified rationalism that moves from a privileged epistemological subject to a more inclusive ideal of rational dialogue between potentially autonomous and reflexive agents, Foucault has been attacked as an 'irrationalist' (Habermas 1986). This charge resonates. Foucault never appears to envisage the possibility of a participative dialogue or 'dialogical self' leading to reasoned causes and agreed outcomes within discourses of knowledge and power (Taylor 1989). Nevertheless, Foucault has always rejected the charge of irrationality and his later work has consistently emphasized the 'indispensability' of modernist ideas of reason and enlightenment, as well as their limits and dangers (1996: 394).

Overall, the conventional notion of reflexivity has served the traditions of rationalism well because it allows for a realist notion of reality 'out there' to which reflexivity can refer in deciding what constitutes knowledge and what makes for effective action. The reflexivity–practice interface therefore allows for the adjudication between knowledge claims, and a self-questioning exploration of the moral presuppositions of knowledge. There are hypothetical causes in the real world and reasons to act and so human agents are not at the mercy of determinism or, worse still, victims of moral impotence in the face of evil (Taylor 1989).

There are, however, considerable problems for a notion of agency if one distances reflexivity from reason and treats it as a self-referential category within discourse. Once the connection between reason and self is broken there are few limits to the possibilities of self-reflective doubt. Everything can be questioned including the once apparently invincible self-certainty of the rational self – '*I think therefore I am*'. In this sense, Foucault inevitably goes much further in challenging the limits of any notion of self-reflexivity. By arguing that ideas of individuality, intentionality, rationality and unconscious motivations are located within the workings of discourse of knowledge and power Foucault historicizes any notion of a truly self-conscious or autonomous subject. Furthermore, Foucault almost totally de-naturalizes the subject by stripping *our* apparently universal notions of 'human nature' and 'humanity' of any hypothetical causal-biological or moral-political foundations. The subject is essentially wiped clean to be historically written and re-written anew.

While Foucault's early work effectively destroys the pretensions of rationalism and scientific naturalism regarding self and human nature, he still appears interested in a notion of self with agency: or an ideal of decentred agency with discursive self-reflexivity. Unlike many postmodernists and constructionists, Foucault somehow wants to keep the hope of an activitistic notion of agency implicit in his work, both as a vaguely therapeutic device and a moral counterforce to self-subjugation. For the destruction of the rational self is designed to create a discursive space for the emergence of a politics of transformation that allows polyvocal selves within new discourses of self-identity (Gergen 1999). By creating a profoundly problematic relation between self and self-reflexivity, however, Foucault appears to give no guidance on how subjects can become agential selves through the creation of new self-identities within discourse. To do so, Foucault would have to specify a link between agency and change, resistance and self-transformation.

These issues are emergent in Foucault's early work. He sometimes describes his methodological task as the strategic analysis of emergent contexts of interaction, concerned with the self-formation of the self or agential selves by processes of action, self-reflexivity and self-discipline, thus allowing the subject to exercise freedom, autonomy and moral choice in a multiplicity of shifting and unique historical contexts (1978: 387). This is an underlying theme that is also captured in Foucault's famous insistence that 'power is only exercised over free subjects' (1992: 221). But it is only in his later 'ethical' writings that one detects a clear shift towards a positive reading of self-constitution and self-creation through 'strategic' (i.e. rational and intentional) modes of self-discipline. The 'negative paradigm' of defaced disciplinary power and self-subjugation is reconfigured as the formation of an autonomous and reflective self through discipline, conceived as an 'aesthetics of existence'.

With this shift Foucault argues that his concern is to develop 'a historical ontology in relation to ethics through which we constitute ourselves as moral agents' (1991: 351). Again, this project is counter-posed as a critical re-engagement with the metaphysical ontology of the rational self proposed by Enlightenment ideals of autonomy and freedom (Chan and Garrick 2002). But unfortunately Foucault never completed this project, although there are clear indications that it was part of a broader attempt to reconnect 'agency' with reflexivity, creativity and change: 'All my analyses are against the idea of universal necessities in human existence. They show the arbitrariness of institutions and show which space of freedom we can still enjoy and how many changes can still be made' (1988: 233).

Discussion: agency and change

Does Foucault's exploration of the 'decentring from (and of) the subject' within discourses of power/knowledge and his related explorations of embodiment and self-reflexivity lead to a coherent theorization of the relations between agency and change – perhaps the central creative ambition of his work? Or, does his conception of decentred agency remain trapped in notions of autonomous discourse, a Panopticon vision of disciplinary power and a politically and morally impotent idea of docile bodies forever entangled in self-reflexive and self-referential discourses?

There are certainly fundamental problems with Foucault's notion of *D/discourse/s* and these become dramatically apparent when discourse is applied to the exploration of self, subjectivity or agency. If the self is constituted within self-referential discourses or shifting discursive practices that appear to have no secure ontological or epistemological foundations, then how can we reconstruct alternative notions of the self that escape the circular entrapments of discourse? Without the narrative idea of an historical continuity to the self, a moral ideal of a 'true self', or an intentional notion of an empirical self somehow made 'real' through rational knowledge, Foucault appears to have no way of reconnecting discourse and self, agency and change.

It is partly because Foucault finds the idea of a self with a rational, intentional or realist centre of gravity to be so deeply unpalatable that he cannot imbue the 'subject' with the moral and political possibilities of changing the world. To search for any epistemological and ontological security of the self, or any realist notion of 'causal agency' is futile. Yet, Foucault wishes to reinstate a new possibility of 'agential selves' that can discursively recreate new discourses and dialogues of self-identity and embodied agency. Is this possible, however, without a concept of intentional action or the causal power of agency, and hence some tentative notion of realism? Foucault never gives clear answers to this question and so his work ends up producing a series of equivocations regarding materiality and discourse, realism and nominalism that continue to haunt postmodernist and constructionist discourses of the self, subjectivity and agency (Newton 1998; Gergen 1999).

Despite Foucault's (1972) many oblique references to materiality his rejection of a return to epistemological realism appears to rule out any serious attempt to reconnect agency and change, rationality and causality. Essentially Foucault wants to argue, contra-naturalism, that there is no reality outside discourse. To suggest that 'things', or 'objects' in the world, or attributes of the self, should be endowed with ontological and epistemological substance or a moral and political reality is a dangerous metaphysical illusion. Ontologically things may appear to exist independently of thought or consciousness, but epistemologically they enter discourses as things we give names to. The analysis of how we mirror, represent and understand the world through discourse is replaced by the analysis of discourse – the mirror itself becomes the object (Deetz 2003: 425).

This nominalist reading of discourse is perhaps most evident in Foucault's (1999) early exploration of the shifting discourses of madness. Ideas of madness are constituted as stable objects of knowledge (epistemology), which are supposed to rest on naturalistic distinctions between reason and madness (ontological) but which are actually shifting objects and classifications derived from discourses in the human sciences and medical psychiatry (Parker 1992: 31). In this sense, Foucault's method of analysing madness is not simply to ask what is regarded as madness within a given historical period, but rather 'to ask how these divisions are operated' within a specific discourse: what methods are used to define it, how does it circulate as a category and how are the distinctions between the sane and insane maintained (Foucault 1999). Ultimately, for Foucault, madness is not a fixed mental condition with pre-discursive biological properties, but the shifting expression of the specific social and historical conditions in which human subjects are 'historically alienated' by the medical discourses of insanity.

At first reading this is a provocative and illuminating position. It punctures the pretensions of science and reason in the face of the shifting pathological 'object' of madness and it allows the 'subject' of madness *itself* to speak (Derrida 1977: 33). Yet, the virtues of scientific classifications that are social-psychologically realist is that they can reflexively expose the presuppositions and potential reifications implicit in objects of knowledge (Archer 2003). Within scientific discourses there are rules of evidence, of what can be claimed as objective or true. Ultimately, this allows prescriptive claims to enter scientific discourse as the aims or goals of knowledge, and this in turn reinstates possibilities of expert knowledge and intervention, as well as agency and change.

For Foucault, however, any realist re-centring of agency and change by connecting expertise and intervention must be treated with considerable caution. Such a connection would be a reflexive extension of the self-defining subject of rationalism from which Foucault wishes to escape. If the relationship between discourse and reality, agency and change can be conceptualized using the expert knowledge of objects or intentions, then how does one ensure that one is not simply reproducing new forms of power/knowledge? Who decides what things or objects belong in each category and how do we know when someone is using realist ontological categories to further moral, political or ideological ends?

Moreover, rationalist and realist notions often have more empirical efficacy in naturalistic discourses of the psychical or biological foundations of behaviour, while their applications to cultural constructs of gender, ethnicity, race or moral and political ideals of agency can be enormously problematic. Push realistic assumptions and intentional categories of action too far and one can end up with crude positivism or unbounded naturalism (Barnes 2000). Instead of exposing the 'order of things' as the 'order of discourse', realism can therefore cover up the self-reflexivity of knowledge that should be part of scientific discourse (Foucault 1972: xi). Ultimately, the danger of shifting the project of Foucauldian studies of society, organizations or the self towards realism is that it may surreptitiously recreate a variety of naturalism.

Foucault, of course, rarely comes close to embracing a version of epistemological realism, despite his various references to 'materiality' and the broader intention of his work to locate discursive practices within social and institutional contexts. Epistemological realism would be a return to the idea that there is an essential self within discourse and that there is an external reality or real entities outside discourse. For Foucault the idea of an existing or pre-discursive self is rejected. Anti-essentialism and anti-realism therefore appear to go together.

Unfortunately, the implications of Foucault's legacy for organizational theory and constructionist discourses are rarely consistent on this matter (Rowlinson and Carter 2002). Anti-essentialism can be a basis of rebuilding a bridge to realism (Parker 1998). This is perfectly understandable. Some Focauldian organizational theorists and constructionists drift back towards some variant of realism because they need to find an ontological and epistemological foundation for the self-constitution of the subject (Newton 1998). For without the translation of the subjectivity of subjugated selves into 'agency', moral and political action becomes problematic – if not impossible.

In contrast to Foucault's ambivalence towards a reinstatement of realism his reading of discourse would appear to drift towards the conventional self-refuting stance of relativism. Foucault claims that his exploration of discourse is an alternative to humanism and scientism because it recognizes that the self-defining subject of rationalism divides the self and the self from nature. Enlightenment discourses of rationalism are also suspect because they limit the possibilities of reflexivity: self-reflexivity is unending and so the search for truth is an illusion. In a world without any metaphysical anchorage, moral certainty or real foundations all discourses and all voices are valid and equal (Foucault 1996).

Foucault, of course, does not formally espouse a position of relativism or constructionism. Rather, he assumes a neutral stance of historical self-understanding towards all discourse, all concepts of reality and all evaluative positions. This represents the exploration of discourse as the historicist equivalent of the metaphysical trans-valuation of all values

(Nietzsche 1974). Questions of what is 'truth, what 'values' should we affirm and how we interpret subjectivity and human agency do not require answers. For all such questions will simply reproduce competing discourses which express their own culturally relative presuppositions of what is true, what is good and how we should act in the world (Foucault 2000: 8–9). In this respect, Foucault appears to be, despite his protestations, an unrelenting relativist in his openness to competing discourses.

Yet here too there are equivocations. The apparently relativistic exploration of discourse also incorporates an undercurrent of monist idealism: the idea of discourse as grand Discourse (Alvessen and Karreman 2000). For Foucault every appeal to words such as 'experience', 'consciousness', 'agency' as ways of capturing what is true or accurate with respect to what there 'is' becomes an infinite regress to other words that refer to other words that ultimately lead to a realization that discourse and reality, self and other, mind and body, experience and nature are inseparable. This curiously holistic notion, beyond the relativism of discourse, suggests that Foucault's seemingly neutral stance towards discourse has more in common with the ambitions of Hegelian idealism to reabsorb the self-defining but self-divided subject of Enlightenment rationalism and scientism into a new embodied self (Taylor 1986). It is no surprise then that some Foucault-inspired constructionists have ended up reinstating various versions of idealism, with strong utopian undertones (Gergen 2001a: 422).

Undoubtedly Foucault would be wary of any attempt to chart a course through relativism to idealism. He would certainly be deeply uncomfortable with an all-enveloping notion of discourse that restored a metaphysical intent to dissolve subject–object dichotomies into each other: a back door to old style Hegelian idealism appears firmly closed (Foucault 2000: 12). In Foucault's post-structuralist worldview the idea of a subject of history or any hint of a subject within discourse is antithetical:

> What is this anonymous system without a subject, what thinks? This 'I' has exploded … this is the discovery of the 'there is'. There is one. In some ways one comes back to the seventeenth century point of view, with this difference: not man but anonymous thought, knowledge without a subject, theory with no identity, in God's place.
>
> (Foucault, cited in Erobon 1991: 161)

Despite Foucault's objections, this curiously hyperbolic and disjointed rejection of any notion of a subject-centred vision of the world has strong transcendent resonances as a counter-memory against Enlightenment rationalism (Habermas 1987). If Hegel was concerned with the final reconciliation of the subject in history, Foucault wishes to banish all reference to any form of subject, to relativize all '*epistemes* of truth' and to dissipate any search for the foundations of *our* cultural identity (Foucault 1977: 162). This is a morally courageous position, but it also carries profound intellectual dangers. Discourse as an anti-metaphysical position invoked to destroy the 'subject' of all discourses of knowledge can itself become a metaphysical inversion of Hegel's Euro-centric world spirit: *Discourse* as the transvaluation of all values. Hegel's humanism in which the subject and object of history are reconciled is replaced by an equally virulent anti-humanism in which subjectivity, identity and the intentional sources of moral and political action are torn asunder.

What allows Foucault partly to escape the dangers of grand Discourse as the metaphysical assent to a new *episteme* of the 'politics of truth' counterpoised to rationalism, is his constant focus on the genealogical exploration of discourses of power/knowledge that define and redefine the different ways in which human beings have been 'made into subjects'. The grand intent may be polemically anti-humanistic and anti-rational, but Foucault often succeeds in historically exposing the multiplicity of historical forms that inhumanity imprints on the face of the human. If Hegel's humanistic rationalism was designed to see beyond the 'slaughterhouse of history' and disclose the 'rose in the cross' of the present, Foucault's anti-humanist history explores the rituals of torture, mutilation and execution that mark the dominance of 'sovereign power' and the transformation of rationality into the disciplinary power of knowledge that subjugates the body, the mind and the self. This allowed Foucault to 'bring *evils* to light' but he refused the humanistic and rationalist assertion that 'the negation or overcoming of these evils will promote a good' (Taylor 1986: 69).

Despite this apparent moral agnosticism, Foucault envisions the possibility that within discourses of knowledge and new forms of disciplinary power, we can recover and rediscover *our-selves*: 'Discourse transmits and produces power; it reinforces it, but it also undermines it, renders it fragile and makes it possible to thwart it' (Foucault 1979: 100). Paradoxically, discourses that make us into subjects also allow the creation of a space for resistance and change. Within discourse Foucault therefore appears to allow for the possibility of self-transformation, despite his assault on the possibilities of intentional agency. By somehow resisting what we have become we create possibilities for defining what we are and what we can become – we rediscover embodied agency. But how does this occur? Does Foucault really engage with the possibility of creative human agency that can change the social world?

If Foucault partly charts the move from reflexivity to self-reflexivity, from disembodied agency to embodied agency and beyond, he gives no guidance on how the polyvocal selves he envisages can become agents of new identities and new discourses of the self. This has created a profound set of difficulties for Focauldian organizational theory and constructionist discourses that seek both critical self-reflexivity and the promise of new identities founded on new acts of refusal and resistance (Newton 1998; Gergen 2001a). For once self-reflexivity starts it appears to have no resting point. Discourses can therefore appear as endless circles of self-reflexivity that can never come to an end (Reed 2000). Acts of self-reflexivity, resistance and change are themselves discursively constituted and therefore potentially infinite. In this sense processes of self-reflexivity and self-explication can never really be complete; they can never specify an end, goal or purpose to which resistance and change are directed. Foucauldian organizational theory and constructionist discourses are therefore constantly in danger of occupying an infinite space of discursive possibilities, filled with nothing but discourse about discourses, possible agential selves with no agency, change without any fixed starting point or outcome.

Conclusion

Four major criticisms of Foucault's conception of agency and change have been made. First, Foucault's most influential works tend to treat agency as an exogenous effect of discourses of power/knowledge. He therefore underplays the central importance of intentional action in any notion of agency. Second, without a distinction between power and knowledge it becomes almost impossible to imbue agency with 'causal power' to transform knowledge into action, or to create a substantive distinction between the powerful and the powerless. As a result agency becomes counteraction identified with resistance to power as an emergent and potentially voluntaristic act. Third, Foucault appears to challenge the conventional mind–body split and naturalism in his temporal treatment of 'docile bodies', but he does not provide a coherent theory of embodied agency or embodiment (McNay 2000). Instead, he simply re-embodies the apparently 'alienated' self of scientific discourse and liberal humanist thought by denaturalizing the body as realm of infinite refashioning; there are no limits beyond the assertion of our will to become 'who we are'. We are, in principle, equally free to choose our bodies, as we are free to choose ourselves. Fourth, Foucault's early attacks on ontological and epistemological dualism lead to the advocacy of a form of hyper-reflexivity in which there is no fixed 'truth' or object to which self-reflexivity can refer. The self as a subject or object of knowledge therefore appears to be determined by discourses of power/knowledge and yet is ultimately free-floating.

While Foucault's vision of the decentring of power and the decentring of agency undoubtedly opens up new possibilities for rethinking agency and change in organizations and societies, it also closes down ideals of agency founded on intentional action, knowledge, autonomy and reflexivity (Giddens 1984). If organizational theory and construction discourses are to seriously rethink 'agency' and 'change' in a post-Panopticon world of organizational networks, increasing global complexity and risk, they will have to reconnect decentred agency with centred agency (Lash 2003). This will require a systematic exploration of four key questions.

First, how can intentional, future-oriented action and forms of discourse be mediated through practice? When Foucault's later work returned to the possibilities of self-formation through 'intentional and voluntary action' he began a belated re-engagement with intentionality and rationalism (Habermas 1986: 107). But this was short-lived and Foucault still remained deeply resistant to the idea that a viable concept of agency should incorporate an intentional notion of rational action that circumscribes the possibilities of practice. Decentred agency appears as the antithesis of rationality and any belief in the translation of theory into practice-discourse is practice. Most varieties of postmodern organizational theory and constructionist discourse have taken this hostility to intentionality and rationality to its logical conclusion and rejected ontological dualism and with it any realist concept of subjectivity, the self or agency (Carr 1997; Chan and Garrick 2002). Even the traces of 'backdoor determinism' (Reed 2000) implicit in Foucault's early work are subsumed into a form of apodictic indeterminism (Gergen 1999, 2003). We confront a world without structures, without 'objective' knowledge, without 'others', and without the possibilities of social or political action informed by reasoned discourse. This carries all the dangers of a return not only to idealism but also to old-style voluntarism.

The second synthetic question further highlights these issues. How can 'knowledge' rather than discourses of power/knowledge provide a basis of self-knowledge and self-creation, of agency and change? Foucault's work rarely faces up to the central importance of separating knowledge from power (Lukes 2002). This is essential if one is to construct a viable concept of the causal power and creative possibilities of agency. In his remorseless attempt to steer clear of epistemological subjectivity and any form of subjectivism, however, Foucault appears to end up removing any causation from individuals by relocating objectivity and practice in a neutral stance towards discourse. Yet it is clear that any synthetic concept of agency must include both the causal power of action and the creative possibilities of agency; each of which requires an epistemological space outside the over-determination of power/knowledge. With such a synthetic conceptualization, agency is not simply an either/or dichotomy: an intentional application of power against resistance, nor a voluntaristic form of resistance against power. Unfortunately, Foucault decentres intentionality while re-centring resistance as a realm of emergent choice beyond power/knowledge. The result is that agency simply becomes the indeterminate emergence of marginalized, transgressive and voluntaristic resistance to power, rather than the creation of alternative definitions of what power is, how it is legitimated and how it can be transformed.

This over-emphasis on counteraction is also reinforced when the third synthetic question is posed. Can the notion of embodied agency include an exploration of an ideal of autonomy and its limits? Foucault's attempt to re-embody the abstract knowing subject of rationalistic thought becomes an attempt to de-naturalize and de-subjectivize the body and the self. But a notion of agency is analytically and morally vacuous unless it engages with the temporal scientific insights into what might define us as biological entities, and what socially limits the possibilities of our autonomy as social beings. Because Foucault brackets these questions his analysis of bodily inscription through disciplinary power and bio-power is unable to clarify a rounded or realistic notion of autonomy (1991: 351). By following Foucault down this path, postmodern organizational theorists and constructionists create an impossible image of autonomy; they go to extremes in denying any traces of naturalism and determinism or any privileging of the social over the individual. This can lead to a wholesale abandonment of 'agency' as a limiting construct (Gergen 1999). Yet even Foucault (1986) realized in his later work that one cannot really subvert subjectivity, rationality and individualist notions of choice, unless one redefines a viable counter-concept of autonomous agency.

Finally, how can self-reflexivity be linked to a positive object of self-knowledge or self-formation that defines new possibilities of identity rather than a negative image of self-subjugation? Foucault (1991) tries to answer this question in his later work by linking self-reflexivity to an ethical ontology of self-formation. However, his notion of self-creation through an 'aesthetics of existence', reproduces a strong undercurrent of voluntarism that again conflates agency with the malleability of the self through ethical self-discipline. Just as his original notion of power/knowledge narrows agency to resistance or counteraction, so correspondingly does his later ethical ideal of self-formation as self-reflexivity end in the possibility of an indeterminate and infinitely malleable self. This sets up an impossible and ultimately utopian mission for self-reflexivity as a source of agency and change.

A synthetic and practice-oriented concept of agency would have to mediate between classical ideas of intentional action, autonomy and choice and ideals of embodied agency as always changing and always open to reinvention. This cannot be achieved by invoking a stand-off between realism and nominalism, faced and de-faced power, stasis and change, a fixed universal self of rationalism and the forever changing and indeterminate subject of a postmodern polyvocal self. Foucault is partly responsible for perpetuating these false dichotomies, even though his later work was inspired by the search for a deeper realm of autonomy and self-reflexivity that would somehow escape the insidious reach of universal reason and disciplinary power. What Foucault managed to rescue, however, from the grand narrative of rationalism and intentional agency was incomplete and theoretically flawed, not because it does not match up to an abstract moral imperative of autonomy, but because it limits agency and change to resistance, counteraction and transgression; to all the forms of agential power that are other to the self and its polymorphous expressions. At the core of Foucault's notion of agency and change is not a moral vision or a programmatic political mission to *make a difference* but an aesthetic, erotic and voluntaristic desire to *act otherwise*.

7 Things fall apart?

- Future research
- Things fall apart?
- Postscript

This book began with a brief analytical overview of Giddens' work and it has ended with a critical appraisal of Foucault and the constructionist challenge of decentred agency. Along the way we have also re-examined Lewin's classic concept of change agency, Pettigrew's sustained contextualist attack on planned change, and the growing challenges posed by complexity theories of organizational change, as a problematic of order/chaos. Where do we go from here?

Overall, the exploration of the four discourses on agency and change in organizations has underscored the growing fragmentation and complexity of the research field. We now confront an enormous diversity of competing discourses on change agency, both individual and team focused, autonomous and decentred, that no longer fit within the conventional rationalist ideals of organizational change theory and practice bequeathed by rational choice theories, models of strategic action and the organizational development tradition. The widespread espousal of the search for learning organizations, ideas of distributed leadership, theories of organizational complexity, concepts of sensemaking agency and contructionist discourses on decentred agency have finally crystallized this shift towards potentially more inclusive and team-based models of leadership, agency and change in organizations.

This new plurality is in many respects a very positive development. All too often the variety of forms of change agency in organizations has been identified with one-dimensional rationalist theories of leadership, managerial models of control or exclusive concepts of change agent expertise (Caldwell 2003). These formulations of singular ideals have both exaggerated the individual autonomy of leaders and managers in organizational change and undermined the various practical roles other human actors can actually play in processes of organizational change. There are, however, new dangers lurking in the breakdown of rationalist discourses and the growing ascendancy of dispersalist and social constructionist ideas.

Some of these dangers can be explored by briefly examining possible research agendas within each of the four sets of discourses and then by speculating on the possibilities for establishing a future direction for interdisciplinary research within an intrinsically multidisciplinary field. In this way we can ask if there is any possibility of establishing a convergence of research pathways or perhaps the prospect of a more integrated research paradigm for the exploration of change agency.

Future research

Rationalist discourses

It is from the pioneering work of Kurt Lewin that the organizational development tradition inherited the modern ideal of the change agent or action researcher as an expert who can rationally and objectively explicate the relationship between knowledge and action. This ideal was central to Lewin's commitment to rational action and democratic values, his belief in expert knowledge as reflexive feedback, and his overall liberal idealism regarding the self-reflective mediation of theory and practice, knowing and doing. But Lewin (1947, 1999) was simply too optimistic about the connections between science and action. He had few doubts regarding the objectivity of scientific knowledge as democratic knowledge because he assumed that the meaning and presuppositions of science are given, and so his model of research *into* action treats the value presuppositions of knowledge as unproblematic. For Lewin science was a universal enterprise that grounded democratic virtues and acted as a bulwark against authoritarian politics. What Lewin failed to realize, however, was that his model of change agency carried the ever-present danger within the action research tradition of transforming expertise, democratic virtues and liberal humanism into rationalist dogmatism – the one best way of designed or planned change managed by experts. Effectively, an ideal of participative inquiry as a form of empowerment or democracy in action is constantly in danger of collapsing into a legitimization of expertise (Reason and Bradbury 2001).

Since Lewin's time the ascendancy of expertise has been accompanied by growing challenges to its efficacy, and this creates new research questions and issues for the OD tradition. As knowledge becomes more specialized, differentiated and distributed within organizational settings that are less hierarchical and more decentralized, the strategic issues of how to manage, develop and exercise 'expertise' have become increasingly problematic. The idea of expertise now extends beyond the action research context and expert/lay boundaries of knowledge are problematic (Beck 1992). This presents an enormously difficult challenge. Faced with changing forms of knowledge creation, new measures of professional 'competence', competing modes of expertise and reflexivity, and the external scrutiny of publics 'overloaded' or disillusioned with competing expert discourses and practices, all claims to expertise are fragile (Willard 1998). Moreover, challenges to expert regimes of 'disciplinary power' are likely to intensify within the workplace, especially under the assault of constructionism and organizational discourse analysis. In this respect, the forces that lead to dependence on expertise can lead to its disintegration as it is devalued in the eyes of its users or rejected by its subalterns. To confront these mounting challenges the OD tradition needs to undertake a far-reaching search for new practice-based and distributive models of expertise, rational inquiry, moral discourse and knowledge creation.

There are, however, few signs that OD practitioners as a professional grouping are willing or able to embark on this task – even in the face of a perceived crisis (Bradford and Burke 2005). Instead, the increasing shift of OD practitioners towards management-driven interventions that can deliver value has led to an even greater emphasis on more instrumental forms of consultancy practice. In these circumstances it is becoming increasingly difficult to differentiate the inclusive models of change agency developed within the OD tradition from more managerial models of change agency emanating from management consultants. As this blurring of boundaries continues it raises new issues and creates new research agendas.

The problematic role of management consultants and other related professions in the creation, diffusion and institutionalization of new expert discourses about knowledge, power and change agency clearly present major possibilities for future research (Kipping and Engwell 2002). As key carrier groups and 'knowledge entrepreneurs' they are often crucial in developing new instrumental product ideas, or the hard and soft technologies of 'managing change' or 'facilitating change' that can be engineered or programmed into organizations as quick fix solutions (Abrahamson and Fairchild 1999). How these interventions are managed is particularly relevant to organizational development practitioners and other change agents, who often use a curious mix of uncodified knowledge, instrumental expertise, project management techniques, practical know-how and political skills to effect change (Buchanan and Boddy 1992; Clark and Salaman 1996; Fincham 2001). But the turnover of ideas and the legacy of re-engineering and change programme failures suggests a need to explore why certain ideas and processes succeed or fail – and how they are reinvented. It is also important to research the dislocation of managers as change agents by management consultants. Moreover, exploration of the ethics of professional conduct and consultancy practice are increasingly required in the face of the recurrent convergence of technocratic expertise and managerial interests and the countervailing need to include broader constituencies of employees and other stakeholders in achieving successful organizational change. Without a recognition of these issues change agency as a concept and mode of practice may become conflated with ideas of instrumental rationality and expertise and therefore lose any connection within the reciprocal ideas of autonomy and reflexivity. This would mark the final eclipse of Lewin's once inspirational image of the change agent.

Contextualist discourses

If rationalist discourses suggest generalizing research agendas around issues of intervention, consultancy practice and professional expertise, then contextualism points in the opposite direction: towards an historical awareness of the empirical particularity of change processes as revealed through the highly intensive exploration of small numbers of discrete case studies (Pettigrew 1997). This focus presents enormous scope for a wide-ranging case research on the context, content and process of change, although there have been few case studies that have emulated the richness of Pettigrew's early work. More research on linking processes of change to a comparative analysis of organizational outcomes is also likely, and this holds out greater possibilities for combining processual analysis with larger scale statistical mapping techniques and an exploration of macro–micro issues (Pettigrew 1997). There are already signs that moves in this direction may lead to a rapprochement between contextualism and causal predictive and contingency theories of organizations, as contextualists begin to moderate their once apparently hostile posture toward positivistic methodologies (Donaldson 2001; Pettigrew et al. 2003). There are also some indications that contextualism may also be willing to appropriate aspects of constructionist discourses in the process-based notions of 'organizing/strategizing', while still remaining deeply sceptical about the claims of postmodernists: 'we can repudiate the overdrawn distinctions and misplaced concreteness of modernism without burdening ourselves with the exaggerated relativism and irresponsible detachment of post-modernism's fringe' (Whittington and Melin 2003: 43).

Despite these tentative crossovers, contextualism is unlikely to trek back towards modernist rationalism, nor is it likely openly to embrace the perplexities of constructionism. Certainly, the overriding historical particularity of processual analysis, its emphasis on the temporal interconnectedness of past, present and future, will mean that it is unlikely to overcome its deep ambivalence towards rationality, systematic theory, causality and the directionality of change. Equally, contextualist discourses are unlikely seriously to engage contructionism because its essentially realist notion of knowledge would begin to undermine the empirical facticity of contextual analysis. If contextualism really wants to move in this direction it would have to contextualize contextualism as a particular form of academic discourse about the embeddedness of agency and change in organizations (see Chapter 3). The difficulty with this move is that contextualism would then have to face up to a disconcerting self-concept of its own discourse as a product of *Homo Academicus* (Bourdieu 1988).

There are also other pressing issues that contextualist research needs to grapple with. Most notably, the idea of the embeddedness of agency as socially bounded action and choice in dynamically complex and shifting contexts is a vital research topic that needs much more clarification. Giddens' (1984) ideas on agency and structure appear partly to underpin the contextualist notion of embeddedness, but it is unclear how the idea of the 'duality of structure' can be translated into an exploration of strategic change and strategic choice in organizations. Giddens provides an essentially 'process' theory of structuration but not a convincing theory of agency. In this respect, Pettigrew's processual focus on the micro-dynamics of organizational politics and power appears to emulate Giddens in emphasizing constraint while simultaneously undermining determinism and reaffirming choice. But in doing so it also reproduces Giddens under-theorization of agency. Paradoxically, contextualism, despite its emphasis on agency and choice, does not offer a contextual theory of leadership or agency, nor an understanding of the processes of 'leading change'. It would be a fascinating challenge for contextualists to extend Giddens' structuration theory to encompass a concept of leadership as a form of embedded agency in organizations (Whittington and Melin 2003: 46). This would also mark an important act of bridge-building between organizational change theory and leadership research.

Finally the continued focus on the all-enveloping complexity of context poses a research challenge in developing a theory of practice, especially given the ambition of contextualism to provide 'practically useful research'. But this challenge is rarely addressed. Instead, contextualist discourses often express their opposition to instrumental tools or prescriptive recipes of practice. This is sometimes presented as a necessary challenge to 'managerialism', although it does not come with alternative conceptions of the theory–practice divide. For example, the notion of *discourse as practice* provides an alternative reading of the theory–practice dichotomy, but this is rarely addressed directly by contextualists (Foucault 1994). Nor has the increasing 'practice turn' within contextualism addressed the challenges of theorizing the 'logic of practice' (Bourdieu 1990). In this respect, the idea of 'embeddedness' as the guiding methodological principle of 'contextual realism' is only likely to provide a temporary safe haven against the perceived ills of postmodernism. In the long run contextualist defences appear unsustainable in a context where expertise, knowledge creation and practice are increasingly problematic (Whittington 2003). Until contextualism seriously confronts these issues it will remain a conventional liberal defence of scholarship and academic virtues in the face of the practice-bias of managerial action, new forms of knowledge creation and the potentially corrosive logic of postmodern discourses of organizational and strategic change.

Dispersalist discourses

It is within dispersalist discourses that new approaches to change agency, leadership, decentred agency and the theory–practice divide have been theorized, although it is difficult to speculate on where research in this area will lead given its growing plurality and fragmentation. The enormous plurality of dispersalist discourses also means that it is very difficult to give any kind of comprehensive overview, and this was one of the main reasons why this book has focused only on one variety of dispersalist discourses: *complexity theories*. Here, however, it may be useful to give a snapshot of the scope and possible research agendas for other varieties of dispersalist discourse (Buchanan 2003). Again, this will have to be selective. Only four areas will be briefly outlined: the learning organization and distributed leadership, communities of practice, sensemaking agency and, finally, chaos or complexity theories (see Chapter 4). All of these discourses have a variety of sources, involve different assumptions and are sometimes contradictory in their implications. They do, however, share some common features in their emphasis on decentred agency, complex system self-organization and the importance of practice.

The learning organization. This concept is currently the most influential and controversial model of a team approach to change agency and organizational change, and it has had a considerable influence on many practitioners (Dierkes *et al.* 2001). The learning organization concept conceives of organizations not as highly formalized hierarchical structures, but as macro-systems and micro-processes of learning and knowledge creation that give primacy to leadership and change agency at all levels. Everyone throughout the organization is therefore expected to work collaboratively by harnessing their knowledge, skills and insights to constantly renew and improve organizational success. This amounts, in principle, to an extension of leadership theory by identifying decentred agency with a distributed yet unified striving to realize collective or system goals (Senge 1996). As such, the 'distributed leadership' idea at the core of the learning organization concept potentially challenges many of the theoretical and prescriptive assumptions underlying conventional leadership paradigms, especially the leader-centrism implied in most leadership–followership dichotomies. Instead, the empirical focus shifts towards far-reaching changes within the workplace that have allowed the increasing emergence of autonomous and devolved forms of 'concertive action' and 'conjoint agency' (Gronn 2002).

There are, however, serious theoretical and empirical problems with the concept of learning organizations (Jackson 2000; Friedman *et al.* 2005). The systemic and 'unitarist' ideal of organizational learning as a collective process raises fundamental research issues of how learning, formal and 'tacit', can be dispersed throughout an organization; who is involved in learning, where does it take place, what is being learnt, how does it accumulate, and how can it be applied (Easterby-Smith *et al.* 2000; Hendry 1996)? Until these research questions are answered, the learning organization remains more rhetorical prescription than realistic practice (Friedman *et al.* 2005).

Partly because of these unresolved questions and issues, it is likely that the related concepts of distributed leadership and 'conjoint agency' provide probably the most immediately fruitful avenues for future research on team-based forms of leadership and change agency in learning organizations. As the tensions between differentiation and integration in organizations intensify, concertive actions by groups provide new ways of accommodating new forms of role interdependence, work coordination and learning. This insight applies equally to organizational change interventions which may involve both a need for synergy between goals and a reciprocal sharing of influence among change agents. But unravelling these links will require much more research work on multiple levels and micro units of analysis of conjoint change agency, while not losing sight of the macro or structural dimensions of organizations as systems, including the ubiquitous counterforces of control. It is often forgotten that moves towards increased autonomy, decentred agency and 'concertive action' are partly sustained by the creation of new systemic logics of electronic surveillance and 'concertive control' within the workplace (Baker 1999). As yet, research on learning organizations has rarely seriously addressed the possibility that distributed forms of agency and leadership are synonymous with the 'dispersal of instrumental rationality' (Grey 1999: 579).

Communities of practice. The concept of 'communities of practice', so persuasively formulated by Wenger (1998), enriches and reformulates the idea of learning organizations by moving towards a 'social theory of learning' founded on practice. Wenger argues that organizations are both designed 'institutions' and emergent 'constellations of practice'. This is a theoretical arbitration of traditional action and structure dichotomies in that practice becomes a mediated realm of mutual engagement and shared meaning (Giddens 1984). But the *duality of meaning* is retained in that 'agency' and 'structure' are conceived as both designed and emergent: products and processes of 'participation' and 'reification' that occur within communities of practice (Wenger 1998). Because communities of practice are relatively autonomous, this allows for the creative reshaping of organizations by participation and mutual engagement: 'The point of design is to make organizations ready for the emergent by serving the inventiveness of practice and the potential for innovation inherent in its emergent structure' (Wenger 1998: 245). Organizational change and redesign are therefore conceptualized as an emergent and iterative process of self-organization within communities of practice, rather than the outcome of a predetermined strategy or the top-down design interventions of experts.

Despite the enormous appeal of Wenger's work as a theorization of practice it leaves some difficult research questions unresolved. The idea that communities of practice are sustained through the ongoing 'negotiation of meaning' is often confusing because it operates through reciprocal processes of 'participation' and 'reification' that lack analytical clarity (1998: 92). Participation appears to depend on an idealized notion of mutual meaning creation in practice, while reification is an amorphous concept covering virtually every form of signification and objectification of human activity (Wenger 1998: 63). Thus while the duality of participation–reification opens up classical organizational issues of autonomy and control, agency and structure, no systemic, structural or institutional categories are offered to explain how workplace control or power is produced and reproduced (Giddens 1984). Instead, Wenger claims that: 'External forces have no direct power over this production because, in the last analysis (i.e. in the doing through mutual engagement in practice), it is the community that negotiates its enterprise' (1998: 80). In this respect, Wenger is in danger of an old-style idealization of the moral community as a form of team-based agency while failing to explore both the limits of communities of practice as a form of decentred agency and the realities of structure as systems of power.

Sensemaking agency and change. Sensemaking discourses have a complex intellectual genealogy and they are enormously diverse, although their common epistemological origins are in pragmatism, symbolic interactionism and cognitive psychology. Karl Weick (1995, 2001) is probably the most influential proponent of sensemaking concepts. He conceives sensemaking as ongoing processes of meaning 'enactment' through which individuals and groups create intersubjective interpretations of the world: 'sensemaking is an attempt to produce micro stability amidst continuing change' (Weick 2001: 22). This involves a number of related assumptions: that organizations are ongoing processes of enactment rather than pregiven structures or functional entities with goals; that enactment occurs through narratives, symbols, talk and labels that create 'plausible stories' of events and causes; that managerial action is informed by self-fulfilling prophesies in which decisions become realized when they are treated as if they were true, or, alternatively, they are treated as rational when they are realized – strategy and intent are self-confirming or post-rationalizing actions (Weick 2001: 170). And finally, it is assumed that human agency is not prescribed by authority, rules or formal roles but is enacted through the pragmatic self-efficacy of practice. Despite this micro construction of the macro and the accompanying decoupling of rationality from intention, sensemaking discourses are rarely relativistic (Weick 2001: 98). Weick certainly embraces some moderate ideas from social constructionist discourses, but his disciplinary grounding of knowledge in pragmatism, symbolic interactionism and cognitive psychology means that he is unwilling to treat sensemaking as a discourse of power/knowledge.

While sensemaking concepts are intrinsically receptive to explorations of innovation and change in less hierarchical, or 'loosely coupled systems', especially in information-intensive and knowledge creating organizations, they also raise questions regarding the nature of change agency. Because sensemaking agency cannot specify strategic ends it is always in danger of becoming its opposite: self-validating action or a self-fulfilling prophecy that may potentially reproduce *more of the same*. Weick (2001) sometimes appears to reinforce this possibility when he suggests that self-belief, optimism, enthusiasm and behavioural commitment are more important in realizing goals than plans, predicted outcomes or expert inferences as to the causality of events:

> Whether people are called fanatics, true believers, or the currently popular phrase *idea champions*, they all embody what looks like strategy in their persistent behaviour. Their persistence carries the strategy; the persistence is the strategy. True believers impose their view on the world and fulfill their own prophecies.
>
> (Weick 2001: 349–350)

Yet, paradoxically, this apparently proactive concept of sensemaking agency as enacted self-belief rather than rationality or expertise tends to be diffuse, therapeutic and passive: 'Actors in a loosely coupled system rely on trust and presumption, persist, are often isolated, find social comparison difficult, have no one to borrow from, seldom imitate, suffer pluralistic ignorance, maintain discretion, improvise, and have less hubris ...' (Weick 2001: 401). Moreover, because organizational change is perceived as continuous, Weick tends to argue that change unfolds through slow iterative or incremental steps: 'Microchanges predominate in loosely coupled systems' (Weick 2001: 400). Weick therefore conceives loosely coupled systems as 'the ultimate neutralizer of managerial hubris' and rationalist models of change agency; an assumption that can again can lead to a reactive–passive image of agency.

Weick's vaguely voluntaristic and yet reactive–passive image of sensemaking agency also has its structurally obverse implications. Sensemaking invariably conflates agency and structure, conceiving both as modes of 'enactment', with the result that one is never sure when 'organizing' as ongoing micro-processes of cognition begin and end. Like the traditions of symbolic interactionism, sensemaking has enormous difficulties in theorizing systemic linkages between episodic streams of meaning and action, mainly because the concept of 'enactment' treats processes of meaning creation as momentary, circular and self-referential (Hendry and Seidl 2003). Organizations are therefore not treated as macro entities with recursive or interactive properties of reproduction that can be analysed, designed or changed, but are rather 'a stream of problems, solutions and people tied together by choices' (Weick 2001:

28). This process of deconstructing structures as systems partly explains why power and control in organizations are rarely examined in sensemaking approaches, except as an ad hoc appendage or incidental afterthought. But if meaning is imposed, controlled or manipulated, then sensemaking and sensegiving may be an effect of power, rather than the ongoing outcome of choice or emergent processes of consensus seeking. This blind spot may also help explain why there appears to be no stable means–ends linkages in organizational decision-making processes that can be subject to some degree of rationality, objectivity or expert knowledge. Instead, the self-referential and self-confirming logic of sensemaking treats interpretations as 'real' causes and rationality as post-rationalization; although, paradoxically, all interpretations are not equally valid (Weick 1995).

Complexity theories. As argued in Chapter 5, complexity theories provide alternative explorations of organizational change and *agential dispersal*. Organizations are conceived as configurations of self-organizing systems within systems, networks within networks, operating without tight hierarchies of strategic control (Anderson 1999). Complexity theories are therefore an attempt to explore the processual and relational dynamics of unpredictability, non-linearity and chaos in organizations. Rather than conceive of organizations as hierarchical or purposeful control systems, the focus shifts to how complex self-organizing systems achieve innovation or change through a diversity of agents operating outside any centrally controlled system: agents simply interact with other agents and are 'free' to follow, ignore or modify rules of interaction. In this sense, 'agency' is a dispersed interactional field of positive feedback loops and discretional rules outside the usual norms of delegated or shared authority and this potentially allows order, cohesion and change to emerge from the *middle* and *bottom* of organizations.

While complexity theories open up new avenues for research on new forms of autonomy and control in organization as well as new possibilities for innovation and knowledge creation, they still leave many issues unresolved. In particular, ideas of agent-based networks or concepts of 'participative self-organizing learning' diffuse any sense of how decentred agency can be managed, controlled or developed in organizations (Stacey 2001; Smith 2003). Complexity theories have been slow to address these issues, focusing instead on the possibilities that *order without control* will emerge from simple rules of behaviour or interaction – a highly problematic idea (Houchin and MacLean 2005). Unfortunately, future research on complexity theory cannot rule out the ever present danger that actor networks and conjoint agency may not be able to cope with the imperatives of organizational integration or act as an effective substitute for leadership and transformation from above. Complexity theories have therefore to consider the more disturbing possibility that new information and communication technologies have led to not simply the creation of open networks within networks, but also subtle and perhaps more coercive forms of centralizing decentralization that can concentrate power and control. The idea that complex systems unambiguously increase autonomy through networks of information and communication without power is simply an illusion.

Undoubtedly, the new discourses on agential dispersal in organizations have grown out of the enormous changes in the workplace over the last three decades. Yet it is unclear where these changes will lead in terms of promoting innovation and change. There are already indications that dispersal can create new dangers for managing change in much the same way as earlier empowering initiatives on quality and 'programmatic' culture change have (Beer *et al.* 1990). This appears to be occurring in two major forms. First, by encouraging a plethora of disparate and unconnected change agent initiatives, the potential coherence and control of change programmes are seriously undermined (Doyle 2001). Second, empowering new and sometimes 'unaccountable' collective leaders and teams, often with no clear focus or agenda for change, can disempower or undermine the fragile interventions of more conventional forms of expert knowledge. In this paradoxical sense, dispersal as an empowerment philosophy may have the opposite effect, creating change fatigue, chaos and perhaps even organizational collapse. Again, these broader issues open up potentially new arenas for further research.

Contructionist discourses

Fundamentally different research agendas of power and control are central to the *change-without-agency problematic* that threatens to envelop discussions of change agent roles within constructionist discourses on organizational change (Gergen 2001a). Constructionist discourses are by definition diffuse because they argue for a perspective image of knowledge, a decentring of the epistemological and moral subject of science, rationalism and humanism, and an accompanying fragmentation of social and organizational life. In its most extreme form, constructionism removes human agents from centre stage by placing them within a multiplicity of autonomous discourses and practices they do not appear to control; they are simply the conduits and bearers of autonomous discourses of power/knowledge that have their own internal efficacy. Yet this decentring of agency within discourse allows an illumination of the nature of power/knowledge as discourse, especially the multiple forms and shifting boundaries of micro-power (Foucault 1994). At first reading this power forms an insidious basis of social control as 'disciplinary power' that 'produces the agent'; effectively robbing human actors of their ability to choose their ends in any rational or intentional sense. But this 'defacing of power' or its decoupling from autonomous rational agents with free will or unconstrained choices can be viewed as a means of creating an opening for marginalized discourses that give voice to the disempowered. This suggests potentially wide-ranging but intrinsically fractured research agendas that lack a critical stance towards practice. If agency and change are discursive constructions it becomes difficult to sustain a concept of expert knowledge or a translation of discourse into action – *discourse is practice*. Paradoxically, the contructionist defacing of power may therefore be unsustainable without an escape from the debilitating nominalism of discourse analysis. In this respect, constructionist research and organizational discourse may have to rebuild an epistemological island of knowledge with a concept of critical realism, or at least a viable methodological distinction between 'knowledge' and 'power'. Only in this way can the decoupling of autonomous agency from power be reconstituted as a connection between decentred agency and change.

Finally, the challenges of creating any coherent research pathways that link or intersect the four discourses should not be underestimated. The idea that change can be managed as a planned or iterative process with stage is key to the action-research concept of the individual change agent as both a rational and 'objective' actor who can create change (Lewin 1947). This is central to the OD tradition and many models of leadership, managerial control and strategic planning which assume a neutral stance towards rational interventions or expertise in the face of competing interests (Ansoff 1991). Contextualists also hold on to an ideal of intentionality, despite their emergent and processual perspectives: they challenge rationalism as a foundation of action, but not the reassertion of agency as choice in the face of uncertainty (Pettigrew 1997). Even some constructionists have embraced a linkage between rationalism and realism as a form of change intervention: 'We can intervene directly in clarifying consequences of discursive

frameworks with speakers (as in training or action research, for
example), as well as commenting on the discursive-political
consequences of discursive clashes and frameworks' (Parker and
Burman 1993: 170). However, in transformed organizational contexts
where changes are emergent, processual, political or the outcome of
competing rhetorical discourses, neutral or expert-centred ideals of
'social rationality' and agency are deeply problematic (Finstad 1998).
Such ideals depend on a corresponding concept of agency as intentional
action by individuals or groups towards a predetermined end or rational
outcome. Without this concept, human actors, both individually and
collectively, may be perceived as the bearers, filters or puppets of
change processes over which they have little or no control. Worse still,
change agency may be conceived as a political mechanism of macro-
power and disciplinary power, rather than a means of realizing the
broader possibilities of shared knowledge or insight.

Things fall apart?

Is there really any prospect of finding a way out of the Babel of
competing discourses? Or should we even look for one? While the four
sets of discourses offer possibilities for clarifying the future theoretical
and empirical research agendas essential for the exploration of agency
and change in organizations, they do not hold out the possibility of a
convergence of research pathways and certainly no synthetic 'theory' or
unified model. There are at least four major reasons for this.

The limits of knowledge. Most of the knowledge articulated within the
competing and diffuse disciplinary paradigms and discourses relevant to
agency and change in organizations lack a *cumulative* logic. After
decades of empirical research and theoretical discussion on leadership,
innovation, organizational change and agency, we appear no nearer to a
widely agreed body of knowledge in these areas. The simple question
'what do we know?' is rarely answered by a convincing list of additive
accomplishments, but rather a narrative retelling of what others say they
knew and believed in specific cultural and historical contexts. This
leaves very little prospect of research progress that is cumulative and
certainly no hope for 'universal' knowledge of agency and change in
organizations. Nor is there currently any prospect of more modest
interdisciplinary paradigms emerging. If anything, the opposite may be
occurring, as social contructionist, postmodernist or cultural and
historically relativist approaches to epistemology and knowledge

creation intensify disciplinary insecurity and the territorial warfare between opposing paradigms (Hacking 1999; Abbott 2001).

The failure of synthesis. There has always been really only one practical guiding principle for the exploration of agency and structure: *agency without structure is blind, structure without agency is empty.* Agency and structure are ontologically inseparable. Yet, there have been no successful attempts to link the micro-level understanding of agency to macro-level structural, institutional, organizational, or 'causal' models of change (Giddens 1984). Instead, there has been a persistent tendency to over-emphasize or privilege one side of the dichotomy. For example, structural, institutional and 'causal process theories' of organizational change often emphasize macro issues, predictive outcomes and even determinism, while various agent-based models emphasize micro-discourses of change (Van de Ven and Poole 1995; Donaldson 1997). One way out of these dualisms would be to argue, as Giddens has done, that the micro versus macro problem is a delusion that can be resolved through a concept of the 'duality of structure': dualism is replaced by duality (Giddens 1984). But Giddens' structuration theory tends to turn structure into process and agency into an affirmation of choice.

More recent attempts to transpose structuration theory into 'organizational discourse' analysis do not overcome Giddens' process-bias and implicit voluntarism. An organizational discourse reading of structuration theory leads to concepts of agency and structure as instantiated manifestations of discursive practices: 'where discourse is seen as a duality of communicative action and structural properties, recursively linked through the modality of actors' interpretative schemes' (Heracleous and Hendry 2000: 1271). While this partly represents an interesting re-working of the duality of structure as the duality of communicative interaction, it does not really resolve the intrinsic tensions between centred–decentred agency and the problematic of structure as both systems and processes. To do so organizational discourse would have to incorporate an iterative notion of agency, a more 'structural' (i.e. system) reading of meaning and action, a theorization of organizational change, and of course a viable notion of theory and practice that is not reducible to discourse. None of these developments are evident at present.

Other alternatives are of course possible. One approach would be to collapse the agency and structure dichotomy into a process ontology of becoming: change is constant and indivisible (Chia 1999). This again appears to make ontological sense, but epistemologically it too comes at the price of analytical clarity as well as the absence of a notion of instrumental practice. Structure and agency lose any analytical or explanatory value. Structure is collapsed into process and agency is potentially dissolved into discourses of temporality and becoming, with the result that all forms of systems ontologies are de-structured and it becomes enormously difficult to connect agency with change, or knowledge with practice.

What all these analytical short-circuits highlight, however, is perhaps a much more intractable problem. Without some kind of systemic, institutional or even larger-scale 'structural' concept of organizational change and development, teleological, causal or otherwise, it is very difficult to have any really coherent models of agency that escape the unresolved problematics of the micro–macro, agency–structure dichotomies. Parsons' (1951: 502–503) classic structural–functional theorizing could not find a way out of these problematics half a century ago and Giddens' (1984) 'structuration' theory has ended in an equally dismal theory of 'agency' that moderates rationalism while lacking analytical specificity or practical efficacy. Some constructionists may think they are heading down a different route by rejecting agency and structure, and by treating change as a purely ontological category, but they are in danger of ending up in the worst of all possible worlds: without agency and without a theory of change. Perhaps we need the delusions of both ontological synthesis *and* epistemological duality, for without the striving for unity or identity we cannot appreciate diversity and difference.

The idea that 'agency' is both centred and decentred and that 'structure' is both systems and processes is one attempt to face up to this dilemma, at least at a meta-theoretical level. Although no synthetic formulation is being proposed here, the old debates on agency and structure are shifted towards the problematic of agency and change. If intentional and rationalist concepts of agency leave us without an understanding of embodied forms of action and practice, the decentring of agency can leave us without a concept of change. Similarly, most attempts to capture the nature of organizational structure have used atemporal or static categories allied to system ontologies and realist epistemologies, while many attempts to explore organizational change tend to use temporal categories allied to process ontologies and 'interpretative' models of action. What we need are analytical schemas, categories and theories that can cope with this complexity by asking more challenging questions. Can we have concepts of structure and organizational change that are both/and, systems and processes, recursive and iterative, ordered and disordered, lineal and non-linear? Can we have concepts of agency and change that are both/and, modes of intentionality and embodied action, forms of rational intervention and enacted practice? By asking such questions we can begin to challenge the either/or dichotomies that have plagued discussions of agency and organizational change.

The eclipse of the subject. Concepts of agency cannot be formally grounded in purely 'rational' or intentional ideals of human action, knowledge, communication or moral discourse. Despite all the heroic efforts of rationalists to achieve such an ideal, rationalism always falls short as a guide to action (Habermas 1971, 1987). One can understand the sources of this limitation. Because the nature of rational action is always externally constrained or internally context dependent, human actors are by definition rational *and* irrational creators of discourses and rhetorics of knowledge and expertise that both legitimize and symbolize a belief in the efficacy of rationality, while their actions simultaneously confirm its impotence in the face of competing knowledge claims and the unintended consequences of rational action. This predicament can engender a debilitating embrace of nominalism and a corresponding rejection of rationalism all together. This is the uncompromising message of radical constructionist discourses in which the subject is potentially subsumed in self-referential discourses of power/knowledge. But if these arguments are taken to their logical conclusion there is really no need for teleological explanations of actions and moral conduct: all action is not chosen, there is no need for a subject at all. Is this destruction of choice the end of agency directed towards rational goals, a fragile ideal of 'discursive ethics' or a concept of 'relational dialogue' (Habermas 1987; Gergen 2001a)? Certainly, agency and organizational change become precarious without a self-fulfilling belief that intention, knowledge and rational action have efficacy in a world enveloped by complexity, uncertainty and risk, even if the goals and outcomes of our actions are often unpredictable (Beck 1992). Paradoxically, theories of change agency may be able to live with the challenges of decentred agency exemplified by constructionism, but it is unlikely that they can live without a belief in individual choice.

The paradoxes of practice. Almost all forms of agency, whether centred or decentred, are modes of enactment in practice that mix intentionality and moral action, habitual behaviour and irrational conduct. This is why all apparently expert or rational interventions in human affairs are subject to ethical scrutiny and self-questioning, both in their formulation, planned outcomes and unintended consequences. This also explains why the ideal of the 'change agent' as an 'unbiased' facilitator of planned change has always been an intellectual and moral illusion, an illusion that has rarely been confronted within the soft scientism of action research or the instrumentalism of managerial agency and consultancy practice (Schön 1983; Schein 1990b). It is not simply claims to expertise that have given the change agent concept a degree of theoretical coherence, but also the evaluative positions it denotes in terms of rationality and the pursuit of moral ends (Argyris 2003). Implicitly all change management interventions are invariably linked to some assumptions or evaluations about the direction of change in organizations and society. These reflexive evaluations may be supported by the search for 'value-relevant' objective knowledge, but they are rarely inseparable from 'value-judgements' in the everyday world of action and involvement (Weber 1949). Without such judgements, the practical intent or moral purpose of knowledge and the role of agency in organizations becomes deeply problematic. Yet without a corresponding sense of the relativity of ethical evaluations and the precarious nature of scientific knowledge of human conduct we lose our sense of the limits of rational interventions. Ultimately, it is only through practice that these ethical paradoxes are both partly resolved and recreated in new forms.

These four issues clearly create profound difficulties in defining the scope and practice of change agency in organizations, as both a form of involvement and an empirical research subject. Taken together, they threaten to achieve the empirical or theoretical equivalent of the constructionist loss of the subject, the prospect that both the disciplinary subject matter and practice of change agency and organizational change theory may fall apart. Confronted with these dilemmas and their implications, the hybrid and eclectic interdisciplinary legacy of organizational change theory and practice must affirm a positive middle way between competing and increasingly fragmented discourses and paradigms for both interpreting and managing change. This middle way will allow us to classify and explore the plurality of newly emerging forms of agency and change within organizations. One could argue that this is in fact the most important future empirical research goal, given the retrospective insight into the fragmented nature of specialist research and the equally diverse nature of forms of agency and modes of practice. Certainly middle range theory has always been a way of avoiding the vortex of 'bottomless empiricism', although it is a poor defence against both paradigm incommensurability and the potentially corrosive logic of nominalism within constructionist discourses. Yet it is perhaps the most reasonable path that we can take. For without our belief in the mediation of knowledge to inform increasingly fragile ideals of 'rational' dialogue, practice and moral action in the face of organizational complexity, risk and uncertainty, all our human interventions may lose their vital centre of gravity: the hope that *we can make a difference.*

Postscript

Endings with a note of hope should always invoke a degree of realistic optimism. There are certainly reasons to be optimistic about the future. The legacy of rationalism and positive change bequeathed by Lewin and the OD tradition may rediscover the core concepts of reflectivity and autonomy and stretch them into new and more inclusive forms of change intervention. The embedding of strategic change and strategic choice in contextualist discourses may eventually lead to a powerful 'practice turn' towards the challenges of making change happen. The increasing dispersal of knowledge creation, power and control through new models of distributed leadership and team-based change agency may lead to new forms of managing innovation and change in the face of increasing chaos, complexity and uncertainty. The decentring of agency within constructionism and organizational discourse analysis may open up new possibilities for exploring agency as discourse and change that creates greater and more genuine forms of workplace empowerment. Within the Babel of discourses there are not only dangers of fragmentation, but also enormous possibilities for creative pluralism and the reinvention of practice.

References

Abbott, A. (2001) *Chaos of Disciplines*, Chicago: University of Chicago Press.

Abrahamson, E. and Fairchild, G. (1999) 'Management fashion: lifecycles, triggers and collective learning processes', *Administrative Science Quarterly*, 44, 4: 708–740.

Alvesson, M. and Karreman, D. (2000) 'Varieties of discourse: on the study of organizations through discourse analysis', *Human Relations*, 53, 9: 1125–1149.

Anderson, P. (1999) 'Complexity theory and organizational science', *Organizational Science*, 10: 233–236.

Ansoff, H. I. (1991) 'A critique of Henry Mintzberg's "The design school: reconsidering the basis premises of strategic management"', *Strategic Management Journal*, 12: 449–461.

Archer, M. (1983) 'Process without system', *European Journal of Sociology*, 24, 1: 196–221.

Archer, M. S. (2003) *Structure, Agency and the Internal Conversation*, Cambridge: University of Cambridge Press.

Argyris, C. (1976) 'Single-loop and double-loop models in research on decision making', *Administrative Science Quarterly*, 21: 363–375.

Argyris, C. (1982) *Reasoning, Learning and Action*, San Francisco, CA: Jossey Bass.

Argyris, C. (1985) *Strategy, Change and Defensive Routines*, Cambridge: MA: Ballinger.

Argyris, C. (2003) 'A life full of learning', *Organization Studies*, 24, 7: 1178–1192.

Argyris, C., Putman, R. and Smith, D. M. (1985) *Action Science, Concepts, Methods and Skills for Research and Intervention*, San Francisco, CA: Jossey Bass.

Armenakis, A. and Bedeian, A. (1999) 'Organizational change: A review of theory and research in the 1990s', *Journal of Management*, 25, 3: 293–315.

Arrow H., McGrath J. E. and Berdahl, J. L. (2000) *Small Groups as Complex Systems: Formation, Coordination, Development and Adaptation*, Newbury Park, CA: Sage.

Baker, J. R. (1999) *The Discipline of Teamwork: Participation and Concertive Control*, London: Sage.

Baker, P. (1993) 'Chaos, order, and sociological theory', *Sociological Inquiry*, 63: 123–149.

Barnes, B. (2000) *Understanding Agency: Social Theory and Responsible Action*, London: Sage Publications.

Beck, U. (1992) *Risk Society: Towards a New Modernity*, London: Sage.

Beck, U. (2000) *The Brave New World of Work*, Cambridge: Polity Press.

Beckhard, R. (1969) *Organizational Development: Strategies and Methods*, Reading, Mass: Addison-Wesley.

Beer, M., Eisenstat, R. A. and Spector, B. (1990) 'Why change programmes don't produce change', *Harvard Business Review*, 68: 158–166.

Bennis, W. (1969) *Organizational Development: its Nature, Origins, and Prospects*, Reading, MA: Addison-Wesley.

Berglund, J. and Werr, A. (2000) 'The invincible character of management consulting rhetoric: how one blends incommensurables while keeping them apart', *Organization*, 7, 4: 633–655.

Blackler, F., Crump, N. and McDonald, S. (2000) 'Organizing processes in complex activity networks', *Organization*, 7, 2: 277–300.

Boal, K. B., Hunt, J. G. J. and Jaros, S. J. (2003) 'Order is free: on the ontological status of organizations', in R. G. Westwood and S. Clegg (eds) *Debating Organizations: Point/CounterPoint in Organizational Studies*, Oxford: Blackwell.

Bokeno, M. R. (2003) 'The works of Chris Argyris as critical organizational practice', *Journal of Organizational Change Management*, 16, 6: 633–640.

Bouchikihi, H. (1998) 'Living with and building on complexity: a constructivist perspective on organizations', *Organization*, 5, 2: 217–322.

Bourdieu, P. (1985) 'The genesis of the concepts of habitus and field', *Sociocriticism*, 2: 11–24.

Bourdieu, P. (1988) *Homo Academicus*, Cambridge: Polity Press.

Bourdieu, P. (1990) *The Logic of Practice*, Cambridge: Polity Press.

Bradford, D. L. and Burke, W. W. (2004) 'Introduction: is OD in crisis?' *Journal of Applied Behavioral Science*, 40, 4: 369–373.

Bradford, D. L. and Burke, W. W. (2005) *The Crisis in OD*, San Francisco: Jossey Bass.

Brown, S. L. and Eisenhardt, K. M. (1997) 'The art of continuous change: linking complexity theory to time-space evolution in relentlessly shifting organizations', *Administrative Science Quarterly*, 42: 1–34.

Buchanan, D. (2003) 'Demands, instabilities, manipulations, careers: the lived experience of driving change', *Human Relations*, 56, 6: 663–684.

Buchanan, D. and Boddy, D. (1992) *The Expertise of the Change Agent*, London: Prentice Hall.

Bunker, B. B. Alban, B. T. and Lewicki, R. J. (2004) 'Ideas in Currency and OD Practice', *Journal of Applied Behavioural Science*, 40, 4: 403–422.

Burke, W. W. (2002) *Organization Change: Theory and Practice*, London: Sage.

Burnes, B. (2004) 'Kurt Lewin and the planned approach to change: a re-appraisal', *Journal of Management Studies*, 41, 6: 977–998.

Burrell, G. (1988) 'Modernism, postmodernism and organizational analysis: the contribution of Michael Foucault', *Organization Studies*, 9, 2: 221–235.

Caldwell, R. (2003) 'Models of change agency: a fourfold classification', *British Journal of Management*, 14, 2: 128–141.

Caldwell, R. (2005a) 'Things fall apart? Discourses on agency and change in organizations', *Human Relations*, 58, 1: 83–114.

Caldwell, R. (2005b) 'Revisiting Giddens: Reformulating agency and change', Discussion Paper, Birbeck College, University of London.

Carley, K. M. and Hill, V. (2001) 'Structural change and learning within organizations', in A. Lomi and E. R. Larsen (eds) *Dynamics of Organizations and Societies: Computational Modeling and Organization Theory*, MA: MIT Press.

Carr, A. (1997) 'Organization theory and postmodern thinking: the uncertain place of human agency', *Policy, Organization and Society*, 13: 82–104.

Castells, M. (2000) *The Rise of the Network Society*, Volume 1, Oxford: Blackwell.

Chan, A. and Garrick, J. (2002) 'Organization theory in turbulent times: the traces of Foucault's ethics', *Organization*, 9, 4: 683–701.

Checkland, P. B. (1981) *Systems Thinking, Systems Practice*, Chichester: Wiley.

Chia, R. (1998) 'From complexity science to complex thinking: organization as simple location', *Organization*, 5, 3: 341–369.

Chia, R. (1999) 'A "rhizomic" model of organizational change and transformation: perspectives from a metaphysics of change', *British Journal of Management*, 10: 209–227.

Chia, R. (2002) '*Essai:* Time, duration and simultaneity: rethinking process and change in organizational analysis', *Organization Studies*, 23, 6: 863–868.

Child, J. (1972) 'Organizational structure, environment and performance: the role of strategic choice', *Sociology*, 6: 1–22.

Child, J. (1997) 'Strategic choice in the analysis of action, structure, organizations and environment', *Organization Studies*, 18, 1: 43–76.

Cilliers, P. (1998) *Complexity and Postmodernism: Understanding Complex Systems*, New York: Routledge.

Clark, T. and Salaman, G. (1996) 'The management consultant as organizational witchdoctor', *Organization*, 1: 85–107.

Clegg, S., Kornberger, M. and Rhodes, C. (2005) 'Learning/Becoming/Organizing', *Organization*, 12, 2: 147–167.

Colander, D., Holt, R. P. F. and Barkley-Rosser, J. (2004) 'The changing face of mainstream economics', *Review of Political Economy*, 16, 4: 485–499.

Cooke, B. (1999) 'Writing the left out of management theory: the historiography of change management', *Organization*, 6, 1: 81–105.

Cummings, T. G. and Worley, C. G. (2005) *Organisational Development and Change* (6th edn), Cincinnati, OH: South Western.

Cyert, R. M. and March, J. G. (1963) *A Behavioural Theory of the Firm*, Englewood Cliffs, NJ: Prentice Hall.

Danziger, K. (1990) *Constructing the Subject: Historical Origins of Psychological Research*, Cambridge: University of Cambridge.

Davidson, D. (2001) 'Agency', in D. Davidson, *Essays on Actions and Events*, Oxford: Oxford University Press, pp. 43–62.

Dawe, A. (1978) 'Theories of social action', in T. B. Bottomore and R. Nisbet (eds) *A History of Sociological Analysis*, New York: Basic Books.

Dawson, P. (1994) *Organizational Change: A Processual Approach,* London: Paul Chapman.

Dawson, P. (2003) *Reshaping Change: A Processual Perspective*, London: Routledge.

Deetz, S. (2003) 'Reclaiming the legacy of the linguistic turn', *Organization*, 10: 421–429.

Dennett, D. C. (1995) *Darwin's Dangerous Idea*, London: Allen Lane, Penguin Press.

Dent, E. R. and Galloway Goldberg, S. (1999) 'Challenging "resistance to change"', *The Journal of Applied Behavioral Science*, 35, 1: 25–41.

Derrida, J. (1977) *Writing and Difference*, Chicago: Chicago University Press.

Descartes, R. (1984) *The Philosophical Writings of Descartes*, Vol. 2, Cambridge: Cambridge University Press.

Dickens, L. (1998) 'Action research: rethinking Lewin', *Management Learning*, 39, 2: 127–140.

Dierkes, M., Berthoin-Antal, A., Child, C. and Nonaka, I. (eds) (2001) *Handbook of Organizational Learning and Knowledge*, Oxford: Oxford University Press.

DiMaggio, P. J. and Powell, W. W. (1983) 'The iron cage revisited: institutional isomorphism and collective rationality in organizational fields', *American Sociological Review*, 48: 147–180.

Donaldson, L. (1997) 'A positivist alternative to the structure-action approach', *Organization Studies*, 18, 1: 77–92.

Donaldson, L. (1999) 'The normal science of structural contingency theory', in S. Clegg and C. Hardy *Studying Organizations: Theory and Methods*, London: Sage.

Donaldson, L. (2001) *The Contingency Theory of Organizations*, Thousand Oaks, CA: Sage.

Dooley, A. and Van de Ven, A. (1999) 'Explaining complex organizational dynamics', *Organizational Science*, 10, 3: 358–372.

Doyle, M. (2001) 'Dispersing change agency in high velocity change organizations: issues and implications', *Leadership and Organizational Development*, 22: 321–329.

Dumphy, D. and Stace, D. (1993) 'The strategic management of corporate change', *Human Relations*, 46: 905–918.

Easterby-Smith, M., Crossan, M. and Nicolini, D. (2000) 'Organizational learning: debates past, present and future', *Journal of Management Studies*, 37, 6: 783–796.

Emirbayer, M. and Mische, A. (1998) 'What is agency'? *American Journal of Sociology*, 103, 4: 962–1023.

Erobon, D. (1991) *Michel Foucault*, Cambridge, Mass: Harvard University Press.

Fincham, R. (2001) 'The consultant-client relationship: critical perspectives on the management of organizational change', *Journal of Management Studies*, 36: 335–351.

Finstad, N. (1998) 'The rhetoric of organizational change', *Human Relations*, 51: 717–740.

Fitzgerald, L. A. and Van Eijnatten, F. M. (2002) 'Reflections: Chaos in organizational change', *Journal of Organizational Change Management*, 15, 4: 402–411.

Flake, G.W. (1998) *The Computational Beauty of Nature: Computer Explorations of Fractals, Chaos, Complex Systems, and Adaptation*, Cambridge, Mass: MIT Press.

Foucault, M. (1972) *The Archaeology of Knowledge*, New York: Pantheon.

Foucault, M. (1977) *Language, Counter-Memory, Practice*, in D. Bouchard (ed.) New York: Cornell University Press.

Foucault, M. (1979) *The History of Sexuality, Volume 1: An Introduction*, London: Allen Lane.

Foucault, M. (1981) 'The order of discourse', in R.Young (ed.) *Untying the Text: a Post-structuralism Reader*, 48–79, London: Routledge.

Foucault, M. (1986) *The History of Sexuality, Volume 2: The Care of the Self*, London: Allen Lane.

Foucault, M. (1988) *Michel Foucault: Politics, Philosophy, Culture: Interviews and Other Writings*, L. Kritzman (ed.), London: Routledge.

Foucault, M. (1991) 'On the genealogy of ethics', in P. Rainbow (ed.) *The Foucault Reader*, London; Penguin.

Foucault, M. (1992) 'Afterword: the subject and power', in H. Dreyfus and P. Rabinow (eds) *Michel Foucault: Beyond Structuralism and Hermeneutics*, Brighton: Harvester, pp. 208–226.

Foucault, M. (1994) *Discipline and Punish: The Birth of the Prison*, London: Penguin.

Foucault, M. (1996) 'What is critique?', in J. Schmidt (ed) *What is Enlightenment?*, Berkeley: University of California Press.

Foucault, M. (1999) *Madness and Civilization*, London: Routledge.

Foucault, M. (2000) *Michel Foucault: The Essential Works: Power*, Vol. 3, Colin Gordon (ed.), London: Allen Lane, Penguin Press.

Freud, S. (1972 [1921]) *Group Psychology and the Analysis of the Ego*, Pelican Freud Library (Vol. 12) Harmondsworth: Pelican.

Freud, S. (1968 [1938]) *An Outline of Psycho-Analysis*, Standard Edition (Vol. 23), New York: Norton.

Freundlieb, D. (1994) 'Foucault's theory of discourse and human agency', in C. Jones and R. Porter (eds) *Reassessing Foucault: Power, Medicine and the Body*, London: Routledge.

Friedman, V. J., Lipshitz, R. and Popper, M. (2005) 'The mystification of organizational learning', *Journal of Management Inquiry*, 14, 1–19.

Garud, R. and Van de Ven, A. (2002) 'Strategic change processes', in A. Pettigrew, H. Thomas and M. Whittington (eds) *The Handbook of Strategic Management*, London: Sage.

Gavetti, G. and Levinthal, D. A. (2004) 'The strategy field from the perspective of Management Science: divergent strands and possible integration', *Management Science*, 50, 10: 1039–1318.

Gergen, K. J. (1992) 'Organization theory in the postmodern era', in M. Reed and M. Hughes, *Rethinking Organizations*, London: Sage.

Gergen, K. J. (1999) *An Invitation to Social Construction*, London: Sage.

Gergen, K. J. (2001a) *Constructionism in Context*, London: Sage.

Gergen, K. J. (2001b) 'Construction in contention: toward consequential resolutions', *Theory & Psychology*, 11: 803–813.

Gergen, K. J. (2003) 'Action research and orders of democracy', *Action Research*, 1, 1, 39–56.

Giddens, A. (1976) *New Rules of Sociological Method*, London: Hutchinson.

Giddens, A. (1979) *Central Problems in Social Theory*, London: Macmillan.

Giddens, A. (1982) *Profiles and Critiques in Social Theory*, London: Macmillan.

Giddens, A. (1984) *The Constitution of Society*, Cambridge: Polity Press.

Giddens, A. (1990a) 'Structuration theory and sociological analysis', in J. Clark *et al.* (eds) *Anthony Giddens: Consensus and Controversy*, Basingstoke: Falmer.

Giddens, A. (1990b) *The Consequences of Modernity*, Cambridge: Polity Press.

Giddens, A. (1992) *The Transformation of Intimacy: Sexuality, Love and Eroticism in Modern Societies*, Cambridge: Polity Press.

Giddens, A. (1993) 'Critique of Foucault', in P. Cassell (ed.) *The Giddens Reader*, London: Macmillan, pp. 228–235.

Giddens, A. (2000) *The Third Way and Its Critics*, Cambridge: Polity Press.

Gould, S. J. (2002) *The Structure of Evolutionary Theory*, Cambridge, Mass: Harvard University Press.

Granovetter, M. (1985) 'Economic action and social structure: the problem of embeddedness', *American Journal of Sociology*, 91, 3: 481–510.

Grant, D., Hardy, C., Oswick, C., Phillips, N. and Putman, L. (2004) *Handbook of Organizational Discourse*, London: Sage.

Gregory, W. J. (1996) 'Discordant pluralism: a new strategy for critical systems thinking?' *Systems Practice*, 9: 605–625.

Greiner, L. E. and Cummings, T. G. (2004) 'Wanted: OD More alive than dead!' *Journal of Applied Behavioural Science*, 40, 4: 374–391.

Grey, C. (1999) '"We are all managers now"'; "We always were": on the development and demise of management', *Journal of Management Studies*, 36, 5: 561–585.

Griffin, D. (2002) *The Emergence of Leadership*, London: Routledge.

Gronn, P. (2002) 'Distributed leadership as a unit of analysis', *Leadership Quarterly*, 13: 423–451.

Habermas, J. (1971) *Toward a Rational Society*, London: Heinemann.

Habermas, J. (1974) *Theory and Practice*, Boston: Beacon Press.

Habermas, J. (1981) 'Modernity versus postmodernity', *New German Critique*, 22 (Winter): 3–18.

Habermas, J. (1984) *The Theory of Communicative Action*: Volume 1, London: Heinemann.

Habermas, J. (1986) 'Taking aim at the heart of the present', in D. C. Hoy (ed.) *Foucault: A Critical Reader*, Oxford: Basil Blackwell, pp. 103–108.

Habermas, J. (1987) 'The critique or reason as an unmasking of the human sciences: Michel Foucault', in J. Habermas, *The Philosophical Discourse of Modernity*, pp. 238–265. Cambridge: Polity Press.

Hacking, I. (1999) *The Social Construction of What?,* Cambridge, MA: Harvard University Press.

Hales, C. (1999) 'Why do managers do what they do? Reconciling evidence and theory in accounts of managerial work', *British Journal of Management*, 10: 335–350.

Hancock, P. and Tyler, M. (2001) *Work, Postmodernism and Organization*, London: Sage.

Hardy, C. (2004) 'Scaling up and bearing down in discourse analysis: questions regarding textual agencies and their context', *Organization*, 11, 3: 415–425.

Hayles, N. K. (1991) *Chaos and Order*, Chicago: Chicago University Press.

Hayward, C. (2000) *De-Facing Power*, Cambridge: Cambridge University Press.

Hendry, J. (1996) 'Understanding and creating whole organizational change through learning theory', *Human Relations*, 48, 5: 621–641.

Hendry, J. and Seidl, D. (2003) 'The structure and significance of strategic episodes: social systems theory and the routine practices of strategic change', *Journal of Management Studies*, 40, 1: 175–196.

Hensmans, M. (2003) 'Social movement organizations: a metaphor for strategic actors in institutional fields', *Organization Studies*, 24, 3: 355–381.

Heracleous, L. and Barrett, M. (2001) 'Organizational change as discourse: communicative actions and deep structures in the context of information technology implementation', *Academy of Management Journal*, 44, 4: 755–778.

Heracleous, L. and Hendry J. (2000) 'Discourse and the study of organizations: towards a structurational perspective', *Human Relations*, 53, 10: 1251–1286.

Hillis, D. (1998) *The Pattern of the Stone*, New York: Basic Books.

Holland, J. (1998) *Emergence from Chaos to Order*, New York: Oxford University Press.

Houchin, K. and MacLean, D. (2005) 'Complexity theory and strategic change: an empirically informed critique', *British Journal of Management*, 16: 149–166.

Jackson, B. (2000) 'A fantasy theme analysis of Peter Senge's learning organization', *Journal of Applied Behavioural Science*, 36, 2: 193–209.

Jackson, M. C. (2003) *Systems Thinking*, London: Wiley.

Johns, G. (2001) 'In praise of context', *Journal of Organizational Behaviour*, 22, 1: 31–42.

Johnson, P. and Duberley, J. (2003) 'Reflexivity in management research', *Journal of Management Studies*, 40 (3), pp. 1279–1303.

Kauffman, S.A. (1993) *The Origins of Order: Self-Organization and Selection in Evolution*, New York: Oxford University Press.

Kemmis, S. (1991) 'Critical action research', in O. Zuber-Skerritt (ed.) *Action Research for Change and Development*, London: Gower.

Kemmis, S. (2001) 'Exploring the relevance of critical theory for action research: emancipatory action research in the footsteps of Habermas', in P. Reason and H. Bradbury (eds) *Handbook of Action Research*, London Sage.

Kiel, D. and Elliott, E. (1997) *Chaos Theory in the Social Sciences: Foundations and Applications*, Ann Arbor: University of Michigan Press.

Kipping, M. and Engwell, L. (2002) *Management Consulting*, Oxford: Oxford University Press.

Knight, D. (1997) 'Organizational theory in the age of deconstruction: dualism, gender and postmodernism revisited', *Organization Studies*, 18, 1: 1–19.

Knight, D. (2004) 'Michel Foucault', in S. Linstead *Organization Theory and Postmodern Thought*, London: Sage.

Kotter, J. P. (1996) 'Leading change: why transformation efforts fail', *Harvard Business Review*, March-April.

Lane, D. (2004) 'Irrational agents or accomplished actors?', *Systems Research and Behavioral Science*, 21, 4: 233–438.

Lash, S. (2003) 'Reflexivity as non-linearity', *Theory, Culture and Society*, 20, 2: 49–57.

Latour, B. (1987) *Science in Action*, Milton Keynes: Open University Press.

Latour, B. (1999) 'On recalling ANT', in J. Law and J. Hassard (eds) *Actor Network Theory and After*, Oxford: Basil Blackwell.

Latour, B. (2005) *Reassembling the Social: An Introduction to Actor Network Theory*, Oxford: Oxford University Press.

Layder, D. (1987) 'Key issues in structuration theory', *Current Perspectives in Social Theory*, 8: 25–46.

Levinthal, D. A. (1997) 'Adaptation on rigged landscapes', *Management Science*, 43: 934–950.

Levinthal, D. A. (2002) 'Organizational capabilities in complex worlds', in G. Dosi., R.R. Nelson and S.G. Winter (eds) *The Nature and Dynamics of Organizational Capabilities*, New York: Oxford University Press, pp. 363–381.

Levi-Strauss, C. (1966) *The Savage Mind*, Chicago: University of Chicago Press.

Lewin, K. (1946) 'Action research and minority problems', *Journal of Social Issues*, 2, 4: 34–46.

Lewin, K. (1947) 'Frontiers in group dynamics: concept, method and reality in social science', *Human Relations*, 1947, 1, 1, 5–40.

Lewin, K. (1951) *Force Field Analysis*, New York: Harper & Row.

Lewin, K. (1997) *Resolving Social Conflicts and Field Theory in Social Science*, (reissue of two previous anthologies) New York: American Psychological Society Press.

Lewin, K. (1999) *The Complete Social Scientist: A Kurt Lewin Reader*, M. Gold (ed.), New York: American Psychological Society Press.

Lindblom, C. E. (1959) 'The science of muddling through', *Public Administration Review*, 19: 79–88.

Linstead, S. (2004) *Organization Theory and Postmodern Thought*, London: Sage.

Loasby, B. J. (1976) *Choice, Complexity and Ignorance: An Inquiry into Economic Theory and Practice in Decision Making*, Cambridge: Cambridge University Press.

Lounsbury, M. and Ventresca, M. (2003) 'The new structuralism in organizational theory'. *Organization*, 10, 3: 457–480.

Luhmann, N. (1976) 'A general theory of organized social systems', in G. Hofstede and M. S. Kassem (eds) *European Contributions to Organization Theory*, Amsterdam: Van Gorcum, pp. 96–113.

Luhmann, N. (1990) *Essays on Self-Reference*, New York: Columbia University Press.

Luhmann, N. (1995) *Social Systems*, Stanford: Stanford University Press.

Luhmann, N. (1997) 'The limits of steering', *Theory, Culture and Society*, 14, 1: 41–57.

Lukes, S. (2002) 'Agency and Power', *British Journal of Sociology*, 53, 3: 491–496.

McKelvey, B. (1999) 'Complexity theory in organizational science: seizing the promise or becoming a fad', *Emergence: Complexity and Organization*, 1, 1: 3–32.

McKinlay, A. and Starkey, K. (1998) *Foucault, Management and Organization Theory: From Panopticon to Technologies of Self*, London: Sage.

McMillan, E. (2004) *Complexity, Organizations and Change*, London: Routledge.

McNay, L. (2000) *Gender and Agency: Reconfiguring the Subject in Feminist Thought and Social Theory*, Cambridge: Polity Press.

McPhee, R. D. (2004) 'Text, agency, and organization in the light of structuration theory', *Organization*, 11, 3: 355–371.

Macy, M. and Willer, R. (2002) 'From factors to actors: computational sociology and agent-based modeling', *Annual Review of Sociology*, 28: 143–166.

Maguire, S. and McKelvey, B. (1999) 'Complexity and management: moving from fad to firm foundations', *Emergence: Complexity and Organization*, 1, 2: 5–49.

March, J. G. (1981) 'Footnotes to organizational change', *Administrative Science Quarterly*, 26: 563–577.

Marrow, A. J. (1969) *The Practical Theorist*, New York: Basic Books.

Metraux, A. (1992) 'Kurt Lewin: Philosopher-psychologist', *Science in Context*, 5, 373–384.

Midgley, G. (2003) 'Five sketches of postmodernism: implications for systems thinking and operational research', *Organizational Transformation and Social Change*, 1, 1: 47–62.

Miller, J. (1993) *The Passion of Michael Foucault*, London: Harper Collins.

Miller, S., Hickson, D. and Wilson, D. (1999) 'Decision-making in organizations', in S. Clegg, C. Hardy and W. Nord. (eds) *Managing Organizations: Current Issues*, London: Sage, pp. 43–62.

Mintzberg, H. (1994) *The Rise and Fall of Strategic Planning*, London: Prentice Hall.

Morcol, G. (2002) 'What is complexity science? Postmodernist or postpositivist?', *Emergence: Complexity and Organization,* 3, 1: 104–119.

Newton, T. J. (1998) 'Theorizing subjectivity in organizations: the failure of Foucauldian studies', *Organization Studies*, 19: 415–447.

Nietzsche, F. (1974) *The Gay Science*, trans. W. Kaufman, New York: Vintage Books.

Nonaka, I. (1994) 'Creating organizational order out of chaos: self-renewal in Japanese firms', *Harvard Business Review*, November–December, 96–104.

Nonaka, I. and Takeuchi, H. (1995) *The Knowledge Creating Company*, New York: Oxford University Press.

Nowotny, H., Scott, P. and Gibbons, M. (2001) *Re-Thinking Science: Knowledge and Science in an Age of Uncertainty*, Cambridge: Polity Press.

Orlikowski, W. (1997) 'Improvising organizational transformation over time: a situated change perspective', *Information Systems Research*, 7, 1: 63–92.

Osborn, R. N., Hunt, J. G. and Jauch, L. R. (2002) 'Toward a contextual theory of leadership', *Leadership Quarterly*, 13: 797–837.

Parker, I. (1992) *Discourse Dynamics,* London: Routledge.

Parker, I. (1998) (ed.) *Social Constructionism: Discourse and Realism*, London: Sage

Parker, I. and Burman, E. (ed.) (1993) *Discourse Analytics Research*, London: Routledge.

Parsons, T. (1951) *The Social System*, Glencoe, IL: Free Press.

Perrow, C. (1961) 'The analysis of goals in complex organizations', *American Sociological Review*, 26: 859–866.

Perrow, C. (1999 [1984]) *Normal Accidents: Living with High-Risk Technologies,* Reissue, Princeton, NJ: Princeton University Press.

Pettigrew, A. M. (1972) 'Information control as a power resource', *Sociology*, 188–204.

Pettigrew, A. M. (1979) 'On studying organizational cultures', *Administrative Science Quarterly*, 24, 4: 570–581.

Pettigrew, A. M. (1985) *The Awaking Giant: Continuity and Change in ICI*, Oxford: Basil Blackwell.

Pettigrew, A. M. (1987) 'Context and action in the transformation of the firm', *Journal of Management Studies*, 24, 6: 649–670.

Pettigrew, A. M. (1990) 'Studying strategic choice and strategic change', *Organization Studies*, 11, 1: 6–11.

Pettigrew, A. M. (1992) 'On studying managerial elites', *Strategic Management Journal*, 6, 16: 163–182.

Pettigrew, A. M. (1997) 'What is processual analysis?', *Scandinavian Journal of Management*, 1997, 13, 4: 337–348.

Pettigrew, A. M. (1998) 'Catching reality in flight', in A. Bedeian (ed.) *Management Laureates*, Vol. 5, pp. 171– 206, Greenwood, CT: JAI Press.

Pettigrew, A. M. (2000) 'Linking change processes to outcomes', in M. Beer and N. Nohria (eds) *Breaking the Code of Change*, Boston, MA: Harvard Business School Press.

Pettigrew, A. M. (2001) 'Management research after modernism', *British Journal of Management*, 12: 61–70.

Pettigrew, A. M. (2002) 'Andrew Pettigrew on executives and strategy: an interview by Kenneth Starkey', *European Journal of Management*, 20, 1: 20–34.

Pettigrew, A. M. (2003a) 'Strategy as process, power and change', in S. Cummings and D. Wilson (eds) *Images of Strategy*, Oxford: Blackwell.

Pettigrew, A. M. (2003b) 'Innovative forms of organizing: progress, performance and process', in A. Pettigrew *et al.* (eds) *Innovative Forms of Organizing*, London: Sage, pp. 331–351.

Pettigrew, A. M. and Whipp, R. (1991) *Managing Change for Competitive Success*, Oxford: Blackwell.

Pettigrew, A. M. and Woodman, R. W. (2001) 'Studying organizational change and development: challenges for future research', *Academy of Management Journal*, 44, 4: 697–713.

Pettigrew, A. E., Ferlie, E. and McKee, L. (1992) *Shaping Strategic Change*, London: Sage.

Pettigrew, A., Whittington, R., Melin, L., Snachez-Runde, C., Van de Bosch, F. and Numagami, T. (2003) *Innovative forms of Organizing*, London: Sage.

Pickart, J. (1997) 'Profile: Chris Argyris', *People Management*, 6 March, pp. 34–35.

Price, R. (1997) 'The myth of a postmodern science', in R. A. Eve, S. Horsfall and M. E. Lee (eds) *Chaos, Complexity, and Sociology: Myths, Models and Theories*, Thousand Oaks, CA: Sage, pp. 3–14.

Prigogine, I. and Nicolis, G. (1989) *Exploring Complexity*, New York: W. H. Freeman.

Quinn, J.B. (1980) *Strategies for Change: Logical Incrementalism*, Homewood, IL: Irwin.

Reason, P. (2003) 'Pragmatist philosophy and action research', *Action Research*, 1, 1: 103–123.

Reason, P. and Bradbury, H. (eds) (2001) *Handbook of Action Research: Participative Inquiry and Practice*, London: Sage.

Reed, M. I. (1997) 'In praise of duality and dualism: rethinking agency and structure in organizational analysis', *Organization Studies*, 18, 1: 21–42.

Reed, M. I. (1998) 'Organizational analysis as discourse analysis', in David Grant, Tom Keenoy and Cliff Oswick (eds) *Discourse and Organization*, London: Sage pp. 193–213.

Reed, M. I. (2000) 'The limits of discourse analysis in organizational analysis', *Organization*, 7: 524–530.

Robertson, P. J., Roberts D. R. and Porras, J. I. (1992) 'A meta-analytic review of the impact of planned organizational change interventions', in J. L. Wall and L. J. Janch (eds) *Academy of Management Best Paper Proceedings,* Briarcliff Manor, NY: Academy of Management.

Rorty, R. (1989) *Contingency, Irony and Solidarity*, Cambridge: Cambridge University Press.

Rorty, R. (1995) *Objectivity, Relativism and Truth*, Cambridge: Cambridge University Press.

Rowlinson, M. and Carter, C. (2002) 'Foucault and history in organization studies', *Organization*, 9, 4: 607–620.

Ruse, M. (2004) *Darwin and Design: Does Evolution Have a Purpose?* Boston: Harvard University Press.

Schein, E. H. (1961) *Coercive Persuasion*, New York: Norton.

Schein, E. H. (1962) 'Man against man: brainwashing', *Corrective Psychiatry and Journal of Social Therapy*, 8, 2: 90–97.

Schein, E. H. (1987) *Process Consultation (Volume 2), Lessons for Managers and Consultants*, Reading, MA: Addison-Wesley.

Schein, E. H. (1988) (2nd edition) *Process Consultation (Volume 1), Its Role in Organizational Development*, Reading, MA: Addison-Wesley.

Schein, E. H. (1990a) *Organizational Culture and Leadership*, San Francisco, CA: Jossey Bass.

Schein, E. H. (1990b) 'Back to the future: recapturing the OD vision', in F. Massarik (ed.) *Advances in Organizational Development* (Vol. 1), Norwood, NJ: Ablex.

Schein, E. H. (1996) 'Kurt Lewin's change theory in the field and in the classroom: notes toward a model of management learning', *Systems Practice*, 9, 1: 27–47.

Schein, E. H. (1999) 'Empowerment, coercive persuasion and organisational learning: Do they connect?', *The Learning Organisation*, 6, 4:163–172.

Schein, E. H. (2002) 'Consulting: what should it mean?', in T. Clark and R. Fincham (eds) *Critical Consulting*, Oxford: Blackwell.

Schön, D. (1983) *The Reflective Practitioner*, London: Temple Smith.

Sen, A. (2004) *Rationality and Freedom*, New York: Belknap Press.

Senge, P.M. (1990) *The Fifth Discipline: The Art and Practice of the Learning Organization*, London: Century Business.

Senge, P. M. (1996) 'Rethinking leadership in the learning organization', *Systems Thinker*, 7, 1: 1–8.

Senge, P. M. (1999) 'Learning for a change', *Fast Company*, 24 (May), 178–185.

Senge, P. M. (2003) 'Taking personal change seriously: the impact of organizational learning on management practice', *Academy of Management Executive*, 17, 2: 47–51.

Simon, H. (1947) *Administrative Behaviour*, New York: Macmillan.

Simon, H. (1991) 'Bounded rationality and organizational learning', *Organization Science*, 2, 1 (February).

Smelser, N. (1992) 'The rational choice perspective: a theoretical assessment', *Rationality and Society*, 4, 4: 381–410.

Smith, P. A. C. (2003) 'Implications of complexity and chaos theories for organizations that learn', *The Learning Organization*, 10, 6: 321–324.

Stacey, R. D. (1993) 'Strategy as order emerging from chaos', *Long Range Planning*, 26, 1: 10–17.

Stacey, R. D. (1995) 'The science of complexity: an alternative perspective for strategic change processes', *Strategic Management Journal*, 16, 6: 477–495.

Stacey, R. D. (2001) *Complex Responsive Processes in Organizations: Learning and Knowledge Creation*, London: Routledge.

Stacey, R.D. (2003) *Strategic Management and Organizational Dynamics: The Challenge of Complexity*, London: Prentice Hall.

Stacey R.D., Griffin, D. and Shaw, P. (2000) *Complexity and Management*, London: Routledge.

Stewart, P. (2001) 'Complexity theories, social theory, and the question of social complexity', *Philosophy of the Social Sciences*, 31: 323–360.

Sturdy, A. and Grey, C. (2003) 'Beneath and beyond organizational change management: exploring alternatives', *Organization*, 10, 4: 651–662.

Styhre, A. (2002) 'Non-linear change in organizations: organizational change management informed by complexity theory', *Leadership and Organisational Development Journal*, 23, 6: 342–351.

Sztompka, P. (1993) *The Sociology of Social Change*, Oxford: Blackwell.

Taylor, C. (1986) 'Foucault on freedom and truth', in D. C. Hoy (ed.) *Foucault: A Critical Reader*, Oxford: Blackwell, pp. 69–103.

Taylor, C. (1989) *Sources of the Self*, Cambridge, MA: Harvard University Press.

Thietart, R. A. and Forgues, B. (1995) 'Chaos theory and organizations', *Organizational Science*, 6, 1: 19–31.

Thrift, N. (1999) 'The place of complexity', *Theory, Culture and Society*, 16: 31–70.

Tichy, N. (1974) 'Agents of planned change: congruence of values, cognitions, and actions', *Administrative Science Quarterly*, 19, 163–182.

Tsoukas, H. (1998) 'Introduction: chaos, complexity theory and organization theory', *Organization*, 5: 291–314.

Tsoukas, H. and Chia, R. (2002) 'On organizational becoming: Rethinking organizational change', *Organization Science*, 13: 567–582.

Ulrich, W. (2003) 'Beyond methodology choice: critical systems thinking as critically systemic discourse', *Journal of the Operational Research Society*, 54: 325–345.

Urry, J. (2003) *Global Complexity*, Cambridge: Polity Press.

Van de Ven, A. H. and Poole, S. P. (1995) 'Explaining development and change in organizations', *Academy of Management Review*, 20: 510–540.

Van de Ven, A. (1987) 'Review essay: four requirements for processual analysis', in A. M. Pettigrew (ed.) *The Management of Strategic Change*, Oxford: Blackwell.

Van de Ven, A. (2002) 'Andrew Pettigrew, the engaged scholar: commentary by Andrew Van de Ven', *European Management Journal*, 20, 1: 20–34.

Van Eijnatten, F. M. and Putnik, G. D. (2004) 'Chaos complexity, learning and the learning organization', *The Learning Organization*, 11, 6: 418–429.

Van Eltern, M. (1992) 'Karl Korsch and Lewinian social psychology: failure of a project', *History of the Human Sciences*, 5, 33–61.

Watson, G. (1978) 'Theory and practice', *Journal of Social Issues*, 34, 4: 168–182.

Weber, M. (1949) *The Methodology of The Social Sciences*, New York: The Free Press.

Weick, K. (1977) 'Organization design: organization as a self-designing system', *Organizational Dynamics*, 6: 31–46.

Weick, K. (1995) *Sensemaking in Organizations*, London: Sage.

Weick, K. (1999) 'Theory construction as disciplined reflexivity: trade offs in the 1990s', *Academy of Management Review*, 24, 4: 797–810.

Weick, K. (2001) *Making Sense of the Organization*, Oxford: Blackwell.

Wenger, E. (1998) *Communities of Practice: Learning, Meaning and Identity*, Cambridge: Cambridge University Press.

Wetherall, M. S. (1996) *Social Psychology*, London: Sage.

White, M. C., Brazeal, D. and Friedman. W. (1997) 'The evolution of organizations: suggestions from complexity theory about the interplay between natural selection and adaptation', *Human Relations*, 50, 11: 1383–1401.

Whitley, R. (2003) 'From the search for universal correlations to the institutional structuring of economic organization and change: the development and future of organization studies', *Organization Studies,* 10, 3: 481–501.

Whittington, R. (1992) 'Putting Giddens into action: social systems and managerial agency', *Journal of Management Studies*, 29, 6: 693–712.

Whittington, R. (2003) 'The work of strategizing and organizing: for a practice perspective', *Strategic Organization*, 1, 1: 117–125.

Whittington, R. and Melin, L. (2003) 'The challenge of organizing/strategizing', in A. M. Pettigrew *et al.* (eds) *Innovative Forms of Organizing*, London: Sage, pp. 35–48.

Willard, C. A. (1998) *Expert Knowledge: Liberalism and the Problem of Knowledge*, Chicago: University of Chicago Press.

Willmott, H. (1997) 'Rethinking management and managerial work: capitalism, control, and subjectivity', *Human Relations*, 50, 11: 1329–1358.

Worley, G. C. and Feyerherm, A. E. (2003) 'Reflections on the future of organizational development', *Journal of Applied Behavioral Science*, 39, 1: 97–115.

Worren, N., Ruddle, K. and Moore, K. (1999) 'From organizational development to change management: the emergence of a new profession', *Journal of Applied Behavioral Science*, 35, 3: 273–286.

Index

Abbott, P. 12, 162–3
actor network theories (ANT) 94
agency: and choice 19–20, *see also* centred
   agency; decentred agency
agency–structure dichotomy 4, 21–2, 26–7,
   114, 121
agent-based interaction 112–114
agential dispersion 159–60
agential selves 140
analyst–patient relationship 35–6
Anderson, P. 2, 6–7, 15, 92, 98, 111, 113, 114,
   159
anti-rationalism/scientism/essentialism/realism
   7–8
Archer, M. 96, 103, 141
Argyris, C. 30, 36–9, 51, 56–7
attractors 98, 105
autonomy 23, 30–1; and group rationality
   45–9; and postmodernism 32, 55–6, 136–7
autopoietic reproduction 99–100, 105–6

Barnes, B. 123
Beck, U. 27, 151, 165
being–becoming 68–9, 103, 106–7, 163–4
Boddy, D. 62
Boolean networks 110
bounded instability 110
Bourdieu, P. 89
Buchanan, D. 62
Burke, W. W. 29, 32–5, 39, 48, 56, 59, 87, 151
butterfly effect 99

Castells, M. 7, 15, 117
causal power 23
causal process theories 69–70
centred agency: and decentred agency 4, 22,
   23–4, 26–7, 115; definition 23; modernist
   components 30–3; and postmodernism 59

change agency 10–11, 28–30, 165–7; and
   postmodernism 53–9; and process
   consultation 44; and rationality 33–9
chaos theories *see* complexity theories
chaotic regimes of behaviour 109
Chia, R. 24, 62, 69, 96, 103, 118, 163
Child, J. 5, 61, 86
choice, and agency 19–20
coercion 48–9
communities of practice 2, 26, 156–7
complex adaptive systems (CAS) 94, 113
complex regimes of behaviour 109
complexity theory 92–7; agent-based
   interaction 112–14; and agential dispersion
   159–60; chaotic time–series 104–5, 106;
   core concepts 97–100; criticisms 120–1; and
   decentred agency 115–16; and dispersalist
   discourses 154; diversity 117–18; edge of
   chaos phenomenon 92–3, 110–11, 116–17;
   ordered unpredictability 97–8;
   organizational questions 94–6; plurality v.
   fragmentation 117–18; and postmodernism
   121; practice and expertise 118–19; small
   changes/large effects 99, 105; strange
   attractors 98–9, 105; systems and processes
   100–7, 118–19, 120; and tightly coupled
   systems 116, *see also* evolutionary theory;
   self-organization
constructionist discourse 7–8, 26–7, 160–2
contextualism 60–6; and competing interests
   65; critical readings 61–2, 84–6; cultural
   origins 88–91; definitions of context 65,
   71–2; engaged scholarship 81–84; goals
   62–3; inner context 75–7; legacy 84–8; and
   liberal individualism 89–91; precursors
   60–1; and strategic change 65–6; strategic
   change/choice 77–81, 87–8; structure and
   change 64, 75–7; theoretical links 85–6;

theory and practice 81–84, 86–7, *see also* leading change; outer context; processual analysis
contextualist discourses 6, 26; future research 152–4
contingency theories 73–4, 89
Cummings, T. G. 29
Cyert, R. M. 61

Darwinian natural selection 109–10
Dawson, P. 62
decentred agency: and centred agency 4, 22–4, 26–7; and complexity theory 114–16; definition 23; embodiment and identity 133–7; and postmodernism/constructionist discourse 122–6, 144–8; and the subject 122–5; theorization 124, *see also* power; power/knowledge; self-reflexivity
defensive routines 37–8
Descartes, R. 133–4
deterministic chaos 98
dialectical theories 68, 102
disciplinary discourses 9–10
discourse 5–13, 23, 26–7; analysis of madness 140–1; constructionist 7, 26–7; discursive practices 127; as general domain 128; as power/knowledge 127; relativism 142–4; self-referential 128, 139–40; sensemaking 157–9; and the subject 126–9
discursive practices 127
dispersalist discourses 6, 26–7; future research 154–60
dissipative structures 100
Dooley, A. 106
double-loop learning 37–8, 56–7

embodiedness 23
embodiment 124; and identity 133–7, 144–5; and sexuality 134–6
empowerment, and persuasion 45–6
equilibrium: punctuated 102; quasi-stationary 33–5; stable/periodic 110
espoused theories 37–8
ethics 138–9
evolutionary theory 68, 102, 103, 105–6; and adaptiveness 107–112; fitness landscapes 108–9, 110; natural selection 109–10; origins of order 110; system-evolutionary formulations 111; and teleology/tautology 107, 109–10, 120–21, *see also* complexity theories
expertise 30; diffusion 39–43; and knowledge 23; and postmodernism 31, 55

feminists 135–6
fitness landscapes 108–9, 110
force field analysis 33–4
Forgues, B. 110
Foucault, M. 122–48; embodiment 133–7; influence 122–6, 139–48; power/knowledge 129–33; self-reflexivity 137–9; use of discourse 126–9
Freud, S. 35–6

Gergen, K. J. 124–5
Giddens, A. 4, 64, 81, 153, 163–4; agency and structure 19–22, 24, 26, 64; and complexity theory 96, 101; and constructionist discourses 123, 134; and inner context 75–7, 87–8
Greiner, L. E. 29
Grey, C. 7, 83, 156

Habermas, J. 137, 146, 165
Hacking, I. 8, 13, 163
Hardy, S. 3, 54–5, 56, 116, 124
Hegel, G. 144
homeostasis 99–100

identity, and embodiment 133–7
inner context 75–7
intentions 19–20

Kauffman, S. A. 108–10
Kemmis, S. 48
knowledge: and expertise 23; limits 162; and practice 49–53
knowledge/power *see* power/knowledge
Kotter, J. P. 83

Latour, B. 10, 94, 119
leading change 77–81; components 77–8; dualisms 79–81; processual models 80–1
learning, single-/double-loop 37–8, 56–7
learning organization 2, 155–6
Levi-Strauss, C. 25
Lewin, K. 1, 5, 28–53, 55, 150, 152, 167; and autonomy 45–9; legacy 28–33; and rationality 33–9; and reflexivity 49–53
life cycle theories 68, 102
Lindblom, C. E. 61
Loasby, B. J. 91
Luhmann, N. 99, 103

McNay, L. 122, 123, 135, 136, 145
madness 140–41
March, J. G. 61
Marxism 89

mind–body split 133
Mintzberg, H. 5, 61
morality 138–9

negative feedback 33

ordered unpredictability 97–8
organisational development (OD) 5–6
organizational discourse analysis 12, 87–8, 123, 161, 163
outer context: and contingency theories 73; as environment 73–5

paradoxes of practice 165–7
Parsons, T. 21, 24, 101, 164
periodic equilibrium 110
Perrow, C. 99, 116
persuasion, and empowerment 45–6
Pettigrew, A. M. 6, 60–91
pluralism 88
plurality, new 149–50
Poole, S. P. 11–12, 68, 102
post-Fordist models 1–2
power: embodied 131; as knowledge 129–30; as nominal construct 130; relational 131–2
power/knowledge 23, 53, 124; and discourse 127, 144; and resistance 131–3
practice: communities of 2, 26, 156–7; and contextualism 81–4, 86–7; emancipatory 36–7; and knowledge 49–53; paradoxes of 165–7; and reflexivity 49–53, 58–9; and research 49–53
practices, discursive 127
process: definitions 25–6, 67–70; and systems 4, 23–6
process consultation 39–44
processual analysis 64; leading change 80–81; structure and change 69–70; and temporality 71
psychoanalytic methodology 35–6
punctuated equilibrium 102

quasi-stationary equilibrium 33–5
Quinn, J. B. 62

rationalist discourses 5–6, 26–7; future research 150–2
rationalist epistemologies 3–4
rationality 23; and autonomy 45–9; and change 33–9; and coercion 47–8; and emancipatory practice 36–7; and postmodernism 31, 54–5; prescriptive 38–9; skilled incompetence 39
Reed, M. 122, 136, 145

reflexivity 31; and postmodernism 32, 56; in research and practice 49–53, 58–9, see also self-reflexivity
research and practice 49–53
Rorty, R. 32, 49, 58

Schein, E. H. 30, 39–45, 46, 48, 57
Schon, D. 30, 52–3
self-organization 99–100, 105–6, 109, 111–12; and agent-based interaction 112–114; complex adaptive systems (CAS) 113; and complexity theory 119–20
self-reflexivity 23, 124, 145; and ethics 138–9; and knowledge/power 137–8
Senge, P. 45
sensemaking discourses 157–9
sexuality 134–6
Simon, H. 1, 6, 60–1, 86
single-loop learning 37–8, 57
skilled incompetence 39
small changes/large effects 99, 105
stable equilibrium 110
Stacey, R. D. 110, 115
stasis and change 24–5
strategic change/choice 77–81, 87–8, 167
structural–functional theory 101
structuration theory 20–2, 101–2, 122, 163
subject, the 122–25; and discourse 126–9; eclipse 165
synthesis, failure 163–5
systems: attractors 98, 105; definition 25; and processes 4, 23–6, 100–7

tautology 107
Taylor, C. 47, 137, 138, 143, 144
teleology 68, 102, 107, 109–10
temporality 70–1, 102–103
Thatcherism 89–90
theories-in-use 37–8
Thietart, R. A. 110
tightly coupled systems 116
time–series 104–5, 106

Urry, J. 2, 93, 95, 116

Van den Ven, A. 11–12, 68, 81, 102, 106
virtuous intelligence 111–12

Weick, K. 158
Whipp, R. 82–3
Wilmott, H. 62